Supplemental Readings for Physical Anthropology

Edited by
Samantha M. Hens
California State University

KENDALL/HUNT PUBLISHING COMPANY
4050 Westmark Drive   Dubuque, Iowa 52002

DNA image courtesy of Photo Disc
Monkey images courtesy of Corel

Copyright © 2004 by Samantha Hens

ISBN 0-7575-1185-6

Kendall/Hunt Publishing Company has the exclusive rights to reproduce this work,
to prepare derivative works from this work, to publicly distribute this work,
to publicly perform this work and to publicly display this work.

All rights reserved. No part of this publication may be reproduced,
stored in a retrieval system, or transmitted, in any form or by any
means, electronic, mechanical, photocopying, recording, or otherwise,
without the prior written permission of Kendall/Hunt Publishing Company.

Printed in the United States of America
10 9 8 7 6 5 4 3 2 1

Preface

This collection of readings is meant to supplement a standard introductory course in physical anthropology. Most courses are divided into three sections: genetics and evolution, primatology, and hominid evolution. The layout of this book follows this standard design, providing additional readings for the student beyond the textbook. Students will find an array of articles, expanding on the topics covered in class. The articles selected were written by scientists and science writers, and taken from the public press. The articles represent both the latest research in each area, as well as relevant articles from the past two decades, chosen for their historical significance.

Section I begins with basic evolutionary theory and the nature of scientific thought. These articles are followed by choices linking genetics and evolutionary forces to our understanding of human adaptation and disease, the race concept and racial diversity. Section II explores the Primate Order in its vast diversity and complexity, covering everything from the potential for primate emotion and intelligence to dietary and social adaptations and the genetic link to humans. Section III covers the most recent significant findings in paleoanthropology, spanning the earliest fossil forms to the rise of modern humans. Interpretations of hominid behavior are covered along with morphological distinctions.

Several people from Kendall/Hunt Publishing deserve my sincere thanks for their hard work in putting this reader together. Special thanks go to my sponsoring editor Kristina Stolte, development editor Emily Cabbage, permissions editor Corinna Vohl, and prepress editor Amanda Smith. I sincerely appreciate their efforts to produce a final product that I may be proud of.

Section I:
Genetics, Evolution and Adaptation

An understanding of genetics and evolutionary theory is the foundation for the biological sciences and is a significant part of our society today. We are inundated by modern technological advances in our everyday lives, especially the use of DNA technology; everything from *CSI* on Thursday night television, to DNA used in court cases, to the diversity of the global world we are living in. The articles chosen for this section represent the latest research on human genetics and adaptation.

The section begins with two selections describing evolutionary theory and the nature of science. In *A Theory Evolves*, the author begins with an excellent discussion of Darwin's contribution to early evolutionary theory, but rapidly moves to the addition of genetics in our understanding of evolution with the modern synthesis. Additionally, the author explores the most recent genetic research and puts evolution in a modern context. The author relates how critical it is to continue teaching evolution in the public schools. *Darwin's Rib* picks up right at this point, describing the first hand experiences of a science lab teacher in assisting students to understand the exploratory nature of science, reminding them to always question their beliefs.

Articles 3-5 explore the forces of evolutionary change: mutation, genetic drift, gene flow, nonrandom mating, and natural selection and relates them to modern human disease patterning and adaptation. In *Curse and Blessing of the Ghetto*, author Jared Diamond examines the high incidence of Tay-Sachs disease in the Ashkenazi Jews, and ties it to a selective advantage in combating tuberculosis in the past. Diamond's ideas are challenged in the next article, *Unfortunate Drift*, wherein Tay-Sachs and other diseases in the Ashkenazi are linked to small population size and nonrandom mating. *The Saltshaker's Curse* provides an excellent example of natural selection as it searches for an explanation for the high incidence of hypertension in African-Americans, and links this to salt intake and retention in West African ancestors.

Articles 6 and 7 continue to explore the idea of natural selection, but in the context of human microevolutionary adaptation to climate and other factors in *Black, White, Other* and *Racial Odyssey*. Both articles discuss the difference between biological and social race, and humans desire to classify themselves, which has become increasingly difficult.

The final selection, *From* Pan *to Pandemic*, continues the topic of disease and looks at the origin of HIV infection in our closest relative, the chimpanzee. We begin to understand how disease may cross the species barrier and the author provides numerous examples as to why we should stop the wholesale butchery of animals for "bush meat" and study the chimpanzees in the wild as opposed to captive environments. This article allows us to see the consequences of our actions on the environment, and pushes for conservation, providing a link to the next section on primatology.

A Theory Evolves

Thomas Hayden

When scientists introduced the world to humankind's earliest known ancestor two weeks ago, they showed us more than a mere museum piece. Peering at the 7 million-year-old skull is almost like seeing a reflection of our earlier selves. And yet that fossil represents only a recent chapter in a grander story, beginning with the first single-celled life that arose and began evolving some 3.8 billion years ago. Now, as the science of evolution moves beyond guesswork, we are learning something even more remarkable: how that tale unfolded.

Scientists are uncovering the step-by-step changes in form and function that ultimately produced humanity and the diversity of life surrounding us. By now, scientists say, evolution is no longer "just a theory." It's an everyday phenomenon, a fundamental fact of biology as real as hunger and as unavoidable as death.

Darwin proposed his theory of evolution based on extensive observations and cast-iron logic. Organisms produce more young than can survive, he noted, and when random changes create slight differences between offspring, "natural selection" tends to kill off those that are less well suited to the environment. But Darwin's evidence was fragmentary, and with the science of genetics yet to be invented, he was left without an explanation for how life might actually change.

The "modern synthesis" of genetics and evolutionary theory in the 1940s began to fill that gap. But until recently, much of evolution still felt to nonscientists like abstract theory, often presented in ponderous tomes like paleontologist Stephen Jay Gould's 1,464-page *Structure of Evolutionary Theory*, published shortly before his death this spring. As theorists argued over arcane points and creationists stressed uncertainties to challenge evolution's very reality, many people were left confused, unsure what to believe.

Nuts and Bolts. But away from heated debates in schools and legislatures, a new generation of scientists has been systematically probing the fossil record, deciphering genomes, and scrutinizing the details of plant and animal development. They are documenting how evolution actually worked, how it continues to transform our world, and even how we can put it to work to fight disease and analyze the wealth of data from genome-sequencing projects. "The big story," says evolutionary biologist E. O. Wilson of Harvard University, "is not in overarching, top-down theory now, but

From *U.S. News & World Report*, July 29, 2002, pp. 42-50. ©2002 U.S. News & World Report, L.P. Reprinted with permission.

in the details of research in the lab and in the field."

Scientists have confirmed virtually all of Darwin's postulates. For example, Ward Watt of Stanford University has demonstrated natural selection in action. In a hot environment, he found, butterflies with a heat-stable form of a metabolic gene outreproduced their cousins with a form that works well only at lower temperatures. "Darwin was more right than he knew," says Watt. Darwin also held that new species evolve slowly, the result of countless small changes over many generations, and he attributed the lack of transitional forms—missing links—to the spotty nature of the fossil record. By now many gaps have been filled. Dinosaur researchers can join hands with bird experts, for example, their once disparate fields linked by a series of fossils that show dinosaurs evolving feathers and giving rise to modern birds. And last year, paleontologists announced that they had recovered fossils from the hills of Pakistan showing, step by step, how hairy, doglike creatures took to the sea and became the first whales.

But new research also shows that evolution works in ways Darwin did not imagine. Many creatures still appear quite suddenly in the fossil record, and the growing suspicion is that evolution sometimes leaps, rather than crawls. For example, the first complex animals, including worms, mollusks, and shrimplike arthropods, show up some 545 million years ago; paleontologists have searched far and wide for fossil evidence of gradual progress toward these advanced creatures but have come up empty. "Paleontologists have the best eyes in the world," says Whitey Hagadorn of Amherst College, who has scoured the rocks of the Southwest and California for signs of the earliest animal life. "If we can't find the fossils, sometimes you have to think that they just weren't there."

A new understanding of Earth's history helps explain why. Scientists have learned that our planet has been rocked periodically by catastrophes: enormous volcanic eruptions that belched carbon dioxide, creating a super greenhouse effect; severe cold spells that left much of the planet enveloped in ice; collisions with asteroids. These convulsions killed off much of life's diversity. Once conditions improved, says Harvard paleontologist Andy Knoll, the survivors found a world of new opportunities. They were freed to fill new roles, "experimenting" with new body plans and evolving too rapidly to leave a record in the fossils.

We may owe our own dominance to the asteroid impact that killed the dinosaurs 65

Life of an idea

1831–36 A young Charles Darwin sails aboard the Beagle to Patagonia, Tierra del Fuego, and the Galápagos, making observations that led to his theory.

1859 Darwin publishes *The Origin of Species*, spelling out natural selection as the mechanism behind "descent with modification," or evolution.

1890s Social Darwinism is on the rise, misusing evolutionary ideas to justify the wealth and power of tycoons like Rockefeller and Carnegie.

1896 Henri Becquerel discovers radioactivity, leading to calculations that put Earth's age at billions of years—enough time for Darwinian evolution to work.

1925 John Scopes is tried in Tennessee—and fined $100—for teaching evolution.

1940s The Modern Synthesis of genetics and evolution provides a mechanism for heritable changes.

1975 Sociobiologists stir controversy by suggesting that many human social behaviors, like those in ants, are biological adaptations.

1981 A 65 million-year-old debris layer points to an asteroid impact at the time of the dinosaurs' extinction, confirming the importance of catastrophes in evolution.

1984 Discovery of homeotic genes, which orchestrate embryonic development. Mutations can produce drastic changes in body plan.

1999 Kansas temporarily drops evolution from its high school science curriculum.

million years ago. As mammals, we like to think that we're pretty darned superior. The sad truth: "Mammals coexisted with dinosaurs for 150 million years but were never able to get beyond little ratlike things," says Knoll. "It was only when the dinosaurs were removed that mammals had the ecological freedom to evolve new features."

Whether evolution worked fast or slow, theorists labored to explain how it could produce dramatic changes in body structure through incremental steps. Half an eye would be worse than none at all, creationists were fond of arguing. But "partial" eyes turn out to be common in nature, and biologists can trace eye evolution from the lensless flatworm eyespot to the complex geometry of vertebrate eyes. Now "evo-devo" biologists, who study how fertilized egg cells develop into adults, are discovering powerful new ways evolution can transform organisms. They are finding that changes in a handful of key genes that control development can be enough to drastically reshape an animal.

Master Switches. The central discovery of evo-devo is that the development and ultimate shape of animal bodies are orchestrated by a small set of genes called homeotic genes. These regulatory genes make proteins that act as master switches. By binding to DNA, they turn on or shut down other genes that actually make tissues. All but the simplest animals are built in segments (most obvious in creatures like centipedes, but also apparent in human vertebrae), and the Hox family of homeotic genes interacts to determine what each segment will look like. By simple genetic tinkering, evo-devo biologist can tweak the controls, making flies with legs where their antennae should be, or eyeballs on their knees.

This might seem like little more than a cruel parlor trick, and the resulting monstrosities would never survive in nature. But small changes in these master-switch genes may help explain some major changes in evolutionary history. This past winter, evo-devo biologists showed that an important animal transition 400 million years ago, when many-legged arthropods (think lobsters) gave rise to six-legged insects, was due to just a few mutations in a Hox gene. In the past few months, researchers have found that a change in the regulation of a growth-factor gene could have resulted in the first vertebrate jaw. And, incredibly, researchers reported in the journal *Science* last week that a single mutation in a regulatory gene was enough to produce mice with brains that had an unusually large, wrinkled cerebral cortex resembling our own. (No word, though, on whether the mutant mice gained smarts.)

Some critics of evolution argue that animals are so complex and their parts so interconnected that any change big enough to produce a new species would cause fatal failures. Call it the Microsoft conundrum. But just as Judge Thomas Penfield Jackson managed to delete that company's Web browser on his own computer without crashing the operating system, evo-devo biologists are learning how evolution can tweak one part of an animal while leaving everything else alone. The key to modifying the machine of life while it's running, says biologist Sean Carroll of the University of Wisconsin-Madison, is mutations in the stretches of DNA that homeotic proteins bind to.

"If you change a Hox protein, you might mess up the whole body," says Carroll. "But if you change a control element, you can change a part as small as a bristle or a fingernail." He explains that genetic accidents can set the stage by duplicating segments, creating spares that are free to evolve while the other segments carry on with their original function. Biologists now believe that appendages like insect wings and the proboscis a mosquito jabs you with evolved from spare leg segments.

Making Do. This process may be rapid, but it's not elegant. Instead of inventing new features from scratch, evolution works with what it has, modifying existing structures by trial and error. The result is a messy legacy of complicated biochemical pathways and body parts that are more serviceable than sleekly designed. Although proponents of intelligent design hold that organisms are too "perfect" to have arisen by chance, science shows that organisms don't work perfectly at all; they just work.

While many scientists busy themselves figuring out the history and mechanics of evolution, others are already putting it to use. Jonathan Eisen of the Institute for Genomic Research in Rockville, Md., deciphers the information stored in organisms' genomes for clues to their ancestry and how they function. For him, evolution is as critical a tool as DNA-sequencing machines and supercomputers. "If I didn't approach everything with an evolutionary perspective," says Eisen, "I'd miss out on most of the information."

That's because genomes are the handiwork of evolution, and their origin can be key to making sense of them. Researchers analyzing the human genome, for example, reported finding a series of human genes that were also common in bacteria but absent from invertebrates like fruit flies. They concluded that bacterial genes had infiltrated vertebrate animals, helping to shape our genetic identity. But the explanation turned out to be more mundane. Knowing how evolution often prunes away unneeded genes, Eisen and several others showed most of the suspect genes had simply been dropped during the evolutionary history of flies. The moral of the story: "I'm begging people to treat evolution as a science and not just tack it on as an explanation afterwards," says Eisen.

Arms Race. For microbiologist Richard Lenski, evolution is an obvious reality. Since 1988, the Michigan State University professor has been following 12 populations of the bacterium E. coli. With a new generation every 3.5 hours or so, this is evolution on fast-forward. The populations were once genetically identical, but each has adapted in its own way to the conditions in its test-tube home. The same speedy adaptation, unfortunately, can be readily seen in hospitals, where powerful antibiotics provide a major selective advantage for bacteria that evolve resistance. As bacterial evolution outwits one antibiotic after another, notes Harvard evolutionary biologist Stephen Palumbi, treating infections has become an evolutionary arms race. "It's a cycle of escalation, and the entity that can make the last turn of the cycle wins," says Palumbi. "So far, there's no indication that it's going to be us." The answer, he says, is not just new antibiotics but new strategies based on evolution.

"The key is to tip the balance of selection in favor of mild organisms," says evolutionary biologist Paul Ewald of Amherst College. That can mean measures as simple as having doctors scrub their hands to prevent the spread of the dangerous, antibiotic-resistant strains from their sickest patients. Making life difficult for virulent microbes can actually guide the species' evolution, weeding out the most harmful variants. In the case of malaria, the trick is keeping mosquitoes away from people bedridden with virulent strains. "If you mosquito-proof houses," says Ewald, "then only people walking around outside can spread the disease, and that will be a mild form."

Evolutionary theorists may be able to guess how specific microbes will evolve, but not the fate of the whole panoply of life. "You can't predict what organisms will look like millions of years from now," says Knoll. Chance events, small and large, make all the difference, as mutations arise at random and unpredictable mass extinctions set life on a new course.

One mass extinction is easy to foresee: the one already underway because of our logging and paving and polluting. Things don't look good for most large mammals—

they can't compete with us for space and resources. The outlook is brighter for species that depend on humans, like farm animals and crop plants, as well as rats and cockroaches. But this mass extinction is different from the last, 65 million years ago. "The day after the meteorite hit," says Knoll, "the planet started to heal. The problem now doesn't go away. It gets bad and it stays bad as long as our evolutionary history continues."

God and Man. Which brings us to one final result of evolution, the odd, upright, and curiously self-obsessed ape in the mirror. We've turned the tables on evolution, curing diseases and changing our environment to suit us, rather than the other way around. But don't think that frees us from further evolutionary changes. Incurable epidemics that strike the young are still a powerful selective force. A mutation that boosted resistance to HIV, for example, could spread quickly by allowing those who have it to survive and have children. "We continue to accumulate mutations," says Sarah Tishkoff, a geneticist at the University of Maryland. "But we're altering evolution." Assisted reproduction allows some people to beat natural selection, she notes, while birth control gives an evolutionary leg up to those who don't use it.

A quick survey of the human condition reveals any number of desirable improvements—surely evolution could take care of hernias and osteoporosis and the appendix, which serves no greater purpose than to become inflamed? But those annoyances usually don't keep the annoyed from passing on their genes. And with precious little geographic isolation—one of the main drivers of speciation—left in our global village, we'll probably have to wait until a space colony gets cut off for several thousand generations before a new human species evolves.

Of course, it's the idea that human beings themselves are products of evolution that provokes most of the attacks on evolution. Such rejections leave most scientists mystified. "The scientific narrative of the history of life is as exciting and imbued with mystery as any other telling of that story," says Knoll. The evidence against evolution amounts to little more than "I can't imagine it," Ewald adds. "That's not evidence. That's just giving up."

Many researchers simply ignore the debates and press on with their work. But as evolution becomes an applied science, others say it's more urgent than ever to defend its place in the schools. "HIV is one of the world's most aggressively evolving organisms," says Palumbi. If it weren't for the virus's adaptability, which helps it foil the body's defenses and many drugs, "we would have kicked HIV in the teeth 15 years ago." But doctors don't learn about evolution in medical school, he says, leaving them about as well prepared to combat HIV as a flat-Earth astronomer would be to plan a moon shot.

"Somewhere in high school in this country is a student who's going to cure AIDS," Palumbi says. "That student is going to have to understand evolution."

With Jessica Ruvinsky, Dan Gilgoff, and Rachel K. Sobel

ID#_____   NAME_____

Article 1: A Theory Evolves

1. What was Darwin unable to explain and how did the "modern synthesis" fill in the gap?

2. Describe two lines of evidence that confirmed Darwin's ideas.

3. What new evidence goes beyond Darwin's understanding of evolution?

4. What contributions do the "evo-devo" biologists make to our understanding of evolution?

5. What is the function of homeotic genes?

6. Describe one example where a small change in a master switch gene explained a significant event in evolutionary history.

7. If evolution doesn't invent new features from scratch, how does it work?

8. How is the current mass extinction, due to logging, paving, and pollution, different from the mass extinction that wiped out the dinosaurs 65 million years ago?

9. Why do many researchers believe it is critical to keep teaching evolution in schools?

Darwin's Rib

Robert S. Root-Bernstein

As all good teachers know, students will work much harder for extra-credit points than at the assigned task. I like to take advantage of this convenient trait in my introductory course on evolution. Once my students—nonscience majors at a midwestern land-grant university—understand the basic terms, I offer additional points for answering the questions I really want them to investigate. Find a dozen differences between the skeletons of a chimpanzee and a human being, I challenge them; tell me how a human female skeleton differs anatomically from a male. The male and female skeletons I display are exemplary in their difference, and since most students should be able to guess what that difference is if they don't already know, I usually feel confident that the final answer is a giveaway. I say "usually" because seven years ago, the first time I taught the course, I got a surprising answer that still crops up with alarming regularity. Five minutes into the lab period, a young woman announced that she could answer the question without even examining the human skeletons.

I waited silently for her to explain that the female pelvis is shaped slightly differently from the male's, with a larger opening for childbearing. That part was the giveaway. The real purpose of the exercise was to make her prove her conjecture with measurements—to translate the theory to practice. I also wanted her to explain why this sexual dimorphism—that is, this sexually determined physical difference—is not nearly so pronounced in nonhuman primates, such as chimpanzees.

She spoke: "Males have one fewer pair of ribs than females."

I was totally unprepared for her answer. My mandible dropped. After a moment's reflection, I realized she must be referring to the biblical story in which God creates Eve from one of Adam's ribs. My student was someone who believed in the literal truth of the Bible, and it was her religious belief, not her previous knowledge of human anatomy, that made her so sure of her answer. This was going to be a challenge.

I believe just as firmly in religious freedom as I do in the scientific search for understanding. Thus, while I adhere rigorously to teaching the best science and showing how scientists recognize it as the best, I never insist the students believe scientific results. On the contrary, I encourage them to be skeptical—as long as their skepticism is based on logic and evidence. Scientific results, in my view, should be compelling

From *Discover Magazine*, September 1995. Copyright © 1995 by Robert S. Root-Bernstein. Reprinted by permission of the author.

because the collected observations and experiments leave room for only one possible rational explanation. To insist that students accept my word (or the word of any scientist) about any fact would undermine the one thing that makes science different from all other belief systems. The acid test of science is the personal one of convincing yourself that you perceive what everyone else perceives, whatever reservations you may start with. The evidence should be so compelling that it convinces even the most serious skeptic—as long as that skeptic retains an open mind. Even more important, science must admit what it does not or cannot know. Questions are what drive science, not answers. A teacher who insists on blind faith might well crush some budding Darwin who sees a higher and more compelling truth about nature than the current dogma admits.

But in this instance, I was dealing with a pretty bare-bones case. The skeletons stood there as mute models of reality. Pedagogical ideals notwithstanding, I saw little hope of enlightening my young friend without attacking her religion outright.

I stalled for time. "Have you actually counted the ribs?" I asked. She admitted that she had not. "Well, since this is a science class," I admonished, "let's treat your statement as a hypothesis. Now you need to test it." So off she went to the back of the room, full of confidence that God would not let her down. The breather gave me a chance to plot out what I hoped would be an enlightened, and enlightening, approach to the crisis her assumption had precipitated.

I began by reviewing my lesson plans to see where I had gone wrong. After all, comparative anatomy lab exercises should be fairly straightforward stuff. The body of the work consists in finding and describing the usual anatomic features essential to understanding basic evolutionary theory. We look for homologies (body parts that spring from the same embryological parts but may have different functions, such as a whale's flipper, a human hand, and a bat's wing) and analogies (body parts that serve the same function but have very different developmental origins, such as the wings of birds and insects).

We go on to examine the evidence for transitional forms, using casts of the series of modifications that begins with the four-toed *Hyracotherium* and ends with the modern one-toed horse. The students generally get a few surprises while learning about divergent evolution—how living things become more and more different through geologic time. Imagine the ribs of a reptile broadening and fusing to become the bony back-plate of a tortoise. If you turn the skeleton over and look at the inside, you can even figure out how the shell evolved.

Convergent evolution is usually an eye-opener, too, since the notion that random mutations might lead to similar outcomes is anything but obvious. We study the point by examining a wonderful display of creatures that eat ants—spiny anteaters, silky anteaters, pangolins, and armadillos—each of which evolved from a different class of animals. Despite their disparate origins, they look generally similar: they all have the same long snouts; long, sticky tongues; and long, sharp claws for prying ants from their nests and eating them, and they all have little eyes and thick fur, spines, or scales to protect them from the bites of their tiny prey. Such examples of convergent evolution are among the best evidence for natural selection, because any animal that is going to eat ants, regardless of its anatomic origins, needs certain adaptations and will therefore end up looking similar to all the other animals that live in the same way.

Finally, we study vestigial traits—leftover parts that seem to serve no present function, such as the useless wings of flightless birds like ostriches and our apparently pointless appendix.

The students are required to understand these terms and be able to use their attendant principles to compare many amphibian, reptile, and mammalian skeletons, as well as a few fossil replicas. Was is really possible to learn all that and still think God created Eve from one of Adam's ribs?

"Are you sure those are male and female skeletons?" My cocksure friend was back, looking a little puzzled.

"They're the bona fide item," I answered. "Not only did they come so labeled from the company from which they were bought, but certain anatomic features that I have verified myself lead me to conclude that the labels are correct. But I'm glad you asked. Skepticism is a very useful scientific tool, and scientists do sometimes make mistakes. Not this time, though."

"Yes, but the skeletons have the same number of ribs," objected my student.

I agreed. "Why did you expect otherwise?" Best to get the argument out in the open. As I had guessed, her information came from the Bible, via Sunday school.

I had a sudden vision of whole classes being taught anatomic nonsense as truth. In my imagination, simple skeletons rose with a clamorous rattle to take on new lives as bones of contention. Wherever they appeared, dozens of Bible-toting students followed, egged on by ossified Sunday school teachers clustering around my desk to demand how I dare question Scripture. I knew my department chair would back me up, but the dean? The board of trustees? Weren't a few of them fundamentalists themselves? The problem was getting more difficult by the minute.

"But what does the Bible actually say?" I asked. Surely there had to be some way out of this mess.

"That God took a rib from Adam to create Eve."

"One rib or two?"

"One," she replied without hesitation.

"Don't forget that ribs come in pairs," I prompted her.

"Oh!" I could almost hear her mind whirring. "So men should be missing only one rib, not a pair—is that what you're saying?"

"I don't know." I shook my head. "Why should they be missing any?"

"Well, if God took a rib from Adam, wouldn't his children also be missing a rib?"

"All his children?" I countered. "Boys and girls?"

My young friend thought for a moment. "Oh, I see," she said. "Why should only males inherit the missing rib—why not females, too? That's a good question."

"I have a better one," I pressed on, a full plan of evolutionary enlightenment now formulated in my mind. "What kind of inheritance would this missing rib represent?"

In class we had discussed the differences between Lamarckian evolution by transmission of inherited somatic modifications and Mendelian inheritance through genes carried in the germ line of reproductive cells, but my student missed the point of my question. I explained. "Essentially, Lamarck maintained that anything that affects your body could affect your offspring. Lift weights regularly, and your daughter could inherit a bigger and stronger body than she would if you never stirred from the sofa. Chop off the tails of generation after generation of mice, and eventually you should end up with tailless mice. Make an antelope put its neck out for high-growing leaves, and its distant descendents will be giraffes.

"The problem is that generations of Jewish and Muslim males have been circumcised, without any effect on the presence or absence of the penile foreskin of later generations. Certain breeds of dogs have had their ears and tails cropped for hundreds of years without affecting the length or shape of the ears and tails of their offspring. In other words, Lamarck was wrong.

"In fact, if you recall from lectures, he couldn't have been right. Lamarckian types of inheritance aren't possible in higher animals. Remember: your egg cells are formed prior to birth and, mutations aside, contain essentially unalterable genetic information. Nothing you do to change your personal physiognomy, from lifting weights to having a nose job, will affect the genetic makeup of your offspring." As I reexplained these basic points, I realized that, lacking a problem to apply the information to, my student had not yet understood the important differences between Lamarck's and Mendel's theories. Information without a problem to which it can be applied is like a body without bones: a shapeless mass of muscle with nothing to work against. With Lamarck and Mendel in their fortuitous, Bible-generated problem context, I tried again.

"Look at it this way. Suppose you had an accident, and your right thumb had to be amputated. Would you expect all your children, assuming you have any, to be born lacking a right thumb?"

"Of course not," said my student. Then, after a pause, "Oh, I see. You mean that for the same reason my children would have thumbs even if I didn't, Adam's children would have the normal number of ribs even though God took one of his. Otherwise, it would be Lamarckian inheritance."

"Right!" I said. "And there is no creditable evidence to support Lamarckian inheritance. So you've actually got several problems here. First, Lamarckian inheritance doesn't work. Why should Adam's loss of a rib affect his children? Second, everyone has ribs, men and women alike. Ribs certainly aren't a sex-linked trait like excessive facial hair or a scrotum. So there's no reason I can think of that Adam's male offspring but not his female ones should be missing a rib. If the sons were missing a rib, wouldn't the daughters be missing one, too?

"Third, there is nothing in the Bible that says exactly how many ribs Adam started out with, or how many ribs we should have, is there? So you have no compelling reason to believe that in taking a rib from Adam, God left all his male offspring one short. That's an inference—and a particularly poor one since it relies on an outdated theory of evolutionary change. You don't really want to use a discarded evolutionary theory to prop up the Bible, do you?"

I was pleased to see that my ploy had worked. My student accepted this rebuff of accepted wisdom with good grace and an active intellect. Her religion was intact, but she was learning to think about her assumptions and to reason a bit more like a scientist. She was soon back at the human skeletons counting and measuring other bones. With some help, and a few broad hints ("How can you tell the difference between a man and a woman from behind, if they are the same height and have equal-length hair?"), she finally realized that the reason she wore a different cut of jeans from the men in the class was because she is built slightly differently. *Vive la différence!*

Most human females have a relatively wider pelvis than males because the human brain (even in a newborn) is too large to pass through a narrow birth canal. Thus, one of the reasons sexual dimorphism is so much more pronounced in humans than in most other primates is relative brain size. ("Don't trust me," I told her, "check it—the skeletons are there!") Bigger brains require bigger hips.

By the end of the course, five more students had reported to me that they too knew without having to look at the skeletons that women have more ribs than men. Some of them trotted off to count the ribs and came back to report that they had verified their preconceived notion. I had to stand beside them and count the ribs two or three times before they would believe that there really are the same number in the two skeletons.

These days I'm better prepared than I was that first year. Sometimes I bring in an extra pair of skeletons or a medical textbook with X-ray photographs of the chest, so that the students can count ribs to their hearts' content. I've come to expect at least 10 percent of the students in each class to tell me that men and women differ in rib count. I have conducted surveys of nearly a thousand first-year college students who either are nonscience majors or have not yet declared a major. More than 25 percent report believing that God created the Earth within the last 10,000 years and that man was formed in God's image exactly as described in the Bible. Another 50 percent report being undecided as to whether evolution is a valid scientific theory or a hoax. Only about 20 percent enter my university having learned enough about science and the evidence for evolution to consider it a valid scientific theory.

My college classroom numbers follow fairly closely those reported in recent national polls. A 1991 Gallup poll, for example, found that 47 percent of the respondents believed that God created man within the last 10,000 years. Forty percent believed that man evolved over millions of years but that God had a direct hand in guiding that process. Only 9 percent said man evolved without God's direct intervention. In many communities, such as mine, there are ongoing, active attempts to exclude evolution from the public school curriculum. Lecturing on evolution is an interesting challenge under these circumstances.

But I always have the last laugh. I share it with my classes after they have counted ribs for themselves and know for themselves the correct answer. You see, I really do have one fewer pair of ribs than my mother.

Don't get me wrong: I'm perfectly normal. I have 12 pairs of ribs, just like almost every other human being, male or female. So, as far as we know, do my father and brother. My mother is the unusual one. She has 13 pairs of ribs.

Oh yes, and that 5,300-year-old man they found frozen in a glacier in the Alps a few years back? He's got only 11 pairs of ribs. It happens. Still, imagine what might happen if the creation "scientists" get hold of a replica of the 5,300-year-old man's skeleton and try to pawn it off as proof of the Bible. Or consider the havoc my mother might wreak if her bones find their way into some science class to be compared with a typical male skeleton.

I chuckle at the thought, but I also check my skeletons twice. You can never be too careful. For example, there's a condition known as polydactyly—literally, "many digits"—in which people have extra fingers or toes. In one town in Spain, there has been so much inbreeding that almost everyone has six or seven fingers on each hand. I don't want any of my students unexpectedly claiming that a significant difference between chimps and us is the number of fingers or toes.

On the other hand, I wouldn't say no to a seven-fingered skeleton with 13 pairs of ribs. What a wonderful extra-credit assignment that would make, and what a wonderful example of how nature evades every generalization we try to impose on it. Take nothing for granted, I counsel my students: that is what makes a scientist. But don't ignore the exceptions, either. I'll make no bones about it: anatomic differences are what drive evolution—and its teaching.

ID#_____   NAME_____

Article 2: Darwin's Rib

1. What did the student, who believed that males had one fewer pair of ribs than females, base her answer on?

2. Does the author believe that students should accept his word on scientific matters? Why or why not?

3. Contrast homology and analogy.

4. If God took a rib from Adam, and Adam passed down this trait to his offspring, what kind of inheritance would this represent?

5. Briefly describe three examples from the reading that refute Lamarkian inheritance.

6. What percentage of students does the author see each year that believe men and women have a different number of ribs?

7. In the author's survey, what percentage of students was undecided as to whether evolution was valid science or a hoax?

17

Curse and Blessing of the Ghetto

Jared Diamond

Marie and I hated her at first sight, even though she was trying hard to be helpful. As our obstetrician's genetics counselor, she was just doing her job, explaining to us the unpleasant results that might come out of the genetic tests we were about to have performed. As a scientist, though, I already knew all I wanted to know about Tay-Sachs disease, and I didn't need to be reminded that the baby sentenced to death by it could be my own.

Fortunately, the tests would reveal that my wife and I were not carriers of the Tay-Sachs gene, and our preparenthood fears on that matter at least could be put to rest. But at the time I didn't yet know that. As I glared angrily at that poor genetics counselor, so strong was my anxiety that now, four years later, I can still clearly remember what was going through my mind: If I were an evil deity, I thought, trying to devise exquisite tortures for babies and their parents, I would be proud to have designed Tay-Sachs disease.

Tay-Sachs is completely incurable, unpreventable, and preprogrammed in the genes. A Tay-Sachs infant usually appears normal for the first few months after birth, just long enough for the parents to grow to love him. An exaggerated "startle reaction" to sounds is the first ominous sign. At about six months the baby starts to lose control of his head and can't roll over or sit without support. Later he begins to drool, breaks out into unmotivated bouts of laughter, and suffers convulsions. Then his head grows abnormally large, and he becomes blind. Perhaps what's most frightening for the parents is that their baby loses all contact with his environment and becomes virtually a vegetable. By the child's third birthday, if he's still alive, his skin will turn yellow and his hands pudgy. Most likely he will die before he's four years old.

My wife and I were tested for the Tay-Sachs gene because at the time we rated as high-risk candidates, for two reasons. First, Marie was carrying twins, so we had double the usual chance to bear a Tay-Sachs baby. Second, both she and I are of Eastern European Jewish ancestry, the population with by far the world's highest Tay-Sachs frequency.

In peoples around the world Tay-Sachs appears once in every 400,000 births. But it

From *Discover Magazine*, March 1991 by Jared Diamond. Copyright © 1991 by Jared Diamond. Reprinted by permission.

appears a hundred times more frequently—about once in 3,600 births—among descendants of Eastern European Jews, people known as Ashkenazim. For descendants of most other groups of Jews—Oriental Jews, chiefly from the Middle East, or Sephardic Jews, from Spain and other Mediterranean countries—the frequency of Tay-Sachs disease is no higher than in non-Jews. Faced with such a clear correlation, one cannot help but wonder: What is it about this one group of people that produces such an extraordinarily high risk of this disease?

Finding the answer to this question concerns all of us, regardless of our ancestry. Every human population is especially susceptible to certain diseases, not only because of its life-style but also because of its genetic inheritance. For example, genes put European whites at high risk for cystic fibrosis, African blacks for sickle-cell disease, Pacific Islanders for diabetes—and Eastern European Jews for ten different diseases, including Tay-Sachs. It's not that Jews are notably susceptible to genetic diseases in general; but a combination of historical factors has led to Jews being intensively studied, and so their susceptibilities are far better known than those of, say, Pacific Islanders.

Tay-Sachs exemplifies how we can deal with such diseases; it has been the object of the most successful screening program to date. Moreover, Tay-Sachs is helping us understand how ethnic diseases evolve. Within the past couple of years discoveries by molecular biologists have provided tantalizing clues to precisely how a deadly gene can persist and spread over the centuries. Tay-Sachs may be primarily a disease of Eastern European Jews, but through this affliction of one group of people, we gain a window on how our genes simultaneously curse and bless us all.

The disease's hyphenated name comes from the two physicians—British ophthalmologist W. Tay and New York neurologist B. Sachs—who independently first recognized the disease, in 1881 and 1887, respectively. By 1896 Sachs had seen enough cases to realize that the disease was most common among Jewish children.

Not until 1962, however, were researchers able to trace the cause of the affliction to a single biochemical abnormality: the excessive accumulation in nerve cells of a fatty substance called G_{M2} ganglioside. Normally G_{M2} ganglioside is present at only modest levels in cell membranes, because it is constantly being broken down as well as synthesized. The breakdown depends on the enzyme hexosaminidase A, which is found in the tiny structures within our cells known as lysosomes. In the unfortunate Tay-Sachs victims this enzyme is lacking, and without it the ganglioside piles up and produces all the symptoms of the disease.

We have two copies of the gene that programs our supply of hexosaminidase A, one inherited from our father, the other from our mother; each of our parents, in turn, has two copies derived from their own parents. As long as we have one good copy of the gene, we can produce enough hexosaminidase A to prevent a buildup of G_{M2} ganglioside and we won't get Tay-Sachs. This genetic disease is of the sort termed recessive rather than dominant—meaning that to get it, a child must inherit a defective gene not just from one parent but from both of them. Clearly, each parent must have had one good copy of the gene along with the defective copy—if either had had two defective genes, he or she would have died of the disease long before reaching the age of reproduction. In genetic terms the diseased child is homozygous for the defective gene and both parents are heterozygous for it.

None of this yet gives any hint as to why the Tay-Sachs gene should be most common among Eastern European Jews. To come to grips with that question, we must take a short detour into history.

From their biblical home of ancient Israel, Jews spread peacefully to other

Mediterranean lands, Yemen, and India. They were also dispersed violently through conquest by Assyrians, Babylonians, and Romans. Under the Carolingian kings of the eighth and ninth centuries Jews were invited to settle in France and Germany as traders and financiers. In subsequent centuries, however, persecutions triggered by the Crusades gradually drove Jews out of Western Europe; the process culminated in their total expulsion from Spain in 1492. Those Spanish Jews—called Sephardim—fled to other lands around the Mediterranean. Jews of France and Germany—the Ashkenazim—fled east to Poland and from there to Lithuania and western Russia, where they settled mostly in towns, as businessmen engaged in whatever pursuit they were allowed.

There the Jews stayed for centuries, through periods of both tolerance and oppression. But toward the end of the nineteenth century and the beginning of the twentieth, waves of murderous anti-Semitic attacks drove millions of Jews out of Eastern Europe, with most of them heading for the United States. My mother's parents, for example, fled to New York from Lithuanian pogroms of the 1880s, while my father's parents fled from the Ukrainian pogroms of 1903–6. The more modern history of Jewish migration is probably well known to you all: most Jews who remained in Eastern Europe were exterminated during World War II, while most the survivors immigrated to the United States and Israel. Of the 13 million Jews alive today, more than three-quarters are Ashkenazim, the descendants of the Eastern European Jews and the people most at risk for Tay-Sachs.

Have these Jews maintained their genetic distinctness through the thousands of years of wandering? Some scholars claim that there has been so much intermarriage and conversion that Ashkenazic Jews are now just Eastern Europeans who adopted Jewish culture. However, modern genetic studies refute that speculation.

First of all, there are those ten genetic diseases that the Ashkenazim have somehow acquired, by which they differ both from other Jews and from Eastern European non-Jews. In addition, many Ashkenazic genes turn out to be ones typical of Palestinian Arabs and other peoples of the Eastern Mediterranean areas where Jews originated. (In fact, by genetic standards the current Arab-Israeli conflict is an internecine civil war.) Other Ashkenazic genes have indeed diverged from Mediterranean ones (including genes of Sephardic and Oriental Jews) and have evolved to converge on genes of Eastern European non-Jews subject to the same local forces of natural selection. But the degree to which Ashkenazim prove to differ genetically from Eastern European non-Jews implies an intermarriage rate of only about 15 percent.

Can history help explain why the Tay-Sachs gene in particular is so much more common in Ashkenazim than in their non-Jewish neighbors or in other Jews? At the risk of spoiling a mystery, I'll tell you now that the answer is yes, but to appreciate it, you'll have to understand the four possible explanations for the persistence of the Tay-Sachs gene.

First, new copies of the gene might be arising by mutation as fast as existing copies disappear with the death of Tay-Sachs children. That's the most likely explanation for the gene's persistence in most of the world, where the disease frequency is only one in 400,000 births—that frequency reflects a typical human mutation rate. But for this explanation to apply to the Ashkenazim would require a mutation rate of at least one per 3,600 births—far above the frequency observed for any human gene. Furthermore, there would be no precedent for one particular gene mutating so much more often in one human population than in others.

As a second possibility, the Ashkenazim might have acquired the Tay-Sachs gene from some other people who already had the gene at high frequency. Arthur Koestler's controversial book *The Thirteenth Tribe*, for example, popularized the view that the Ashkenazim are really not a Semitic people but are instead descended from the Khazar, a Turkic tribe whose rulers converted to Judaism in the eighth century. Could the Khazar have brought the Tay-Sachs gene to Eastern Europe? This speculation makes good romantic reading, but there is no evidence to support it. Moreover, it fails to explain why deaths of Tay-Sachs children didn't eliminate the gene by natural selection in the past 1,200 years, nor how the Khazar acquired high frequencies of the gene in the first place.

The third hypothesis was the one preferred by a good many geneticists until recently. It invokes two genetic processes, termed the founder effect and genetic drift, that may operate in small populations. To understand these concepts, imagine that 100 couples settle in a new land and found a population that then increases. Imagine further that one parent among those original 100 couples happens to have some rare gene, one, say, that normally occurs at a frequency of one in a million. The gene's frequency in the new population will now be one in 200 as a result of the accidental presence of that rare founder.

Or suppose again that 100 couples found a population, but that one of the 100 men happens to have lots of kids by his wife or that he is exceptionally popular with other women, while the other 99 men are childless or have few kids or are simply less popular. That one man may thereby father 10 percent rather than a more representative one percent of the next generation's babies, and their genes will disproportionately reflect that man's genes. In other words, gene frequencies will have drifted between the first and second generation.

Through these two types of genetic accidents a rare gene may occur with an unusually high frequency in a small expanding population. Eventually, if the gene is harmful, natural selection will bring its frequency back to normal by killing off gene bearers. But if the resultant disease is recessive—if heterozygous individuals don't get the disease and only the rare, homozygous individuals die of it—the gene's high frequency may persist for many generations.

These accidents do in fact account for the astonishingly high Tay-Sachs gene frequency found in one group of Pennsylvania Dutch: out of the 333 people in this group, 98 proved to carry the Tay-Sachs gene. Those 333 are all descended from one couple who settled in the United States in the eighteenth century and had 13 children. Clearly, one of that founding couple must have carried the gene. A similar accident may explain why Tay-Sachs is also relatively common among French Canadians, who number 5 million today but are descended from fewer than 6,000 French immigrants who arrived in the New World between 1638 and 1759. In the two or three centuries since both these founding events, the high Tay-Sachs gene frequency among Pennsylvania Dutch and French Canadians has not yet had enough time to decline to normal levels.

The same mechanisms were one proposed to explain the high rate of Tay-Sachs disease among the Ashkenazim. Perhaps, the reasoning went, the gene just happened to be overrepresented in the founding Jewish population that settled in Germany or Eastern Europe. Perhaps the gene just happened to drift up in frequency in the Jewish populations scattered among the isolated towns of Eastern Europe.

But geneticists have long questioned whether the Ashkenazim population's history was really suitable for these genetic accidents to have been significant. Remember, the founder effect and genetic drift become significant only in small populations, and the founding populations of Ashkenazim may have been quite large.

Moreover, Ashkenazic communities were considerably widespread; drift would have sent gene frequencies up in some towns but down in others. And, finally, natural selection has by now had a thousand years to restore gene frequencies to normal.

Granted, those doubts are based on historical data, which are not always as precise or reliable as one might want. But within the past several years the case against those accidental explanations for Tay-Sachs disease in the Ashkenazim has been bolstered by discoveries by molecular biologists.

Like all proteins, the enzyme absent in Tay-Sachs children is coded for by a piece of our DNA. Along that particular stretch of DNA there are thousands of different sites where a mutation could occur that would result in no enzyme and hence in the same set of symptoms. If molecular biologists had discovered that all cases of Tay-Sachs in Ashkenazim involved damage to DNA at the same site, that would have been strong evidence that in Ashkenazim the disease stems from a single mutation that has been multiplied by the founder effect or genetic drift—in other words, the high incidence of Tay-Sachs among Eastern European Jews is accidental.

In reality, though, several different mutations along this stretch of DNA have been identified in Ashkenazim, and two of them occur much more frequently than in non-Ashkenazim populations. It seems unlikely that genetic accidents would have pumped up the frequency of the same gene not once but twice in the same population.

And that's not the sole unlikely coincidence arguing against accidental explanations. Recall that Tay-Sachs is caused by the excessive accumulation of one fatty substance, G_{M2} ganglioside, from a defect in one enzyme, hexosaminidase A. But Tay-Sachs is one of ten genetic diseases characteristic of Ashkenazim. Among those other nine, two—Gaucher's disease and Niemann-Pick disease—result from the accumulation of two other fatty substances similar to G_{M2} ganglioside, as a result of defects in two other enzymes similar to hexosaminidase A. Yet our bodies contain thousands of different enzymes. It would have been an incredible roll of the genetic dice if, by nothing more than chance, Ashkenazim had independently acquired mutations in three closely related enzymes—and had acquired mutations in one of those enzymes twice.

All these facts bring us to the fourth possible explanation of why the Tay-Sachs gene is so prevalent among Ashkenazim: namely, that something about them favored accumulation of G_{M2} ganglioside and related fats.

For comparison, suppose that a friend doubles her money on one stock while you are getting wiped out with your investments. Taken alone, that could just mean she was lucky on that one occasion. But suppose that she doubles her money on each of two different stocks and at the same time rings up big profits in real estate while also making a killing in bonds. That implies more than lady luck; it suggests that something about your friend—like shrewd judgment—favors financial success.

What could be the blessings of fat accumulation in Eastern European Jews? At first this question sounds weird. After all, that fat accumulation was noticed only because of the curses it bestows: Tay-Sachs, Gaucher's, or Niemann-Pick disease. But many of our common genetic diseases may persist because they bring both blessings and curses (see "The Cruel Logic of Our Genes," *Discover*, November 1989). They kill or impair individuals who inherit two copies of the faulty gene, but they help those who receive only one defective gene by protecting them against other diseases. The best understood example is the sickle-cell gene of African blacks, which often kills homozygotes but protects heterozygotes against malaria. Natural selection sustains such genes because more heterozygotes than normal individuals survive to pass on their genes, and those extra gene copies offset the copies lost through the deaths of homozygotes.

So let us refine our question and ask, What blessing could the Tay-Sachs gene bring to those individuals who are heterozygous for it? A clue first emerged back in 1972, with the publication of the results of a questionnaire that had asked U.S. Ashkenzaic parents of Tay-Sachs children what their own Eastern European-born parents had died of. Keep in mind that since these unfortunate children had to be homozygotes, with two copies of the Tay-Sachs gene, all their parents had to be heterozygotes, with one copy, and half of the parents' parents also had to be heterozygotes.

As it turned out, most of those Tay-Sachs grandparents had died of the usual causes: heart disease, stroke, cancer, and diabetes. But strikingly, only one of the 306 grandparents had died of tuberculosis, even though TB was generally one of the big killers in these grandparents' time. Indeed, among the general population of large Eastern European cities in the early twentieth century, TB caused up to 20 percent of all deaths.

This big discrepancy suggested that Tay-Sachs heterozygotes might somehow have been protected against TB. Interestingly, it was already well known that Ashkenazim in general had some such protection: even when Jews and non-Jews were compared within the same European city, class, and occupational group (for example, Warsaw garment workers), Jews had only half the TB death rate of non-Jews, despite their being equally susceptible to infection. Perhaps, one could reason, the Tay-Sachs gene furnished part of that well-established Jewish resistance.

A second clue to a heterozygote advantage conveyed by the Tay-Sachs gene emerged in 1983, with a fresh look at the data concerning the distributions of TB and the Tay-Sachs gene within Europe. The statistics showed that the Tay-Sachs gene was nearly three times more frequent among Jews originating from Austria, Hungary, and Czechoslovakia—areas where an amazing 9 to 10 percent of the population were heterozygotes—than among Jews from Poland, Russia, and Germany. At the same time records from an old Jewish TB sanatorium in Denver in 1904 showed that among patients born in Europe between 1860 and 1910, Jews from Austria and Hungary were overrepresented.

Initially, in putting together these two pieces of information, you might be tempted to conclude that because the highest frequency of the Tay-Sachs gene appeared in the same geographic region that produced the most cases of TB, the gene in fact offers no protection whatsoever. Indeed, this was precisely the mistaken conclusion of many researchers who had looked at these data before. But you have to pay careful attention to the numbers here: even at its highest frequency the Tay-Sachs gene was carried by far fewer people than would be infected by TB. What the statistics really indicate is that where TB is the biggest threat, natural selection produces the biggest response.

Think of it this way: You arrive at an island where you find that all the inhabitants of the north end wear suits of armor, while all the inhabitants of the south end wear only cloth shirts. You'd be pretty safe in assuming that warfare is more prevalent in the north—and that war-related injuries account for far more deaths there than in the south. Thus, if the Tay-Sachs gene does indeed lend heterozygotes some protection against TB, you would expect to find the gene most often precisely where you find TB most often. Similarly, the sickle-cell gene reaches its highest frequencies in those parts of Africa where malaria is the biggest risk.

But you may believe there's still a hole in the argument: If Tay-Sachs heterozygotes are protected against TB, you may be asking, why is the gene common just in the

Ashkenazim? Why did it not become common in the non-Jewish populations also exposed to TB in Austria, Hungary, and Czechoslovakia?

At this point we must recall the peculiar circumstances in which the Jews of Eastern Europe were forced to live. They were unique among the world's ethnic groups in having been virtually confined to towns for most of the past 2,000 years. Being forbidden to own land, Eastern European Jews were not peasant farmers living in the countryside, but business-people forced to live in crowded ghettos, in an environment where tuberculosis thrived.

Of course, until recent improvements in sanitation, these towns were not very healthy places for non-Jews, either. Indeed, their populations couldn't sustain themselves: deaths exceeded births, and the number of dead had to be balanced by continued emigration from the countryside. For non-Jews, therefore, there was no genetically distinct urban population. For ghetto-bound Jews, however, there could be no emigration from the countryside; thus the Jewish population was under the strongest selection to evolve genetic resistance to TB.

Those are the conditions that probably led to Jewish TB resistance, whatever particular genetic factors prove to underlie it. I'd speculate that G_{M2} and related fats accumulate at slightly higher-than-normal levels in heterozygotes, although not at the lethal levels seen in homozygotes. (The fat accumulation in heterozygotes probably takes place in the cell membrane, the cell's "armor.") I'd also speculate that the accumulation provides heterozygotes with some protection against TB, and that's why the genes for Tay-Sachs, Gaucher's, and Niemann-Pick disease reached high frequencies in the Ashkenazim.

Having thus stated the case, let me make clear that I don't want to overstate it. The evidence is still speculative. Depending on how you do the calculation, the low frequency of TB deaths in Tay-Sachs grandparents either barely reaches or doesn't quite reach the level of proof that statisticians require to accept an effect as real rather than as one that's arisen by chance. Moreover, we have no idea of the biochemical mechanism by which fat accumulation might confer resistance against TB. For the moment, I'd say that the evidence points to some selective advantage of Tay-Sachs heterozygotes among the Ashkenazim, and that TB resistance is the only plausible hypothesis yet proposed.

For now Tay-Sachs remains a speculative model for the evolution of ethnic diseases. But it's already a proven model of what to do about them. Twenty years ago a test was developed to identify Tay-Sachs heterozygotes, based on their lower-than-normal levels of hexosaminidase A. The test is simple, cheap, and accurate: all I did was to donate a small sample of my blood, pay $35, and wait a few days to receive the results.

If that test shows that at least one member of a couple is not a Tay-Sachs heterozygote, then any child of theirs can't be a Tay-Sachs homozygote. If both parents prove to be heterozygotes, there's a one-in-four chance of their child being a homozygote; that can then be determined by other tests performed on the mother early in pregnancy. If the results are positive, it's early enough for her to abort, should she choose to. That critical bit of knowledge has enabled parents who had gone through the agony of bearing a Tay-Sachs baby and watching him die to find the courage to try again.

The Tay-Sachs screening program launched in the United States in 1971 was targeted at the high-risk population: Ashkenazic Jewish couples of childbearing age. So successful has this approach been that the number of Tay-Sachs babies born each year in this country has declined tenfold. Today, in fact, more Tay-Sachs cases appear here in non-Jews than in Jews, because only the latter couples are routinely tested. Thus, what used to be the classic genetic disease of Jews is so no longer.

There's also a broader message to the Tay-Sachs story. We commonly refer to the United States as a melting pot, and in many ways that metaphor is apt. But in other ways we're not a melting pot, and we won't be for a long time. Each ethnic group has some characteristic genes of its own, a legacy of its distinct history. Tuberculosis and malaria are not major causes of death in the United States, but the genes that some of us evolved to protect ourselves against them are still frequent. Those genes are frequent only in certain ethnic groups, though, and they'll be slow to melt through the population.

With modern advances in molecular genetics, we can expect to see more, not less, ethnically targeted practice of medicine. Genetic screening for cystic fibrosis in European whites, for example, is one program that has been much discussed recently; when it comes, it will surely be based on the Tay-Sachs experience. Of course, what that may mean someday is more anxiety-ridden parents-to-be glowering at more dedicated genetics counselors. It will also mean fewer babies doomed to the agonies of diseases we may understand but that we'll never be able to accept.

ID#_____   NAME_____

Article 3: Curse and Blessing of the Ghetto

1. How does Tay-Sachs disease progress in children?

2. In non-Jewish populations, the frequency of Tay-Sachs is _____, however in Ashkenazi Jews the frequency of Tay-Sachs is _____.

3. How is Tay-Sachs inherited?

4. Is the diseased child a homozygote or a heterozygote?

5. Briefly describe the four possible explanations for the persistence of the Tay-Sachs gene.

6. Why does the author think that genetic drift does not explain the persistence of Tay-Sachs in the Ashkenazi (name two reasons)?

7. Briefly describe the relationship between Tay-Sachs and tuberculosis.

8. What evidence does the author provide explaining why Tay-Sachs did not become common in non-Ashkenazi Eastern Europeans?

9. What questions remain to be answered?

Unfortunate Drift

Josie Glausiusz

Ashkenazi Jews—those of Central and Eastern European origin, which includes most American Jews—are prey to a unique set of genetic diseases. The best known is Tay-Sachs, which kills in early infancy, but there are at least nine other inherited disorders that are especially prevalent among Ashkenazim. Why? The pattern of inheritance offers a clue: most of the diseases are caused by recessive genes, meaning that symptoms appear only if two copies of the mutant gene are inherited, one from each parent. One copy does no harm, and might even do some good—which would cause natural selection to spread the mutation through a human population instead of weeding it out. Many researchers believe the Ashkenazi burden has this sort of flip side; they argue, for instance, that the Tay-Sachs gene protects its carriers against tuberculosis, a disease that was endemic in the crowded ghettos of Eastern Europe.

But there has always been an alternative theory, says Stanford population geneticist Neil Risch: mutant genes may have become concentrated in the Ashkenazi population purely by chance or historical accident. Now Risch and his colleagues have found evidence that such "genetic drift" does indeed underlie the high incidence among Ashkenazim of idiopathic torsion dystonia (ITD), a disease that causes involuntary muscle contractions. The researchers think drift may explain or help explain the other Ashkenazi diseases as well. The mutant genes may have achieved their high frequency, says Risch, not so much because they confer a selective advantage but because they happened to arise among a relatively small number of Jews who produced a large number of descendants.

ITD, however, is a special case—as Risch and his colleagues discovered when they started analyzing its pattern of inheritance in their study group of 59 Ashkenazi families in the United States. Unlike all the other Ashkenazi diseases, they found, ITD isn't recessive—it's dominant, meaning that a single copy of the gene is enough to transmit the disease. For reasons unknown, though, it usually doesn't. Between one in 1,000 and one in 3,000 Ashkenazim carry the ITD gene, Risch estimates, but only 30 percent of them show symptoms—muscles that cramp and twist a part of the body into contorted positions—and only 10 percent have incapacitating ones. The low incidence of disease allows the gene to survive in the population; most of its carriers can

From *Discover Magazine*, June 1995 by Josie Glausiusz. Copyright © 1995 by Discover Magazine. Reprinted by permission.

still have children. On the other hand, the gene doesn't seem to confer any type of advantage that would explain why it became so common among Ashkenazi Jews.

Another clue that genetic drift rather than natural selection might explain the spread of ITD is the history of the Ashkenazim. *Ashkenazi* is a Hebrew term for "German." Beginning in the fourteenth century, a wave of German Jews fleeing east to escape persecution established new homes in Eastern Europe. The immigrant Jews generally didn't marry members of the surrounding communities, and although historical evidence from the period is sketchy, there is some evidence that their initial population was small. If so, it was an ideal candidate for a type of genetic drift known as the founder effect: when a small group of immigrants founds a new population, isolated from others, whatever mutations the founders happen to have, good or bad, will necessarily be more concentrated in that new, smaller population than they were in the old, larger one the founders came from.

That's just what happened with ITD, says Risch. He and his colleagues have found that a single genetic mutation is responsible for most cases of the disease, and they have traced it to its source. They did so by showing that 90 percent of the families in their study had an identical pattern of genetic markers—recognizable bits of noncoding DNA—flanking the ITD gene on chromosome 9. Since chromosomes swap pieces of DNA each time a sex cell is formed by meiosis, marker patterns tend to get scrambled over time. That 90 percent of the families still had identical markers showed they all inherited the same mutation—and also that the mutation had arisen in a single individual fairly recently.

Knowing the rate at which chromosomes swap DNA, Risch could estimate when the original ITD mutation occurred: around 1650, plus or minus a century or two—but probably after the Ashkenazi Jews migrated to Eastern Europe. When Risch started asking the people in his study about their grandparents and great-grandparents, he found that more than two-thirds of the oldest ITD carriers who could be traced hailed from Lithuania and Belorussia. The most likely scenario, Risch concludes, is that the progenitor of the ITD mutation lived in one of those two places some 350 years ago. That person's descendants spread the mutation to other parts of what came to be known as the Jewish Pale of Settlement—a region that included Poland, the Ukraine, and parts of Russia. (From the late eighteenth century on, Jews living under the Russian czar were confined to the Pale.) In the late nineteenth century, Jews fleeing pogroms in Eastern Europe carried the mutation to other parts of the world, including the United States.

By 1900 there were 5 million Jews living in the Pale of Settlement; in spite of repeated persecutions, the population had grown explosively since at least 1765, when the earliest reliable census put it at 560,000. Extrapolating that growth rate backward in time, Risch estimates that in the mid-seventeenth century, when the ITD mutation most likely appeared, the Ashkenazi population in the Pale was around 100,000. The mutation's initial frequency, then, would have been around one in 100,000. How could the frequency have risen to at least one in 3,000 among today's Ashkenazim?

The answer, Risch thinks, is a second type of genetic drift. In the seventeenth century and later, he says, not all Ashkenazi Jews left equal numbers of children. Family genealogies suggest that the more affluent classes—business and community leaders as well as scholars and rabbis, who were considered desirable marriage partners—had between four and nine children who reached adulthood. In contrast, poorer Jewish families, who were more subject to overcrowding and thus more at risk from epidemics, left fewer surviving descendants. Risch thinks the original ITD mutation just happened to arise in an affluent family, and that it spread rapidly because the affluent Jews tended to marry one another and to have many children. ITD is so common among the Ashkenazim today, he argues, because most of the world's 11 million Ashkenazim are descended from just a few thousand people who lived in the Pale of Settlement in the seventeenth century.

What about the other Ashkenazi diseases? They are all recessive, which means natural selection could more easily have influenced their frequency. Typically only 1 percent or so of the carriers of a rare recessive mutation get sick (because they have two copies of the mutated gene), compared with 30 percent of the carriers of ITD. As a result, even a small selective advantage might be enough to spread a recessive mutation through the population. Risch points out that natural selection and genetic drift could have worked together to spread the Ashkenazi diseases; the two are not mutually exclusive. But he also thinks further studies will show that most or all of the diseases are, like ITD, of recent origin—too recent for the slow grind of evolution to be the main reason they have achieved such high frequency.

There is another population, Risch points out, whose history makes for an instructive comparison with the Ashkenazim. "The French Canadians have Tay-Sachs also—a different mutation, but almost at the same frequency as the Ashkenazim," he says. "I've never heard anybody arguing that Tay-Sachs gives them an advantage against tuberculosis in crowded ghettos! In fact, the French Canadians are well known for having their own, unique genetic diseases. Their demography is remarkably similar to that of the Ashkenazi Jews—there are currently about 5 million French Canadians who are descended from a relatively small founder population, in the thousands or tens of thousands, dating to 300 or 400 years ago.

"And in Eastern Europe, tuberculosis was quite common in non-Jews also, and you don't see them with these genetic diseases. But our study confirms that the conditions for the operation of genetic drift existed there. You would expect it to apply not just to the ITD gene but to others also." If Risch turns out to be right, the diseases that plague the Ashkenazim will no longer be seen as an example of the cruel beauty of evolution. They'll just be an example of bad luck.

ID#_____   NAME_____

Article 4: Unfortunate Drift

1. Why are so many inherited disorders prevalent in the Ashkenazi?

2. How does this explanation differ from that provided by Risch?

3. What is ITD? Include in your answer: how it is inherited and the symptoms.

4. Define: founder effect.

5. How might founder effect have affected the Ashkenazi?

6. What is the second type of genetic drift?

7. Why does Risch think the ITD mutation occurred in an affluent family?

8. Why might natural selection have more influence in other Ashkenazi diseases?

9. In what way are French-Canadians similar to Ashkenazi?

The Saltshaker's Curse

Jared Diamond

On the walls of the main corridor at UCLA Medical School hang thirty-seven photographs that tell a moving story. They are the portraits of each graduating class, from the year that the school opened (Class of 1955) to the latest crop (Class of 1991). Throughout the 1950s and early 1960s the portraits are overwhelmingly of young white men, diluted by only a few white women and Asian men. The first black student graduated in 1961, an event not repeated for several more years. When I came to UCLA in 1966, I found myself lecturing to seventy-six students, of whom seventy-four were white. Thereafter the numbers of blacks, Hispanics, and Asians exploded, until the most recent photos show the number of white medical students declining toward a minority.

In these changes of racial composition, there is of course nothing unique about UCLA Medical School. While the shifts in its student body mirror those taking place, at varying rates, in other professional groups throughout American society, we still have a long way to go before professional groups truly mirror society itself. But ethnic diversity among physicians is especially important because of the dangers inherent in a profession composed of white practitioners for whom white biology is the norm.

Different ethnic groups face different health problems, for reasons of genes as well as of life style. Familiar examples include the prevalence of skin cancer and cystic fibrosis in whites, stomach cancer and stroke in Japanese, and diabetes in Hispanics and Pacific islanders. Each year, when I teach a seminar course in ethnically varying disease patterns, these by-now-familiar textbook facts assume a gripping reality, as my various students choose to discuss some disease that affects themselves or their relatives. To read about the molecular biology of sickle-cell anemia is one thing. It's quite another thing when one of my students, a black man homozygous for sickle-cell gene, describes the pain of his own sickling attacks and how they have affected his life.

Sickle-cell anemia is a case in which the evolutionary origins of medically important genetic differences among peoples are well understood. (It evolved only in malarial regions because it confers resistance against malaria.) But in many other cases the evolutionary origins are not nearly so transparent. Why is it, for example, that only some human populations have a high

From *Natural History*, October 1991 by Jared Diamond. Copyright © 1991 by Jared Diamond. Reprinted by permission.

frequency of the Tay-Sachs gene or of diabetes?. . .

Compared with American whites of the same age and sex, American blacks have, on the average, higher blood pressure, double the risk of developing hypertension, and nearly ten times the risk of dying of it. By age fifty, nearly half of U.S. black men are hypertensive. For a given age and blood pressure, hypertension more often causes heart disease and especially kidney failure and strokes in U.S. blacks than whites. Because the frequency of kidney disease in U.S. blacks is eighteen times that in whites, blacks account for about two-thirds of U.S. patients with hypertensive kidney failure, even though they make up only about one-tenth of the population. Around the world, only Japanese exceed U.S. blacks in their risk of dying from stroke. Yet it was not until 1932 that the average difference in blood pressure between U.S. blacks and whites was clearly demonstrated, thereby exposing a major health problem outside the norms of white medicine.

What is it about American blacks that makes them disproportionately likely to develop hypertension and then to die of its consequences? While this question is of course especially "interesting" to black readers, it also concerns all Americans, because other ethnic groups in the United States are not so far behind blacks in their risk of hypertension. If *Natural History* readers are a cross section of the United States, then about one-quarter of you now have high blood pressure, and more than half of you will die of a heart attack or stroke to which high blood pressure predisposes. Thus, we all have valid reasons for being interested in hypertension.

First, some background on what those numbers mean when your doctor inflates a rubber cuff about your arm, listens, deflates the cuff, and finally pronounces, "Your blood pressure is 120 over 80." The cuff device is called a sphygmomanometer, and it measures the pressure in your artery in units of millimeters of mercury (that's the height to which your blood pressure would force up a column of mercury in case, God forbid, your artery were suddenly connected to a vertical mercury column). Naturally, your blood pressure varies with each stroke of your heart, so the first and second numbers refer, respectively, to the peak pressure at each heartbeat (systolic pressure) and to the minimum pressure between beats (diastolic pressure). Blood pressure varies somewhat with position, activity, and anxiety level, so the measurement is usually made while you are resting flat on your back. Under those conditions, 120 over 80 is an average reading for Americans.

There is no magic cutoff between normal blood pressure and high blood pressure. Instead, the higher your blood pressure, the more likely you are to die of a heart attack, stroke, kidney failure, or ruptured aorta. Usually, a pressure reading higher than 140 over 90 is arbitrarily defined as constituting hypertension, but some people with lower readings will die of a stroke at age fifty, while others with higher readings will die in a car accident in good health at age ninety.

Why do some of us have much higher blood pressure than others? In about 5 percent of hypertensive patients there is an identifiable single cause, such as hormonal imbalance or use of oral contraceptives. In 95 percent of such cases, though, there is no such obvious cause. The clinical euphemism for our ignorance in such cases is "essential hypertension."

Nowadays, we know that there is a big genetic component in essential hypertension, although the particular genes involved have not yet been identified. Among people living in the same household, the correlation coefficient for blood pressure is 0.63 between identical twins, who share all of their genes. (A correlation coefficient of 1.00 would mean that the twins share identical blood pressures as well and would suggest that pressure is determined entirely by genes and not at all by environment.) Fraternal twins or ordinary siblings or a parent and child, who share half their genes and whose blood pressure would therefore show a correlation coefficient of 0.5 if purely determined genetically, actually have a coefficient of about 0.25. Finally, adopted siblings or a parent and adopted child, who have no direct genetic connection, have a correlation coefficient of only 0.05. Despite the shared household environment, their blood pressures are barely more similar than those of two people pulled randomly off the street. In agreement with this evidence for genetic factors underlying blood pressure itself, your risk of actually developing hypertensive disease increases from 4 percent to 20 percent to 35 percent if, respectively, none or one or both of your parents were hypertensive.

But these same facts suggest that environmental factors also contribute to high blood pressure, since identical twins have similar but not identical blood pressures. Many environmental or life style factors contributing to the risk of hypertension have been identified by epidemiological studies that compare hypertension's frequency in groups of people living under different conditions. Such contributing factors include obesity, high intake of salt or alcohol or saturated fats, and low calcium intake. The proof of this approach is that hypertensive patients who modify their life styles so as to minimize these putative factors often succeed in reducing their blood pressure. Patients are especially advised to reduce salt intake and stress, reduce intake of cholesterol and saturated fats and alcohol, lose weight, cut out smoking, and exercise regularly.

Here are some examples of the epidemiological studies pointing to these risk factors. Around the world, comparisons within and between populations show that both blood pressure and the frequency of hypertension increase hand in hand with salt intake. At the one extreme, Brazil's Yanomamö Indians have the world's lowest-known salt consumption (somewhat above 10 milligrams per day!), lowest average blood pressure (95 over 61!), and lowest incidence of hypertension (no cases!). At the opposite extreme, doctors regard Japan as the "land of apoplexy" because of the high frequency of fatal strokes (Japan's leading cause of death, five times more frequent than in the United States), linked with high blood pressure and notoriously salty food. Within Japan itself these factors reach their extremes in Akita Prefecture, famous for its tasty rice, which Akita farmers flavor with salt, wash down with salty miso soup, and alternate with salt pickles between meals. Of 300 Akita adults studied, not one consumed less than five grams of salt daily, the average consumption was twenty-seven grams, and the most salt-loving individual consumed an incredible sixty-one grams—enough to devour the contents of the usual twenty-six-ounce supermarket salt container in a mere twelve days. The average blood pressure in Akita by age fifty is 151 over 93, making hypertension (pressure higher than 140 over 90) the norm. Not surprisingly, Akitas' frequency of death by stroke is more than double even the Japanese average, and in some Akita villages 99 percent of the population dies before age seventy.

Why salt intake often (in about 60 percent of hypertensive patients) leads to high blood pressure is not fully understood. One possible interpretation is that salt intake triggers thirst, leading to an increase in blood volume. In response, the heart increases its output and blood pressure rises, causing the kidneys to filter more salt and water under that increased pressure. The result is a new steady state, in which salt and water excretion again equals intake, but more salt and water are stored in the body and blood pressure is raised.

At this point, let's contrast hypertension with a simple genetic disease like Tay-Sachs disease. Tay-Sachs is due to a defect in a single gene; every Tay-Sachs patient has a defect in that same gene. Everybody in whom that gene is defective is certain to die of Tay-Sachs, regardless of their life style or environment. In contrast, hypertension involves several different genes whose molecular products remain to be identified. Because there are many causes of raised blood pressure, different hypertensive patients may owe their condition to different gene combinations. Furthermore, whether someone genetically predisposed to hypertension actually develops symptoms depends a lot on life style. Thus, hypertension is not one of those uncommon, homogeneous, and intellectually elegant diseases that geneticists prefer to study. Instead, like diabetes and ulcers, hypertension is a shared set of symptoms produced by heterogeneous causes, all involving an interaction between environmental agents and a susceptible genetic background.

Since U.S. blacks and whites differ on the average in the conditions under which they live, could those differences account for excess hypertension in U.S. blacks? Salt intake, the dietary factor that one thinks of first, turns out on the average not to differ between U.S. blacks and whites. Blacks do consume less potassium and calcium, do experience more stress associated with more difficult socioeconomic conditions, have much less access to medical care, and are therefore much less likely to be diagnosed or treated until it is too late. Those factors surely contribute to the frequency and severity of hypertension in blacks.

However, those factors don't seem to be the whole explanation: hypertensive blacks aren't merely like severely hypertensive whites. Instead, physiological differences seem to contribute as well. On consuming salt, blacks retain it on average far longer before excreting it into the urine, and they experience a greater rise in blood pressure on a high-salt diet. Hypertension is more likely to be "salt-sensitive" in blacks than in whites, meaning that blood pressure is more likely to rise and fall with rises and falls in dietary salt intake. By the same token, black hypertension is more likely to be treated successfully by drugs that cause the kidneys to excrete salt (the so-called thiazide diuretics) and less likely to respond to those drugs that reduce heart rate and cardiac output (so-called beta blockers, such as propanolol). These facts suggest that there are some qualitative differences between the causes of black and white hypertension, with black hypertension more likely to involve how the kidneys handle salt.

Physicians often refer to this postulated feature as a "defect": for example, "kidneys of blacks have a genetic defect in excreting sodium." As an evolutionary biologist, though, I hear warning bells going off inside me whenever a seemingly harmful trait that occurs frequently in an old and large human population is dismissed as a "defect." Given enough generations, genes that greatly impede survival are extremely unlikely to spread, unless their net effect is to increase survival and reproductive success. Human medicine has furnished the best examples of seemingly defective genes being propelled to high frequency by counterbalancing benefits. For example, sickle-cell hemoglobin protects far more people against malaria than it kills of anemia, while the Tay-Sachs gene may have protected far more Jews against tuberculosis than it killed of neurological disease. Thus, to understand why U.S. blacks now are prone to die as a result of their kidneys' retaining salt, we need to ask under what conditions people might have benefited from kidneys good at retaining salt.

That question is hard to understand from the perspective of modern Western society, where saltshakers are on every dining table, salt (sodium chloride) is cheap, and our bodies' main problem is getting rid of it. But imagine what the world used to be like before saltshakers became ubiquitous. Most plants contain very little sodium, yet animals require sodium at high concentrations in all their extracellular fluids. As a result, carnivores readily obtain their needed sodium by eating herbivores, but herbivores themselves face big problems in acquiring that sodium. That's why the animals that one sees coming to salt licks are deer and antelope, not lions and tigers. Similarly, some human hunter-gatherers obtained enough salt from the meat that they ate. But when we began to take up farming ten thousand years ago, we either had to evolve kidneys superefficient at conserving salt or learn to extract salt at great effort or trade for it at great expense.

Examples of these various solutions abound. I already mentioned Brazil's Yanomamö Indians, whose staple food is low-sodium bananas and who excrete on the average only 10 milligrams of salt daily—barely one-thousandth the salt excretion of the typical American. A single Big Mac hamburger analyzed by *Consumer Reports* contained 1.5 grams (1,500 milligrams) of salt, representing many weeks of intake for a Yanomamö. The New Guinea highlanders with whom I work, and whose diet consists up to 90 percent of low-sodium sweet potatoes, told me of the efforts to which they went to make salt a few decades ago, before Europeans brought it as trade goods. They gathered leaves of certain plant species, burned them, scraped up the ash, percolated water through it to dissolve the solids, and finally evaporated the water to obtain small amounts of bitter salt.

Thus, salt has been in very short supply for much of recent human evolutionary history. Those of us with efficient kidneys able to retain salt even on a low-sodium diet were better able to survive our inevitable episodes of sodium loss (of which more in a moment). Those kidneys proved to be a detriment only when salt became routinely available, leading to excessive salt retention and hypertension with its fatal consequences. That's why blood pressure and the frequency of hypertension have shot up recently in so many populations around the world as they have made the transition from being self-sufficient subsistence farmers to members of the cash economy and patrons of supermarkets.

This evolutionary argument has been advanced by historian-epidemiologist Thomas Wilson and others to explain the current prevalence of hypertension in American blacks in particular. Many West African blacks, from whom most American blacks originated via the slave trade, must have faced the chronic problem of losing salt through sweating in their hot environment. Yet in West Africa, except on the coast and certain inland areas, salt was traditionally as scarce for African farmers as it has been for Yanomamö and New Guinea farmers. (Ironically, those Africans who sold other Africans as slaves often took payment in salt traded from the Sahara.) By this argument, the genetic basis for hypertension in U.S. blacks was already widespread in many of their West African ancestors. It required only the ubiquity of saltshakers in twentieth-century America for that genetic basis to express itself as hypertension. This argument also predicts that as Africa's life style becomes increasingly Westernized, hypertension could become as prevalent in West Africa as it now is among U.S. blacks. In this view, American blacks would be no different from the many Polynesian, Melanesian, Kenyan, Zulu, and other populations that have recently developed high blood pressure under a Westernized life style.

But there's an intriguing extension to this hypothesis, proposed by Wilson and physician Clarence Grim, collaborators at the Hypertension Research Center of Drew University in Los Angeles. They suggest a scenario in which New World blacks may now be at more risk for hypertension than their African ancestors. That scenario involves very recent selection for superefficient kidneys, driven by massive mortality of black slaves from salt loss.

Grim and Wilson's argument goes as follows. Black slavery in the Americas began about 1517, with the first imports of slaves from West Africa, and did not end until Brazil freed its slaves barely a century ago in 1888. In the course of the slave trade an estimated 12 million Africans were brought to the Americas. But those imports were winnowed by deaths at many stages, from an even larger number of captives and exports.

First, slaves captured by raids in the interior of West Africa were chained together, loaded with heavy burdens, and marched for one or two months, with little food and water, to the coast. About 25 percent of the captives died en route. While awaiting purchase by slave traders, the survivors were held on the coast in hot, crowded buildings called barracoons, where about 12 percent of them died. The traders went up and down the coast buying and loading slaves for a few weeks or months until a ship's cargo was full (5 percent more died). The dreaded Middle Passage across the Atlantic killed 10 percent of the slaves, chained together in a hot, crowded, unventilated hold without sanitation. (Picture to yourself the result of those toilet "arrangements.") Of those who lived to land in the New World, 5 percent died while awaiting sale, and 12 percent died while being marched or shipped from the sale yard to the plantation. Finally, of those who survived, between 10 and 40 percent died during the first three years of plantation life, in a process euphemistically called seasoning. At that stage, about 70 percent of the slaves initially captured were dead, leaving 30 percent as seasoned survivors.

Even the end of seasoning, however, was not the end of excessive mortality. About half of slave infants died within a year of birth because of poor nutrition and heavy workload of their mothers. In plantation terminology, slave women were viewed as either "breeding units" or "work units," with a built-in conflict between those uses: "These Negroes breed the best, whose labour is least," as an eighteenth-century observer put it. As a result, many New World slave populations depended on continuing slave imports and couldn't maintain their own numbers because death rates exceeded birth rates. Since buying new slaves cost less than rearing slave children for twenty years until they were adults, slave owners lacked economic incentive to change this state of affairs.

Recall that Darwin discussed natural selection and survival of the fittest with respect to animals. Since many more animals die than survive to produce offspring, each generation becomes enriched in the genes of those of the preceding generation that were among the survivors. It should now be clear that slavery represented a tragedy of unnatural selection in humans on a gigantic scale. From examining accounts of slave mortality, Grim and Wilson argue that death was indeed selective: much of it was related to unbalanced salt loss, which quickly brings on collapse. We think immediately of salt loss by sweating under hot conditions: while slaves were working, marching, or confined in unventilated barracoons or ships' holds. More body salt may have been spilled with vomiting from seasickness. But the biggest salt loss at every stage was from diarrhea due to crowding and lack of sanitation—ideal conditions for the spread of gastrointestinal infections. Cholera and other bacterial diarrheas kill us by causing sudden massive loss of salt and water. (Picture your most recent bout of *turista*, multiplied to a diarrheal fluid output of twenty quarts in one day, and you'll understand why.) All contemporary accounts of slave ships and plantation life emphasized diarrhea, or "fluxes" in eighteenth-century terminology, as one of the leading killers of slaves.

Grim and Wilson reason, then, that slavery suddenly selected for superefficient kidneys surpassing the efficient kidneys already selected by thousands of years of

West African history. Only those slaves who were best able to retain salt could survive the periodic risk of high salt loss to which they were exposed. Salt supersavers would have had the further advantage of building up, under normal conditions, more of a salt reserve in their body fluids and bones, thereby enabling them to survive longer or more frequent bouts of diarrhea. Those superkidneys became a disadvantage only when modern medicine began to reduce diarrhea's lethal impact, thereby transforming a blessing into a curse.

Thus, we have two possible evolutionary explanations for salt retention by New World blacks. One involves slow selection by conditions operating in Africa for millennia; the other, rapid recent selection by slave conditions within the past few centuries. The result in either case would make New World blacks more susceptible than whites to hypertension, but the second explanation would, in addition, make them more susceptible than African blacks. At present, we don't know the relative importance of these two explanations. Grim and Wilson's provocative hypothesis is likely to stimulate medical and physiological comparisons of American blacks with African blacks and thereby to help resolve the question.

While this piece has focused on one medical problem in one human population, it has several large morals. One, of course, is that our differing genetic heritages predispose us to different diseases, depending on the part of the world where our ancestors lived. Another is that our genetic differences reflect not only ancient conditions in different parts of the world but also recent episodes of migration and mortality. A well-established example is the decrease in the frequency of the sickle-cell hemoglobin gene in U.S. blacks compared with African blacks, because selection for resistance to malaria is now unimportant in the United States. The example of black hypertension that Grim and Wilson discuss opens the door to considering other possible selective effects of the slave experience. They note that occasional periods of starvation might have selected slaves for superefficient sugar metabolism, leading under modern conditions to a propensity for diabetes.

Finally, consider a still more universal moral. Almost all people alive today exist under very different conditions from those under which every human lived 10,000 years ago. It's remarkable that our old genetic heritage now permits us to survive at all under such different circumstances. But our heritage still catches up with most of us, who will die of life style related diseases such as cancer, heart attack, stroke, and diabetes. The risk factors for these diseases are the strange new conditions prevailing in modern Western society. One of the hardest challenges for modern medicine will be to identify for us which among all those strange new features of diet, life style, and environment are the ones getting us into trouble. For each of us, the answers will depend on our ancestry. Only with such individually tailored advice can we hope to reap the benefits of modern living while still housed in bodies designed for life before saltshakers.

ID#_____   NAME_____

Article 5: The Saltshaker's Curse

1. How do American blacks differ from American whites in terms of:

    a. blood pressure

    b. hypertension

    c. heart disease

    d. kidney failure

    e. strokes

2. Name three environmental factors related to high blood pressure.

3. How might salt intake lead to high blood pressure?

4. What physiological differences are there between blacks and whites in relation to salt and hypertension?

5. Why are American blacks at more risk of hypertension than their West African ancestors?

Black, White, Other

Jonathan Marks

While reading the Sunday edition of the *New York Times* one morning last February, my attention was drawn by an editorial inconsistency. The article I was reading was written by attorney Lani Guinier. (Guinier, you may remember, had been President Clinton's nominee to head the civil rights division at the Department of Justice in 1993. Her name was hastily withdrawn amid a blast of criticism over her views on political representation of minorities.) What had distracted me from the main point of the story was a photo caption that described Guinier as being "half-black." In the text of the article, Guinier had described herself simply as "black."

How can a person be black and half black at the same time? In algebraic terms, this would seem to describe a situation where $x = 1/2x$, to which the only solution is $x = 0$.

The inconsistency in the *Times* was trivial, but revealing. It encapsulated a long-standing problem in our use of racial categories—namely, a confusion between biological and cultural heredity. When Guinier is described as "half-black," that is a statement of biological ancestry, for one of her two parents is black. And when Guinier describes herself as black, she is using a cultural category, according to which one can either be black or white, but not both.

Race—as the term is commonly used—is inherited, although not in a strictly biological fashion. It is passed down according to a system of folk heredity, an all-or-nothing system that is different from the quantifiable heredity of biology. But the incompatibility of the two notions of race is sometimes starkly evident—as when the state decides that racial differences are so important that interracial marriages must be regulated or outlawed entirely. Miscegenation laws in this country (which stayed on the books in many states through the 1960s) obliged the legal system to define who belonged in what category. The resulting formula stated that anyone with one-eighth or more black ancestry was a "Negro." (A similar formula, defining Jews, was promulgated by the Germans in the Nuremberg Laws of the 1930s.)

Applying such formulas led to the biological absurdity that having one black great-grandparent was sufficient to define a person as black, but having seven white great grandparents was insufficient to define a person as white. Here, race and biology are demonstrably at odds. And the

From *Natural History*, December 1994 by Jonathan Marks. Copyright © 1994 by Jonathan Marks. Reprinted by permission.

problem is not semantic but conceptual, for race is presented as a category of nature.

Human beings come in a wide variety of sizes, shapes, colors, and forms—or, because we are visually oriented primates, it certainly seems that way. We also come in larger packages called populations; and we are said to belong to even larger and more confusing units, which have long been known as races. The history of the study of human variation is to a large extent the pursuit of those human races—the attempt to identify the small number of fundamentally distinct kinds of people on earth.

This scientific goal stretches back two centuries, to Linnaeus, the father of biological systematics, who radically established *Homo sapiens* as one species within a group of animals he called Primates. Linnaeus's system of naming groups within groups logically implied further breakdown. He consequently sought to establish a number of subspecies within *Homo sapiens*. He identified five: four geographical species (from Europe, Asia, Africa, and America) and one grab-bag subspecies called *monstrosus*. This category was dropped by subsequent researchers (as was Linnaeus's use of criteria such as personality and dress to define his subspecies).

While Linnaeus was not the first to divide humans on the basis of the continents on which they lived, he had given the division a scientific stamp. But in attempting to determine the proper number of subspecies, the heirs of Linnaeus always seemed to find different answers, depending upon the criteria they applied. By the mid-twentieth century, scores of anthropologists—led by Harvard's Earnest Hooton—had expended enormous energy on the problem. But these scholars could not convince one another about the precise nature of the fundamental divisions of our species.

Part of the problem—as with the *Time's* identification of Lani Guinier—was that we humans have two constantly intersecting ways of thinking about the divisions among us. On the one hand, we like to think of "race"—as Linnaeus did—as an objective, biological category. In this sense, being a member of a race is supposed to be the equivalent of being a member of a species or of a phylum—except that race, on the analogy of subspecies, is an even narrower (and presumably more exclusive and precise) biological category.

The other kind of category into which we humans allocate ourselves—when we say "Serb" or "Hutu" or "Jew" or "Chicano" or "Republican" or "Red Sox fan"—is cultural. The label refers to little or nothing in the natural attributes of its members. These members may not live in the same region and may not even know many others like themselves. What they share is neither strictly nature nor strictly community. The groupings are constructions of human social history.

Membership in these *un*biological groupings may mean the difference between life and death, for they are the categories that allow us to be identified (and accepted or vilified) socially. While membership in (or allegiance to) these categories may be assigned or adopted from birth, the differentia that mark members from nonmembers are symbolic and abstract; they serve to distinguish people who cannot be readily distinguished by nature. So important are these symbolic distinctions that some of the strongest animosities are often expressed between very similar-looking peoples. Obvious examples are Bosnian Serbs and Muslims, Irish and English, Huron and Iroquois.

Obvious natural variation is rarely so important as cultural difference. One simply does not hear of a slaughter of the short people at the hands of the tall, the glabrous at the hands of the hairy, the red-haired at the hands of the brown-haired. When we do encounter genocidal violence between different looking peoples, the two groups are invariably socially or culturally distinct as well. Indeed, the tragic frequency of hatred and genocidal violence between biologically indistinguishable peoples implies that biological differences such as skin color are not motivations but, rather, excuses. They allow nature to be invoked to reinforce group identities and antagonisms that would exist without these physical distinctions. But are there any truly "racial" biological distinctions to be found in our species?

Obviously, if you compare two people from different parts of the world (or whose ancestors came from different parts of the world), they will differ physically, but one cannot therefore define three or four or five basically different kinds of people, as a biological notion of race would imply. The anatomical properties that distinguish people—such as pigmentation, eye form, body build—are not clumped in discrete groups, but distributed along geographical gradients, as are nearly all the genetically determined variants detectable in the human gene pool.

These gradients are produced by three forces. Natural selection adapts populations to local circumstances (like climate) and thereby differentiates them from other populations. Genetic drift (random fluctuations in a gene pool) also differentiates populations from one another, but in non-adaptive ways. And gene flow (via intermarriage and other child-producing unions) acts to homogenize neighboring populations.

In practice, the operations of these forces are difficult to discern. A few features, such as body build and the graduated distribution of the sickle cell anemia gene in populations from western Africa, southern Asia, and the Mediterranean can be plausibly related to the effects of selection. Others, such as the graduated distribution of a small deletion in the mitochondrial DNA of some East Asian, Oceanic, and Native American peoples, or the degree of flatness of the face, seem unlikely to be the result of selection and are probably the results of random biohistorical factors. The cause of the distribution of most features, from nose breadth to blood group, is simply unclear.

The overall result of these forces is evident, however. As Johann Friedrich Blumenbach noted in 1775, "you see that all do so run into one another, and that one variety of mankind does so sensibly pass into the other, that you cannot mark out the limits between them." (Posturing as an heir to Linnaeus, he nonetheless attempted to do so.) But from humanity's gradations in appearance, no defined groupings resembling races readily emerge. The racial categories with which we have become so familiar are the result of our imposing arbitrary cultural boundaries in order to partition gradual biological variation.

Unlike graduated biological distinctions, culturally constructed categories are ultra-sharp. One can be French or German, but not both; Tutsi or Hutu, but not both; Jew or Catholic, but not both; Bosnian Muslim or Serb, but not both; black or white, but not both. Traditionally, people of "mixed race" have been obliged to choose one and thereby identify themselves unambiguously to census takers and administrative bookkeepers—a practice that is now being widely called into question.

A scientific definition of race would require considerable homogeneity within each group, and reasonably discrete differences between groups, but three kinds of data militate against this view: First, the groups traditionally described as races are not at all homogeneous. Africans and Europeans, for instance, are each a collection of biologically diverse populations. Anthropologists of the 1920s widely recognized *three* European races: Nordic, Alpine, and Mediterranean. This implied that races could exist within races. American anthropologist Carleton Coon identified *ten* European races in 1939. With such protean use, the term race came to have little value in describing actual biological entities within *Homo sapiens*. The scholars were not only grappling with a broad north-south gradient in human appearance across Europe, they were trying to bring the data into line with their belief in profound and fundamental constitutional differences between groups of people.

But there simply isn't one European race to contrast with an African race, nor three, nor ten; the question (as scientists long posed it) fails to recognize the actual patterning of diversity in the human species. Fieldwork revealed, and genetics later quantified, the existence of far more biological diversity within any group than between groups. Fatter and thinner people exist everywhere, as do people with type O and type A blood. What generally varies from one population to the next is the *proportion* of people in these groups expressing the trait or gene. Hair color varies strikingly among Europeans and native Australians, but little among other peoples. To focus on discovering differences between presumptive races, when the vast majority of detectable variants do not help differentiate them, was thus to define a very narrow—if not largely illusory—problem in human biology. (The fact that Africans are biologically more diverse than Europeans, but have rarely been split into so many races, attests to the cultural basis of these categorizations.)

Second, differences between human groups are only evident when contrasting geographical extremes. Noting these extremes, biologists of an earlier era sought to identify representatives of "pure," primordial races presumably located in Norway, Senegal, and Thailand. At no time, however, was our species composed of a few populations within which everyone looked pretty much the same. Ever since some of our ancestors left Africa to spread out through the Old World, we humans have always lived in the "in-between" places. And human populations have also always been in genetic contact with one another. Indeed, for tens of thousands of years, humans have had trade networks; and where goods flow, so do genes. Consequently, we have no basis for considering *extreme* human forms the most pure, or most representative, of some ancient primordial populations. Instead, they represent populations adapted to the most disparate environments.

And third, between each presumptive "major" race are unclassifiable populations and people. Some populations of India, for example, are darkly pigmented (or "black"), have Europeanlike ("Caucasoid") facial features, but inhabit the continent of Asia (which should make them "Asian"). Americans might tend to ignore these "exceptions" to the racial categories, since immigrants to the United States from West Africa, Southeast Asia, and northwest Europe far outnumber those from India. The very existence of unclassifiable peoples undermines the idea that there are just three human biological groups in the Old World. Yet acknowledging the biological distinctiveness of such groups, leads to a rapid proliferation of categories. What about Australians? Polynesians? The Ainu of Japan?

Categorizing people is important to any society. It is, at some basic psychological level, probably necessary to have group identity about who and what you are, in contrast to who and what you are not. The concept of race, however, specifically involves the recruitment of biology to validate those categories of self-identity.

Mice don't have to worry about that the way humans do. Consequently, classifying them into subspecies entails less of a responsibility for a scientist than classifying humans into sub-species does. And by the 1960s, most anthropologists realized they could not defend any classification of *Homo sapiens* into biological subspecies or races that could be considered reasonably objective. They therefore stopped doing it, and stopped identifying the endeavor as a central goal of the field. It was a biologically intractable problem—the old square-peg-in-a-round-hole enterprise; and people's lives, or welfares, could well depend on the ostensibly scientific pronouncement. Reflecting on the social history of the twentieth century, that was a burden anthropologists would no longer bear.

This conceptual divorce in anthropology—of cultural from biological phenomena was one of the most fundamental scientific revolutions of our time. And since it affected assumptions so rooted in our everyday experience, and resulted in conclusions so counterintuitive—like the idea that the earth goes around the sun, and not vice-versa—it has been widely underappreciated.

Kurt Vonnegut, in *Slaughterhouse Five*, describes what he remembered being taught about human variation: "At that time, they were teaching that there was absolutely no difference between anybody. They may be teaching that still." Of course there are biological differences between people, and between populations. The question is: How are those differences patterned? And the answer seems to be: Not racially. Populations are the only readily identifiable units of humans, and even they are fairly fluid, biologically similar to populations nearby, and biologically different from populations far away.

In other words, the message of contemporary anthropology is: You may group humans into a small number of races if you want to, but you are denied biology as a support for it.

ID#_____   NAME_____

Article 6: Black, White, Other

1. What is the difference between biological and social race?

2. The author describes membership in "unbiological groupings" that allows individuals to be identified socially. What differentiates members from nonmembers in these groups?

3. Genocidal violence between different looking peoples is also based on what type of differences?

4. The anatomical features that distinguish people are distributed as _____ , not discrete groups.

5. What three forces influence these anatomical differences?

6. Why does the term race have such little value in describing human biological variation?

7. Briefly describe the three kinds of data that contradict the idea of a scientific definition of race.

8. Does the author believe there are biological differences between people? If so, in what way?

Racial Odyssey

Boyce Rensberger

The human species comes in an artist's palette of colors: sandy yellows, reddish tans, deep browns, light tans, creamy whites, pale pinks. It is a rare person who is not curious about the skin colors, hair textures, bodily structures and facial features associated with racial background. Why do some Africans have dark brown skin, while that of most Europeans is pale pink? Why do the eyes of most "white" people and "black" people look pretty much alike but differ so from the eyes of Orientals? Did one race evolve before the others? If so, is it more primitive or more advanced as a result? Can it be possible, as modern research suggests, that there is no such thing as a pure race? These are all honest, scientifically worthy questions. And they are central to current research on the evolution of our species on the planet Earth.

Broadly speaking, research on racial differences has led most scientists to three major conclusions. The first is that there are many more differences among people than skin color, hair texture and facial features. Dozens of other variations have been found, ranging from the shapes of bones to the consistency of ear wax to subtle variations in body chemistry.

The second conclusion is that the overwhelming evolutionary success of the human species is largely due to its great genetic variability. When migrating bands of our early ancestors reached a new environment, at least a few already had physical traits that gave them an edge in surviving there. If the coming centuries bring significant environmental changes, as many believe they will, our chances of surviving them will be immeasurably enhanced by our diversity as a species.

There is a third conclusion about race that is often misunderstood. Despite our wealth of variation and despite our constant, everyday references to race, no one has ever discovered a reliable way of distinguishing one race from another. While it is possible to classify a great many people on the basis of certain physical features, there are no known feature or groups of features that will do the job in all cases.

Skin color won't work. Yes, most Africans from south of the Sahara and their descendants around the world have skin that is darker than that of most Europeans. But there are millions of people in India, classified by some anthropologists as members of the Caucasoid, or "white," race who have darker skins than most Americans who call themselves black. And there are many Africans living in sub-Sahara Africa

From *Science Digest*, January/February 1981. © 1981 by Boyce Rensberger. Reprinted by permission.

today whose skins are no darker than the skins of many Spaniards, Italians, Greeks or Lebanese.

What about stature as a racial trait? Because they are quite short, on the average, African Pygmies have been considered racially distinct from other dark-skinned Africans. If stature, then, is a racial criterion, would one include in the same race the tall African Watusi and the Scandinavians of similar stature?

The little web of skin that distinguishes Oriental eyes is said to be a particular feature of the Mongoloid race. How, then, can it be argued that the American Indian, who lacks this epicanthic fold, is Mongoloid?

Even more hopeless as racial markers are hair color, eye color, hair form, the shapes of noses and lips or any of the other traits put forth as typical of one race or another.

No Norms

Among the tall people of the world there are many black, many white and many in between. Among black people of the world there are many with kinky hair, many with straight or wavy hair, and many in between. Among the broad-nosed, full-lipped people of the world there are many with dark skins, many with light skins and many in between.

How did our modern perceptions of race arise? One of the first to attempt a scientific classification of peoples was Carl von Linné, better known as Linnaeus. In 1735, he published a classification that remains the standard today. As Linnaeus saw it there were four races, classifiable geographically and by skin color. The names Linnaeus gave them were *Homo sapiens Africanus nigrus* (black African human being), *H. sapiens Americanus rubescens* (red American human being), *H. sapiens Asiaticus fuscusens* (brownish Asian human being), and *H. sapiens Europaeus albescens* (white European human being). All, Linnaeus recognized, were members of a single human species.

A species includes all individuals that are biologically capable of interbreeding and producing fertile offspring. Most matings between species are fruitless, and even when they succeed, as when a horse and a donkey interbreed and produce a mule, the progeny are sterile. When a poodle mates with a collie, however, the offspring are fertile, showing that both dogs are members of the same species.

Even though Linnaeus's system of nomenclature survives, his classifications were discarded, especially after voyages of discovery revealed that there were many more kinds of people than could be pigeonholed into four categories. All over the world there are small populations that don't fit. Among the better known are:

- The so-called Bushmen of southern Africa, who look as much Mongoloid as Negroid.
- The Negritos of the South Pacific, who do look Negroid but are very far from Africa and have no known links to that continent.
- The Ainu of Japan, a hairy aboriginal people who look more Caucasoid than anything else.
- The Lapps of Scandinavia, who look as much like Eskimos as like Europeans.
- The aborigines of Australia, who often look Negroid but many of whom have straight or wavy hair and are often blond as children.
- The Polynesians, who seem to be a blend of many races, the proportions differing from island to island.

To accommodate such diversity, many different systems of classification have been proposed. Some set up two or three dozen races. None has ever satisfied all experts.

Classification System

Perhaps the most sweeping effect to impose a classification upon all the peoples of the world was made by the American

> ## Disease Origins
>
> The gene for sickle cell anemia, a disease found primarily among black people, appears to have evolved because its presence can render its bearer resistant to malaria. Such a trait would have obvious value in tropical Africa.
>
> A person who has sickle cell anemia must have inherited genes for the disease from both parents. If a child inherits only one sickle cell gene, he or she will be resistant to malaria but will not have the anemia. Paradoxically, inheriting genes from both parents does not seem to affect resistance to malaria.
>
> In the United States, where malaria is practically nonexistent, the sickle cell gene confers no survival advantage and is disappearing. Today only about 1 out of every 10 American blacks carries the gene.
>
> Many other inherited diseases are found only in people from a particular area. Tay-Sachs disease, which often kills before the age of two, is almost entirely confined to Jews from parts of Eastern Europe and their descendants elsewhere.
>
> Paget's disease, a bone disorder, is found most often among those of English descent. Impacted wisdom teeth are a common problem among Asians and Europeans but not among Africans. Children of all races are able to digest milk because their bodies make lactase, the enzyme that breaks down lactose, or milk sugar. But the ability to digest lactose in adulthood is a racially distributed trait.
>
> About 90 percent of Orientals and blacks lose this ability by the time they reach adulthood and become quite sick when they drink milk.
>
> Even African and Asian herders who keep cattle or goats rarely drink fresh milk. Instead, they first treat the milk with fermentation bacteria that break down lactose, in a sense predigesting it. They can then ingest the milk in the form of yogurt or cheese without any problem.
>
> About 90 percent of Europeans and their American descendants, on the other hand, continue to produce the enzyme throughout their lives and can drink milk with no ill effects.

anthropologist Carleton Coon. He concluded there are five basic races, two of which have major subdivisions: Caucasoids; Mongoloids; full-size Australoids (Australian aborigines); dwarf Australoids (Negritos—Andaman Islanders and similar peoples); full-size Congoids (African Negroids); dwarf Congoids (African Pygmies); and Capoids (the so-called Bushmen and Hottentots).

In his 1965 classic, *The Living Races of Man*, Coon hypothesized that before A.D. 1500 there were five pure races—five centers of human population that were so isolated that there was almost no mixing.

Each of these races evolved independently, Coon believed, diverging from a pre-*Homo sapiens* stock that was essentially the same everywhere. He speculated that the common ancestor evolved into *Homo sapiens* in five separate regions at five different times, beginning about 35,000 years ago. The populations that have been *Homo sapiens* for the shortest period of time, Coon said, are the world's "less civilized" races.

The five pure races remained distinct until A.D. 1500; then Europeans started sailing the world, leaving their genes—as sailors always have—in every port and planting distant colonies. At about the same time, thousands of Africans were captured and forcibly settled in many parts of the New World.

That meant the end of the five pure races. But Coon and other experts held that this did not necessarily rule out the idea of distinct races. In this view, there *are* such things as races; people just don't fit into them very well anymore.

The truth is that there is really no hard evidence to suggest that five or any particular number of races evolved independently. The preponderance of evidence today suggests that as traits typical of fully modern people arose in any one place, they spread quickly to all human populations. Advances in intelligence were almost certainly the fastest to spread. Most anthropologists and geneticists now believe that human beings have always been subject to migrating and mixing. In other words, there probably never were any such things as pure races.

Race mixing has not only been a fact of human history but is, in this day of unprecedented global mobility, taking place at a more rapid rate than ever. It is not farfetched to envision the day when, generations hence, the entire "complexion" of major population centers will be different. Meanwhile, we can see such changes taking place before our eyes, for they are a part of everyday reality.

Hybrid Vigor

Oddly, those who assert scientific validity for their notions of pure and distinct races seem oblivious of a basic genetic principle that plant and animal breeders know well: too much inbreeding can lead to proliferation of inferior traits. Crossbreeding with different strains often produces superior combinations of "hybrid vigor."

The striking differences among people may very well be a result of constant genetic mixing. And as geneticists and ecologists know, in diversity lies strength and resilience.

To understand the origin and proliferation of human differences, one must first know how Darwinian evolution works.

Evolution is a two-step process. Step one is mutation: somehow a gene in the ovary or testes of an individual is altered, changing the molecular configuration that stores instructions for forming a new individual. The children who inherit that gene will be different in some way from their ancestors.

Step two is selection: for a racial difference, or any other evolutionary change to arise, it must survive and be passed through several generations. If the mutation confers some disadvantage, the individual dies, often during embryonic development. But if the change is beneficial in some way, the individual should have a better chance of thriving than relatives lacking the advantage.

Natural Selection

If a new trait is beneficial, it will bring reproductive success to its bearer. After several generations of multiplication, bearers of the new trait may begin to outnumber nonbearers. Darwin called this natural selection to distinguish it from the artificial selection exercised by animal breeders.

Skin color is the human racial trait most generally thought to confer an evolutionary advantage of this sort. It has long been obvious in the Old World that the farther south one goes, the darker the skin color. Southern Europeans are usually somewhat darker than northern Europeans. In North Africa, skin colors are darker still, and, as one travels south, coloration reaches its maximum at the Equator. The same progressions holds in Asia, with the lightest skins to the north. Again, as one moves south, skin color darkens, reaching in southern India a "blackness" equal to that of equatorial Africans.

This north-south spectrum of skin color derives from varying intensities of the same dark brown pigment called melanin. Skin cells simply have more or less melanin granules to be seen against a background that is pinkish because of the underlying blood vessels. All races can increase their melanin concentration by exposure to the sun.

What is it about northerly latitudes in the Northern Hemisphere that favors less pigmentation and about southerly latitudes that favors more? Exposure to intense sunlight is not the only reason why people living in southerly latitudes are dark. A person's susceptibility to rickets and skin cancer, his ability to withstand cold and to see in the dark may also be related to skin color.

The best-known explanation says the body can tolerate only a narrow range of intensities of sunlight. Too much causes sunburn and cancer, while too little deprives the body of vitamin D, which is synthesized in the skin under the influence of sunlight. A dark complexion protects the skin from the harmful effects of intense sunlight. Thus, albinos born in equatorial regions have a high rate of skin cancer. On the other hand, dark skin in northerly latitudes screens out sunlight needed for the synthesis of vitamin D. Thus, dark-skinned children living in northern latitudes had high rates of rickets—a bone-deforming disease caused by a lack of vitamin D—before their milk was routinely fortified. In the sunny tropics, dark skin admits enough light to produce the vitamin.

Recently, there has been some evidence that skin colors are linked to differences in the ability to avoid injury from the cold. Army researchers found that during the Korean War blacks were more susceptible to frostbite than were whites. Even among Norwegian soldiers in World War II, brunettes had a slightly higher incidence of frostbite than did blonds.

Eye Pigmentation

A third link between color and latitude involves the sensitivity of the eye to various wavelengths of light. It is known that dark-skinned people have more pigmentation in the iris of the eye and at the back of the eye where the image falls. It has been found that the less pigmented the eye, the more sensitive it is to colors at the red end of the spectrum. In situations illuminated with reddish light, the northern European can see more than a dark African sees.

It has been suggested that Europeans developed lighter eyes to adapt to the longer twilights of the North and their greater reliance on firelight to illuminate caves.

Although the skin cancer-vitamin D hypothesis enjoys wide acceptance, it may well be that resistance to cold, possession of good night vision and other yet unknown factors all played roles in the evolution of skin colors.

Most anthropologists agree that the original human skin color was dark brown, since it is fairly well established that human beings evolved in the tropics of Africa. This does not, however, mean that the first people were Negroids, whose descendants, as they moved north, evolved into light-skinned Caucasoids. It is more likely that the skin color of various populations changed several times from dark to light and back as people moved from one region to another.

Consider, for example, that long before modern people evolved, *Homo erectus* had spread throughout Africa, Europe and Asia. The immediate ancestor of *Homo sapiens, Homo erectus*, was living in Africa 1.5 million years ago and in Eurasia 750,000 years ago. The earliest known forms of *Homo sapiens* do not make their appearance until somewhere between 250,000 and 500,000 years ago. Although there is no evidence of the skin color of any hominid fossil, it is probable that the *Homo erectus* population in Africa had dark skin. As subgroups spread into northern latitudes, mutations that reduced pigmentation conferred survival advantages on them and lighter skins came to predominate. In other words, there were probably black *Homo erectus* peoples in Africa and white ones in Europe and Asia.

Did the black *Homo erectus* populations evolve into today's Negroids and the white ones in Europe into today's Caucasoids? By all the best evidence, nothing like this happened. More likely, wherever *Homo sapiens* arose it proved so superior to the *Homo erectus* populations that it eventually replaced them everywhere.

If the first *Homo sapiens* evolved in Africa, they were probably dark-skinned; those who migrated northward into Eurasia lost their pigmentation. But it is just as possible that the first *Homo sapiens* appeared in northern climes, descendants of white-skinned *Homo erectus*. These could have migrated southward toward Africa, evolving darker skins. All modern races, incidentally, arose long after the brain had reached its present size in all parts of the world.

North-south variations in pigmentation are quite common among mammals and birds. The tropical races tend to be darker in fur and feather, the desert races tend to be brown, and those near the Arctic Circle are lighter colored.

There are exceptions among humans. The Indians of the Americas, from the Arctic to the southern regions of South America, do not conform to the north-south scheme of coloration. Though most think of Indians as being reddish-brown, most Indians tend to be relatively light skinned, much like their presumed Mongoloid ancestors in Asia. The ruddy complexion that lives in so many stereotypes of Indians is merely what years of heavy tanning can produce in almost any light-skinned person. Anthropologists explain the color consistency as a consequence of the relatively recent entry of people into the Americas—probably between 12,000 and 35,000 years ago. Perhaps they have not yet had time to change.

Only a few external physical differences other than color appear to have adaptive significance. The strongest cases can be made for nose shape and stature.

What's in a Nose

People native to colder or drier climates tend to have longer, more beak-shaped noses than those living in hot and humid regions. The nose's job is to warm and humidify air before it reaches sensitive lung tissues. The colder or drier the air is, the more surface area is needed inside the nose to get it to the right temperature or humidity. Whites tend to have longer and beakier noses than blacks or Orientals. Nevertheless, there is great variation within races. Africans in the highlands of East Africa have longer noses than Africans from the hot, humid lowlands, for example.

Stature differences are reflected in the tendency for most northern peoples to have shorter arms, legs and torsos and to be stockier than people from the tropics. Again, this is an adaptation to heat or cold. One way of reducing heat loss is to have less body surface, in relation to weight or volume, from which heat can escape. To avoid overheating, the most desirable body is long limbed and lean. As a result, most Africans tend to be lankier than northern Europeans. Arctic peoples are the shortest limbed of all.

Hair forms may also have a practical role to play, but the evidence is weak. It has been suggested that the more tightly curled hair of Africans insulates the top of the head better than does straight or wavy hair. Contrary to expectation, black hair serves better in this role than white hair. Sunlight is absorbed and converted to heat at the outer surface of the hair blanket; it radiates directly into the air. White fur, common on Arctic animals that need to absorb solar heat, is actually transparent and transmits light into the hair blanket, allowing the heat to form within the insulating layer, where it is retained for warmth.

Aside from these examples, there is little evidence that any of the other visible differences among the world's people provide any advantage. Nobody knows, for example, why Orientals have epicanthic eye folds or flatter facial profiles. The thin lips of Caucasoids and most Mongoloids have no known advantages over the Negroid's full lips. Why should middle-aged and older Caucasoid men go bald so much more frequently than the men of other races? Why does the skin of Bushmen wrinkle so heavily in the middle and later years? Or why does the skin of Negroids resist wrinkling so well? Why do the Indian men in one part of South America have blue penises? Why do Hottentot women have such unusually large buttocks?

There are possible evolutionary explanations for why such apparently useless differences arise.

One is a phenomenon known as sexual selection. Environmentally adaptive traits arise, Darwin thought, through natural selection—the environment itself chooses who will thrive or decline. In sexual selection, which Darwin also suggested, the choice belongs to the prospective mate.

In simple terms, ugly individuals will be less likely to find mates and reproduce their genes than beautiful specimens will. Take the blue penis as an example. Women might find it unusually attractive or perhaps believe it to be endowed with special powers. If so, a man born with a blue penis will find many more opportunities to reproduce his genes than his ordinary brothers.

Sexual selection can also operate when males compete for females. The moose with the larger antlers or the lion with the more imposing mane will stand a better chance of discouraging less well-endowed males and gaining access to females. It is possible that such a process operated among Caucasoid males, causing them to become markedly hairy, especially around the face.

Attractive Traits

Anthropologists consider it probable that traits such as the epicanthic fold or the many regional differences in facial features were selected this way.

Yet another method by which a trait can establish itself involves accidental selection. It results from what biologists call genetic drift.

Suppose that in a small nomadic band a person is born with perfectly parallel fingerprints instead of the usual loops, whorls or arches. That person's children would inherit parallel fingerprints, but they would confer no survival advantages. But if our family decides to strike out on its own, it will become the founder of a new band consisting of its own descendants, all with parallel fingerprints.

Events such as this, geneticists and anthropologists believe, must have occurred many times in the past to produce the great variety within the human species. Among the apparently neutral traits that differ among populations are:

Ear Wax

There are two types of ear wax. One is dry and crumbly and the other is wet and sticky. Both types can be found in every major population, but the frequencies differ. Among northern Chinese, for example, 98 percent have dry ear wax. Among American whites, only 16 percent have dry ear wax. Among American blacks the figure is 7 percent.

Scent Glands

As any bloodhound knows, every person has his or her own distinctive scent. People vary in the mixture of odoriferous compounds exuded through the skin—most of it coming from specialized glands called apocrine glands. Among whites, these are concentrated in the armpits and near the genitals and anus. Among blacks, they may also be found on the chest and abdomen. Orientals have hardly any apocrine glands at all. In the words of the Oxford biologist John R. Baker, "The Europids and Negrids are smelly, the Mongoloids scarcely or not at all." Smelliest of all are northern European, or so-called Nordic, whites. Body odor is rare in Japan. It was once thought to indicate a European in the ancestry and to be a disease requiring hospitalization.

Blood Groups

Some populations have a high percentage of members with a particular blood group. American Indians are overwhelmingly group O—100 percent in some regions. Group A is most common among Australian aborigines and the Indians in western Canada. Group B is frequent in northern India, other parts of Asia and western Africa.

Advocates of the pure-race theory once seized upon blood groups as possibly unique to the original pure races. The proportions of groups found today, they thought, would indicate the degree of mixing. It was subsequently found that chimpanzees, our closest living relatives, have the same blood groups as humans.

Taste

PTC (phenylthiocarbamide) is a synthetic compound that some people can taste and others cannot. The ability to taste it has no known survival value, but it is clearly an inherited trait. The proportion of persons who can taste PTC varies in different populations: 50 to 70 percent of Australian aborigines can taste it, as can 60 to 80 percent of all Europeans. Among East Asians, the percentage is 83 to 100 percent, and among Africans, 90 to 97 percent.

Urine

Another indicator of differences in body chemistry is the excretion of a compound known as BAIB (beta-amino-isobutyric acid) in urine. Europeans seldom excrete large quantities, but high levels of excretion are common among Asians and American Indians. It has been shown that the differences are not due to diet.

No major population has remained isolated long enough to prevent any unique genes from eventually mixing with those of neighboring groups. Indeed, a map showing the distribution of so-called traits would have no sharp boundaries, except for coastlines. The intensity of a trait such as skin color, which is controlled by six pairs of genes and can therefore exist in many shades, varies gradually from one population to another. With only a few exceptions, every known genetic possibility possessed by the species can be found to some degree in every sizable population.

Ever-Changing Species

One can establish a system of racial classification simply by listing the features of populations at any given moment. Such a concept of race is, however, inappropriate to a highly mobile and ever-changing species such as *Homo sapiens*. In the short view, races may seem distinguishable, but in biology's long haul, races come and go. New ones arise and blend into neighboring groups to create new and racially stable populations. In time, genes from these groups flow into other neighbors, continuing the production of new permutations.

Some anthropologists contend that at the moment American blacks should be considered a race distinct from African blacks. They argue that American blacks are a hybrid of African blacks and European whites. Indeed, the degree of mixture can be calculated on the basis of a blood component known as the Duffy factor.

In West Africa, where most of the New World's slaves came from, the Duffy factor is virtually absent. It is present in 43 percent of American whites. From the number of American blacks who are now "Duffy positive" it can be calculated that whites contributed 21 percent of the genes in the American black population. The figure is higher for blacks in northern and western states and lower in the South. By the same token, there are whites who have black ancestors. The number is smaller because of the tendency to identify a person as black even if only a minor fraction of his ancestors were originally from Africa.

The unwieldiness of race designations is also evident in places such as Mexico where most of the people are, in effect, hybrids of Indians (Mongoloid by some classifications) and Spaniards (Caucasoid). Many South American populations are trihybrids—mixtures of Mongoloid, Caucasoid and Negroid. Brazil is a country where the mixture has been around long enough to constitute a racially stable population. Thus, in one sense, new races have been created in the United States, Mexico and Brazil. But in the long run, those races will again change.

Sherwood Washburn, a noted anthropologist, questions the usefulness of racial classification: "Since races are open systems which are intergrading, the number of races will depend on the purpose of the classification. I think we should require people who propose a classification of races to state in the first place why they wish to divide the human species."

The very notion of a pure race, then, makes no sense. But, as evolutionists know full well, a rich genetic diversity within the human species most assuredly *does*.

ID#_____   NAME_____

Article 7: Racial Odyssey

1. What three major conclusions have been drawn from the research on racial differences?

2. Why can't we use skin color to classify people into races?

3. Define: species.

4. Describe two of the "small populations that don't fit" into strict racial categories.

5. What contributions did Coon make?

63

6. What does the author mean by "hybrid vigor?"

7. What is the relationship between skin color and distance to the equator?

8. What is the relationship between sunlight and vitamin D?

9. How does sexual selection work? Provide one possible example.

10. Describe one of the "neutral traits" that differ among populations? How might this be an example of genetic drift?

From Pan to Pandemic

Robin A. Weiss and Richard W. Wrangham

The origin of human immunodeficiency virus type 1 (HIV-1), the retrovirus that is the main cause of AIDS, has been a puzzle ever since it was discovered by Barré-Sinoussi and her colleagues[1] in 1983. *Gao et al.[2] [have provided] the most persuasive evidence yet that HIV-1 came to humans from the chimpanzee, *Pan troglodytes*, which harbours a related simian immunodeficiency virus, SIV cpz. Moreover, by genetic typing of mitochondrial DNA, it is clear that the three strains of SIV cpz most closely related to HIV-1 come from a single subspecies, *Pan troglodytes troglodytes*, which lives in the same part of central Africa where AIDS is thought to have arisen.

There are three principal groups of HIV-1: the main (M) group comprises the majority of subtypes that have spread across the world; an outlier (O) group is found in Cameroon, Gabon and Equatorial Guinea; and a new group (N) was last year identified in two people in Cameroon[3]. HIV genetic sequences from a Congolese serum sample, originally taken in 1959, showed that the diversification of all the M subtypes has occurred in very recent times, say the past 50 years[4]. Gao and colleagues' evolutionary analysis of the M, N and O groups in comparison to SIV cpz isolates indicates that these HIV-1 groups represent three separate transfers from chimpanzees to humans (such inter-species transmissions of infectious disease are known as zoonoses).

It has been shown[5,6] previously that several strains of HIV-2 in West Africa were independently derived from SIVsm, the virus endemic in the sooty mangabey monkeys of that region. The other human retroviral pathogen, human T-lymphotropic virus type 1 (HTLV-1), has also originated more than once from related simian viruses, including STLV-1 of chimpanzees[7,8]. And a new paper[9] reporting a parallel zoonosis to that of Gao et al.[2] has demonstrated that human pygmies in Gabon are infected with a strain of HTLV-1 that is virtually indistinguishable from STLV-1 of mandrills living in the same forest. Finally, a survey of people who handle primates in captivity recorded several instances of foamy retrovirus transmission and one transfer of SIVmac[10], the strain that causes AIDS in macaques.

So cross-species transmission of primate retroviruses to humans through hunting or husbandry probably occurs relatively frequently, although—thankfully—the subsequent epidemic spread in the human

Reprinted by permission from *Nature*, February 4, 1999, Volume 397, copyright 1999, Macmillan Publishers Ltd.

population is a much rarer event. Such zoonoses have heightened the concern that retroviruses might also cross to humans from more distant species, such as pigs, if their tissues were used for xenotransplantation[11].

Gao et al.[2] also show that a chimpanzee called Noah, from which a highly divergent strain, SIVcpzANT, was isolated, actually belongs to the different subspecies *Pan troglodytes schweinfurthii**. Gao et al. argue that SIVcpz is an ancient chimpanzee infection that has co-evolved with its host during subspeciation. They previously followed the same logic for the diversification of SIVagm among the various subspecies of African green monkey[12]. But these monkeys, like the chimpanzee subspecies, have largely non-overlapping habitats, so it is also conceivable that SIVs were more recently introduced and owe their diversity to geography rather than co-evolution.

Indeed, the ability of SIV to jump host species, together with the demonstration by Gao et al. that one strain of SIVcpz is (like HIV-1E in Thailand) derived from genetic recombination between two distinct parent strains, suggests that the co-evolution hypothesis needs to be viewed with a little caution. To bolster Gao and colleagues' conclusion that chimpanzees are a natural reservoir population for the precursor of HIV-1, serological surveys for the prevalence of SIVcpz infection are required in wild populations in Africa.

The ramifications of the new findings[2] extend well beyond the evolution of HIV-1, and zoonotic transmission of disease, to chimpanzee conservation and welfare. Like the other great apes, chimpanzees are in trouble. In most of the 21 African countries where they live in the wild, their numbers are plummeting—partly because of habitat loss, and partly because ape-hunting has become big business. Hunters are paid by timber companies to provision logging camps, while the kills of freelance hunters are traded as far as the cities. Ape meat can fetch premium prices in middle-class restaurants.

The "ape bushmeat crisis" cannot last long. Numbers are hard to come by, but some estimates of the annual chimpanzee kill are in the thousands, which is an unsustainably high figure when as long as a decade ago the world population was estimated at around 200,000. In the face of such an onslaught, populations of the large, slowly reproducing apes will be swiftly eradicated[13].

Hunters dismember chimpanzees with primitive butchery, and so expose themselves to the risk of zoonotically transmitted disease. Conservationists, therefore, are debating the merits of a campaign that would publicize the disease-transmitting dangers of treating apes as food. Some are concerned that this could backfire, and result in intensified slaughter of the primates, whereas others think the situation could hardly get worse. Later this month, a meeting hosted by the American Zoological Association aims to turn discussion into action. In the long term, apes will survive in the wild only where they are not eaten, a prospect that depends on the acceptance of new values by which apes are treated as too human-like to kill or eat. Many believe that new ethics are also needed in the scientific world. To some AIDS researchers, the use of chimpanzees is constrained merely by their high cost and scarcity[14]. By 1996, 198 chimpanzees had been experimentally infected with HIV in six of the major research institutions in the United States[15], although HIV seldom causes disease in these animals.

Worldwide, there are now about 35 million carriers of HIV-1, and with the increased evidence that the virus is linked to SIVcpz there may be calls for more use of chimpanzees in AIDS research. But according to a growing constituency, evidence of ape possession of human-like

---

*Editorial omission.

cognition and emotions should reduce our willingness to infect them, and condemn them to solitary confinement for life (which lasts for 60 years or more)[16].

The approach of Gao et al. may prompt fresh thinking. Fieldwork with free-living apes provided information for the evolutionary history of chimpanzee subspecies that was critical to their results. Further fieldwork linking demographic data to biomedical monitoring could be even more productive. The four chimpanzee subspecies have deep evolutionary roots, and may yield further types of SIV beyond the two already identified. These are best studied in the place where the host-virus systems evolved. Chimpanzees in captivity are mostly taken from the wild before they become sexually active, and so rarely harbour SIV. Infection can be expected at higher frequencies in wild adults[17], and such individuals would offer research opportunities that simply do not pertain in captivity, where experimenters cannot know how virus strains match to genetic lineages.

Two other ways forward are these. Field researchers intermittently find fresh corpses of individual apes, often with well-documented life-histories, which offer untapped possibilities for virological analysis. And DNA studies of faeces might allow noninvasive monitoring of virus infection.

Biomedical researchers have the prospect of collaborating with fieldworkers in a synthesis that would benefit conservation. The link between HIV-1 and SIVcpz may open a door for research that helps both humans and apes.

References

1. Barré-Sinoussi, F. et al. Science **220,** 868–871 (1983).
2. Gao, F. et al. Nature **397,** 436–441 (1999).
3. Simon, F. et al. Nature Med. **4,** 1032–1037 (1998).
4. Zhu, T. et al. Nature **391,** 594–597 (1998).
5. Gao, F. et al. Nature **358,** 495–499 (1992).
6. Chen, Z. et al. J. Virol. **71,** 3953–3960 (1997).
7. Koralnik, I. J. et al. J. Virol. **68,** 2693–2707 (1994).
8. Voevodin, A. et al. Virology **238,** 212–220 (1997).
9. Mahieux, R. et al. J. Virol. **72,** 10316–10322 (1998).
10. Heneine, W. et al. Nature Med. **4,** 403–407 (1998).
11. Weiss, R. A. Nature **391,** 327–328 (1998).
12. Sharp, P. M., Robertson, D. L. & Hahn, B. H. Phil. Trans. R. Soc. B **349,** 41–47 (1995).
13. Wilkie, D. S. & Carpenter, J. Biodivers. Conserv. (in the press).
14. Letvin, N. L. Science **280,** 1875–1880 (1997).
15. National Research Council Chimpanzees in Research: Strategies for Their Ethical Care, Management, and Use (NRC, Washington, DC, 1996).
16. Singer, P. & Cavalieri, P. (eds) The Great Ape Project (St. Martin's, New York, 1994).
17. Jolly, C. J. et al. J. Med. Primatol. **25,** 78–83 (1996).

ID#_____   NAME_____

Article 8: From *Pan* to Pandemic

1. Why do scientists think HIV-1 came to humans from the chimpanzee?

2. What is the origin of HIV-2?

3. Define: zoonoses.

4. In what two ways are primate retroviruses transmitted to humans?

5. List two reasons why chimpanzee numbers are rapidly declining.

6. While some might argue that chimps should be studied in captivity, many others argue that apes possess _____ and _____ , which should reduce our willingness to infect chimpanzees for study.

7. Name three ways in which studying chimpanzees in the wild would be more beneficial than in captivity.

Section II:
The Primates

The Primate Order is a diverse and fascinating array of animals to which humans belong. Linked by our reliance on vision as opposed to smell, our grasping hands and feet with five digits, long prenatal care, long life, complex social structures and interpersonal relationships, and the importance of learning and the mother infant bond, primates provide us with insight into our own place in the world and are an interesting field of study in their own right. Much of what we have learned about the non-human primates over the past decades has challenged our understanding of what it means to be human. The articles selected for this section explore the rich diversity found in primates, focusing primarily on behavior and adaptation. Many primates are highly endangered, and must be protected if we want their legacy to survive.

The first article by Frans de Waal, *Are We in Anthropodenial?*, discusses anthropomorphism and explores the idea that animals have human qualities and emotions. This is followed by a series of articles (#10-12, 14-15) covering all major groups in the primate order: prosimians, New World monkeys, Old World monkeys, and the apes.

In *Prosimians Find a Home Far from Home*, the mission of the Duke University Primate Research Center is explained along with an excellent discussion of how the prosimians differ from the so-called "higher primates" the monkeys and apes. The article also takes a look at some of the unique behaviors and adaptations of the prosimians housed at their center.

The next two articles explore some adaptations and interesting behaviors in the monkeys. In *Menu for a Monkey*, author and primatologist Karen Strier describes her research with the South American muriqui monkey. She links the dietary adaptations of the muriqui with their social structure and social behavior in an excellent exploration of local environmental adaptation. As an added benefit, Strier also describes how the muriqui differs from other New World monkeys in similar environments. Barbara Smuts describes her long field research with the savanna baboons of East Africa in *What are Friends For?* As an early field primatologist, Smuts describes how she became interested in the role of females in the society. Traditional views had stated that baboon society was male dominated and what Smuts learned through her observations challenges this notion and introduces us to the concept of female choice and friendship in animals.

Article 13, *Called "Trimates," Three Bold Women Shaped Their Field*, introduces us to the three pioneers of primate field research: Jane Goodall, Dian Fossey, and Birute Galdikas. Each woman's challenges, contributions and controversies are discussed, providing insight into the maturing field of primate observation in the wild. This article also introduces us to the great apes, which are the focus of the remaining selections in Section II. *Got Culture?* and *Tooling Through the Trees* explore the concept of primate intelligence and tool use in the wild. The authors put forward convincing arguments that the behavioral variations seen in chimpanzee and orangutan society may represent the early stages of culture as we know it in human society.

Finally, I have included two articles that provide a link to the final section of the book: *Which of our Genes Makes us Human?* and *98% Alike? What Our Similarity to Apes Tells Us About Our Understanding of Genetics*. These articles explore the percentage of the genome that is shared with the apes and discuss the latest findings from the genetics lab in defining what it means exactly to be human. Armed with the knowledge of how different humans and chimpanzees really are, and what it means, we are ready to explore the origin of our lineage.

Are We in Anthropodenial?

Frans de Waal

When guests arrive at the Yerkes Regional Primate Research Center in Georgia, where I work, they usually pay a visit to the chimpanzees. And often, when she sees them approaching the compound, an adult female chimpanzee named Georgia will hurry to the spigot to collect a mouthful of water. She'll then casually mingle with the rest of the colony behind the mesh fence, and not even the sharpest observer will notice anything unusual. If necessary, Georgia will wait minutes, with her lips closed, until the visitors come near. Then there will be shrieks, laughs, jumps—and sometimes falls—when she suddenly sprays them.

I have known quite a few apes that are good at surprising people, naive and otherwise. Heini Hediger, the great Swiss zoo biologist, recounts how he—being prepared to meet the challenge and paying attention to the ape's every move—got drenched by an experienced chimpanzee. I once found myself in a similar situation with Georgia; she had taken a drink from the spigot and was sneaking up to me. I looked her straight in the eye and pointed my finger at her, warning in Dutch, "I have seen you!" She immediately stepped back, let some of the water dribble from her mouth, and swallowed the rest. I certainly do not wish to claim that she understands Dutch, but she must have sensed that I knew what she was up to, and that I was not going to be an easy target.

Now, no doubt even a casual reader will have noticed that in describing Georgia's actions, I've implied human qualities such as intentions, the ability to interpret my own awareness, and a tendency toward mischief. Yet scientific tradition says I should avoid such language—I am committing the sin of anthropomorphism, of turning nonhumans into humans. The word comes from the Greek, meaning "human form," and it was the ancient Greeks who first gave the practice a bad reputation. They did not have chimpanzees in mind: the philosopher Xenophanes objected to Homer's poetry because it treated Zeus and the other gods as if they were people. How could we be so arrogant, Xenophanes asked, as to think that the gods should look like us? If horses could draw pictures, he suggested mockingly, they would no doubt make their gods look like horses.

From *Discover Magazine*, July 1997 by Frans de Waal. Copyright © 1997 by Frans de Waal, PhD. Reprinted by permission.

Nowadays the intellectual descendants of Xenophanes warn against perceiving animals to be like ourselves. There are, for example, the behaviorists, who follow psychologist B. F. Skinner in viewing the actions of animals as responses shaped by rewards and punishments rather than the result of internal decision making, emotions, or intentions. They would say that Georgia was not "up to" anything when she sprayed water on her victims. Far from planning and executing a naughty plot, Georgia merely fell for the irresistible reward of human surprise and annoyance. Whereas any person acting like her would be scolded, arrested, or held accountable, Georgia is somehow innocent.

Behaviorists are not the only scientists who have avoided thinking about the inner life of animals. Some sociobiologists—researchers who look for the roots of behavior in evolution—depict animals as "survival machines" and "pre-programmed robots" put on Earth to serve their "selfish" genes. There is a certain metaphorical value to these concepts, but it has been negated by the misunderstanding they've created. Such language can give the impression that only genes are entitled to an inner life. No more delusively anthropomorphizing idea has been put forward since the pet-rock craze of the 1970s. In fact, during evolution, genes—a mere batch of molecules—simply multiply at different rates, depending on the traits they produce in an individual. To say that genes are selfish is like saying a snowball growing in size as it rolls down a hill is greedy for snow.

Logically, these agnostic attitudes toward a mental life in animals can be valid only if they're applied to our own species as well. Yet it's uncommon to find researchers who try to study human behavior as purely a matter of reward and punishment. Describe a person as having intentions, feelings, and thoughts and you most likely won't encounter much resistance. Our own familiarity with our inner lives overrules whatever some school of thought might claim about us. Yet despite this double standard toward behavior in humans and animals, modern biology leaves us no choice other than to conclude that we *are* animals. In terms of anatomy, physiology, and neurology we are really no more exceptional than, say, an elephant or a platypus is in its own way. Even such presumed hallmarks of humanity as warfare, politics, culture, morality, and language may not be completely unprecedented. For example, different groups of wild chimpanzees employ different technologies—some fish for termites with sticks, others crack nuts with stones—that are transmitted from one generation to the next through a process reminiscent of human culture.

Given these discoveries, we must be very careful not to exaggerate the uniqueness of our species. The ancients apparently never gave much thought to this practice, the opposite of anthropomorphism, and so we lack a word for it. I will call it anthropodenial: a blindness to the human-like characteristics of other animals, or the animal-like characteristics of ourselves.

Those who are in anthropodenial try to build a brick wall to separate humans from the rest of the animal kingdom. They carry on the tradition of René Descartes, who declared that while humans possessed souls, animals were mere automatons. This produced a serious dilemma when Charles Darwin came along: If we descended from such automatons, were we not automatons ourselves? If not, how did we get to be so different?

Each time we must ask such a question, another brick is pulled out of the dividing wall, and to me this wall is beginning to look like a slice of Swiss cheese. I work on a daily basis with animals from which it is about as hard to distance yourself as from "Lucy," the famed 3.2-million-year-old fossil australopithecine. If we owe Lucy the respect of an ancestor, does this not force a different look at the apes? After all, as far as we can tell, the most significant difference between Lucy and modern chimpanzees is found in their hips, not their craniums.

As soon as we admit that animals are far more like our relatives than like machines, then anthropodenial becomes impossible and anthropomorphism becomes inevitable—and scientifically acceptable. But not *all* forms of anthropomorphism, of course. Popular culture bombards us with examples of animals being humanized for all sorts of purposes, ranging from education to entertainment to satire to propaganda. Walt Disney, for example, made us forget that Mickey is a mouse, and Donald a duck. George Orwell laid a cover of human societal ills over a population of livestock. I was once struck by an advertisement for an oil company that claimed its propane saved the environment, in which a grizzly bear enjoying a pristine landscape had his arm around his mate's shoulders. In fact, bears are nearsighted and do not form pair-bonds, so the image says more about our own behavior than theirs.

Perhaps that was the intent. The problem is, we do not always remember that, when used in this way, anthropomorphism can provide insight only into human affairs and not into the affairs of animals. When my book *Chimpanzee Politics* came out in France, in 1987, my publisher decided (unbeknownst to me) to put François Mitterrand and Jacques Chirac on the cover with a chimpanzee between them. I can only assume he wanted to imply that these politicians acted like "mere" apes. Yet by doing so he went completely against the whole point of my book, which was not to ridicule people but to show that chimpanzees live in complex societies full of alliances and power plays that in some ways mirror our own.

You can often hear similar attempts at anthropomorphic humor in the crowds that form around the monkey exhibit at a typical zoo. Isn't it interesting that antelopes, lions, and giraffes rarely elicit hilarity? But people who watch primates end up hooting and yelling, scratching themselves in exaggeration, and pointing at the animals while shouting, "I had to look twice, Larry. I thought it was you!" In my mind, the laughter reflects anthropodenial: it is a nervous reaction caused by an uncomfortable resemblance.

That very resemblance, however, can allow us to make better use of anthropomorphism, but for this we must view it as a means rather than an end. It should not be our goal to find some quality in an animal that is precisely equivalent to an aspect of our own inner lives. Rather, we should use the fact that we are similar to animals to develop ideas we can test. For example, after observing a group of chimpanzees at length, we begin to suspect that some individuals are attempting to "deceive" others—by giving false alarms to distract unwanted attention from the theft of food or from forbidden sexual activity. Once we frame the observation in such terms, we can devise testable predictions. We can figure out just what it would take to demonstrate deception on the part of chimpanzees. In this way, a speculation is turned into a challenge.

Naturally, we must always be on guard. To avoid making silly interpretations based on anthropomorphism, one must always interpret animal behavior in the wider context of a species' habits and natural history. Without experience with primates, one could imagine that a grinning rhesus monkey must be delighted, or that a chimpanzee running toward another with loud grunts must be in an aggressive mood. But primatologists know from many hours of observation that rhesus monkeys bare their when intimidated, and that chimpanzees often grunt when they meet and embrace. In other words, a grinning rhesus monkey signals submission, and a chimpanzee's grunting often serves as a greeting. A careful observer may thus arrive at an informed anthropomorphism that is at odds with extrapolations from human behavior.

One must also always be aware that some animals are more like ourselves than others. The problem of sharing the experiences of organisms that rely on different senses is a profound one. It was expressed most famously by the philosopher Thomas Nagel when he asked, "What is it like to be a bat?" A bat perceives its world in pulses of reflected sound, something we creatures of vision would have a hard time imagining. Perhaps even more alien would be the experience of an animal such as the star-nosed mole. With 22 pink, writhing tentacles around its nostrils, it is able to feel microscopic textures on small objects in the mud with the keenest sense of touch of any animal on Earth.

Humans can barely imagine a star-nosed mole's *Umwelt*—a German term for the environment as perceived by the animal. Obviously, the closer a species is to us, the easier it is to enter its *Umwelt*. This is why anthropomorphism is not only tempting in the case of apes but also hard to reject on the grounds that we cannot know how they perceive the world. Their sensory systems are essentially the same as ours.

Last summer, an ape saved a three-year-old boy. The child, who had fallen 20 feet into the primate exhibit at Chicago's Brookfield Zoo, was scooped up and carried to safety by Binti Jua, an eight-year-old western lowland female gorilla. The gorilla sat down on a log in a stream, cradling the boy in her lap and patting his back, and then carried him to one of the exhibit doorways before laying him down and continuing on her way.

Binti became a celebrity overnight, figuring in the speeches of leading politicians who held her up as an example of much-needed compassion. Some scientists were less lyrical, however. They cautioned that Binti's motives might have been less noble than they appeared, pointing out that this gorilla had been raised by people and had been taught parental skills with a stuffed animal. The whole affair might have been one of a confused maternal instinct, they claimed.

The intriguing thing about this flurry of alternative explanations was that nobody would think of raising similar doubts when a person saves a dog hit by a car. The rescuer might have grown up around a kennel, have been praised for being kind to animals, have a nurturing personality, yet we would still see his behavior as an act of caring. Why then, in Binti's case, was her background held against her? I am not saying that I know what went through Binti's head, but I do know that no one had prepared her for this kind of emergency and that it is unlikely that, with her own 17-month-old infant on her back, she was "maternally confused." How in the world could such a highly intelligent animal mistake a blond boy in sneakers and a red T-shirt for a juvenile gorilla? Actually, the biggest surprise was how surprised most people were. Students of ape behavior did not feel that Binti had done anything unusual. Jörg Hess, a Swiss gorilla expert, put it most bluntly, "The incident can be sensational only for people who don't know a thing about gorillas."

Binti's action made a deep impression mainly because it benefited a member of our own species, but in my work on the evolution of morality and empathy, I have encountered numerous instances of animals caring for one another. For example, a chimpanzee consoles a victim after a violent attack, placing an arm around him and patting his back. And bonobos (or pygmy chimpanzees) have been known to assist companions new to their quarters in zoos, taking them by the hand to guide them through the maze of corridors connecting parts of their building. These kinds of cases don't reach the newspapers but are consistent with Binti's assistance to the unfortunate boy and the idea that apes have a capacity for sympathy.

The traditional bulwark against this sort of cognitive interpretation is the principle of parsimony—that we must make as few assumptions as possible when trying to construct a scientific explanation, and that assuming an ape is capable of something like sympathy is too great a leap. But doesn't that same principle of parsimony argue against assuming a huge cognitive gap when the evolutionary distance between humans and apes is so small? If two closely related species act in the same manner, their underlying mental processes are probably the same, too. The incident at the Brookfield Zoo shows how hard it is to avoid anthropodenial and anthropomorphism at the same time: in trying to avoid thinking of Binti as a human being, we run straight into the realization that Binti's actions make little sense if we refuse to assume intentions and feelings.

In the end we must ask: What kind of risk we are willing to take—the risk of underestimating animal mental life or the risk of overestimating it? There is no simple answer. But from an evolutionary perspective, Binti's kindness, like Georgia's mischief, is most parsimoniously explained in the same way we explain our own behavior—as the result of a complex, and familiar, inner life.

ID#_____ NAME_____

Article 9: Are We in Anthropodenial?

1. What human qualities does the author ascribe to Georgia, the chimpanzee?

2. Define: anthropomorphism.

3. How do the behaviorists describe the activities of animals?

4. Define: anthropodenial.

5. When does the author feel anthropomorphism is not appropriate?

6. How does the author feel we can make use of anthropomorphism?

7. How does the author suggest we avoid silly interpretations based on anthropomorphism?

8. Describe at least one example of animals caring for one another. How do Binti's actions relate to this idea?

Prosimians Find a Home Far from Home

Doug J. Stewart

In North Carolina, researchers are gaining insight into the behavior of some of the world's most unusual primates.

When you go to the trouble of importing Coquerel's sifakas from tropical Madagascar to a facility in North Carolina, the last thing you want to see is one of the exotic creatures sailing over a fence. That's why Duke University Primate Center recently increased the no-tree zone around some of its outdoor enclosures from 30 feet to 40 feet. Before the modifications, says center director Ken Glander, "the sifakas were popping right over."

On the ground, sifakas are hoppers. In a tree, however, they operate like trapeze artists, but without a trapeze. "These guys reportedly are able to leap 60 feet horizontally," says Glander, also a biological anthropologist and Duke University professor. "I've never seen that, but I've seen them jump 40 feet." In an enclosure behind him, several of the fuzzy, maroon-and-white primates leap nonchalantly from branch to branch while holding their wiry bodies erect and staring at their human visitors.

Rarest of all sifakas is the golden-crowned species, of which anywhere from 1,000 to 10,000 may exist, but nobody knows for sure. The Duke primate center has the only mating pair in captivity—"our crown jewels," says Glander. Their tiny home range, a patch of forest in Madagascar barely 30 miles square, is the site of a recent gold strike, and miners unfortunately have taken to hunting the animals for food. Duke plans to mount a joint rescue mission with the Malagasy government to bring back more pairs as soon as possible. Their progeny could return once the gold rush peters out.

Helping to keep sifakas and other endangered prosimians from disappearing for good is the Duke facility's primary mission. Hidden in the wilds of Duke Forest near downtown Durham, the center is home to the largest captive population of endangered primates in the world. All are prosimians, members of the oldest living branch of the primate family tree, a suborder of its own. The other primate suborder, the anthropoids, includes monkeys, apes

From *National Wildlife*, Feb–March 1998 by Doug J. Stewart. Copyright © 1998 by Doug J. Stewart. Reprinted by permission.

and humans. Most prosimians at Duke are native to Madagascar, where slash-and-burn agriculture, charcoal-making, logging, livestock raising and erosion have drastically shrunk tropical-forest habitat. Of the 21 species represented here, 16 are listed by IUCN—The World Conservation Union as endangered. The center also hosts a half-dozen less-threatened species.

Like the sifakas, many of the other prosimians now thriving at Duke also may one day help restock their ancestral wilderness homes. The facility is more than a breeding station, however. Despite a humble $900,000 annual budget, the private nonprofit center has quietly grown since its founding in 1966 into a major scientific center.

"We're considered to be the world authority on prosimians. When people in zoos have questions, they come to us for answers," says Glander. "Of course, we don't always have them." Research here is largely noninvasive, and even blood samples are taken sparingly. "We do research to benefit the animals, not humans—at least not directly," he adds. The indirect benefit to humans is a better understanding of our own mysterious origins. All modern primates are related to long-ago prosimians (hence their name, meaning "pre-monkey"). "Today's prosimians are really a window on the past," says Glander. As he talks, ring-tailed lemurs festoon a branch on the other side of a fence topped with electrified wire. As they creep, jump and chatter, their bushy striped tails curl and uncurl like animated barber poles.

Compared to monkeys and apes, prosimians have smaller brains, less dexterous fingers and a greater reliance on smell. Prosimians divide into several subgroups. Lorises and galagos inhabit tropical forests of Asia and Africa. Tarsiers are native to the Philippines and other parts of East Asia. Lemurs are native only to Madagascar.

The largest and most plentiful animals at Duke are the lemurs. As they squat in the trees, the larger lemurs like the ring-tailed and the red-fronted could sooner be mistaken for raccoons than relatives of chimps. The black-and-white ruffed lemur, with its long snout protruding from a pouf of white fur, calls to mind a tree-climbing poodle.

The center's nocturnal species occupy indoor cages during the colder months. In one, an aye-aye mother and infant peer down placidly from a branch. Their bulging orange-yellow eyes, beaverish teeth, coarse opossum-like fur and big ears suggest a koala crossed with a squirrel. A slender loris maneuvering around another enclosure calls to mind a rat on stilts.

Nearby, a slow loris has just woken up. It languidly stretches one hand toward a branch, grasps it and begins pulling itself over. No, it's not still sleepy, Glander says. "That's top speed for a slow loris." Sluggishness is a defense: The loris avoids attracting attention. Another novel defense is practiced by the potto, which curls itself into a ball so that a row of unusually sharp vertebrae protrude at the back of its neck. If a weasel or other predator bites down the vertebrae often will penetrate the roof of the predator's mouth. The potto, of course, is dead at that point, but the predator learns to avoid others.

Glander, an expert on the diets of wild primates, is especially intrigued by the center's bamboo-eating lemurs. These were thought to be extinct after 1900—until a French naturalist found a live one for sale in 1964 in a village market in Madagascar. Like pandas (which they resemble somewhat), bamboo-eating lemurs eat virtually nothing else. To make the best use of the island's limited stands, each of three species of bamboo lemur munches on a different part of the plant: One eats the stalk, another the leaves, a third the green shoots. No other animal eats the shoots, which are laden with cyanide. "The golden bamboo lemur eats enough cyanide every day to kill a person several times over," Glander says. He assumes the animal's diet has medicinal benefits, but he hasn't worked out what those might be.

Duke's captive-breeding program is more sophisticated than the laissez-faire approach that most zoos took as recently as 20 years ago. "In the old days, a male in a zoo might be a really good breeder, so the zoo would breed him a lot and sell his offspring to a lot of other zoos," says Barbara Coffman, a former research associate at the Duke center. For endangered animals, this strategy resulted in genetic sameness that left a species ill-equipped to cope with new diseases or environmental changes.

Now Duke and other breeding facilities have joined forces to keep exhaustive genealogies of their captives, tracing the animals' bloodlines back to wild-caught forebears. Coordinated by the IUCN, a detailed Species Survival Plan sets breeding guidelines for each of 134 endangered species, from black rhinos to pygmy lorises. Prospective mates or their sperm are shipped from zoo to zoo as needed. The overriding consideration is to keep each population's genetic deck as well shuffled as possible, generation after generation.

For behavioral scientists Duke's roomy, natural-habitat enclosures are a passable substitute for true field conditions. Ken Glander refers to the colony of lemurs in the largest, 23-acre enclosure as "almost free-ranging." In Madagascar, the same group would roam at most 200 acres. "You can study group dynamics in Madagascar, but you can't get as close to the animals," says Glander. "Here, they don't get spooked by humans. And we have 30 years of genetic history on some of these animals. All this means we can get much more information in a much shorter time."

One of the information gatherers is Frances White, a behavioral ecologist. She has been studying lemurs here for more than 10 years, especially larger diurnal animals like ruffed lemurs and ring-tails. One of the unusual characteristics of lemur society she is studying is female dominance. "Female lemurs get the best food. They do much of the mate choice. Males are often deferent." She hypothesizes that the females' dominance serves to ensure their young are well nourished despite limited resources. In ongoing experiments, males seem to lose their deference when food is widely available.

Like Darwin's finches, Madagascar's lemurs have evolved in remarkably distinctive ways. Consider the aye-aye's middle finger: Thin and knobby, it can bend almost snakelike in any direction. The animals use it for everything from tapping for grubs to splashing water into their mouths. In the wild, this appendage has almost been the species' undoing. "Many villagers in Madagascar thing aye-ayes can put curses on them," says Carl Erickson, a Duke experimental psychologist. "They think that if an aye-aye points its weird middle finger at you, you have to kill it to lift the curse."

Superstition, compounded by habitat loss, has nearly wiped out the aye-aye in the wild. No one knows how many remain in Madagascar's shrinking forests. Until recently, the species was considered on the verge of extinction, but lately several small and widely scattered pockets of aye-ayes have turned up on the island. Even so, the aye-aye may be the most endangered primate in the world.

Erickson's fascination with aye-ayes began when the first aye-aye arrived at Duke in the late 1980s. "He had his nose down over a piece of galvanized pipe in his enclosure, his ears were forward and he was tapping on the pipe with that bizarre middle finger," Erickson recalls. He guessed the aye-aye had mistaken the pipe for a tree branch and was tapping it to find insects. In a series of experiments since then, Erickson has proved his hunch correct: Aye-ayes listen to the tapping with their huge ears to locate cavities likely to contain prey. "If we're going to be the custodian of this species," he says, "it's important that we don't let skills like this deteriorate over generations."

Luckily, captive-born animals seen to inherit at least some survival skills. In a test, a Doberman pinscher was walked outside a fence containing captive-born lemurs. The animals climbed high into the trees and gave the ground-predator cry. When large birds have flown overhead, the lemurs have given the aerial-predator call and dropped down to the lower branches, just as wild lemurs do. "They have an instinctive reaction to these things," says Glander. "It's totally hard-wired."

The real test is now underway. Last fall, Duke and Malagasy scientists for the first time released captive-bred prosimians into the wild—five radio-collared black-and-white ruffed lemurs. A second group of lemurs will join them later this year. Old World primates have never been successfully reintroduced to the wild before, but Glander is confident. "I'm convinced this will work. In fact, I know it will work. But we have to convince the world."

Further Reading

"S.O.S. Lemurs! A New Biosphere Reserve in Madagascar" by Edouard Bailby, *UNESCO Courier*, August 1990 p. 46(3). The author discusses the destruction of the natural habitat of the lemurs of Madagascar and the possible life-saving establishment of a biosphere reserve.

"Madagascar's Lemurs" by Alison Jolly, *National Geographic*, Aug. 1988 v. 174, n. 2 pp. 132–160. This piece presents a comprehensive overview of the variety of lemurs in their native habitat, Madagascar. The pictures are very captivating.

An inexpensive video entitled "Marathon Wildlife Collection: Lemurs of Madagascar" produced by Universal Pictures/Walt Disney. Information on the video can be accessed via the website: http://www.vcvideo.com/documentary/lemurs_of_madagascar.html

For further information on the lemurs housed at the Duke Primate Center, access their website: http://farmer.acpub.edu/web/primate/psimians.html

ID#_____   NAME_____

Article 10: Prosimians Find a Home Far from Home

1. What is the primary mission of the Duke University Primate Research Center?

2. Why are the tropical forests of Madagascar disappearing?

3. How do prosimians differ from monkeys and apes?

4. What is unusual about the bamboo eating lemur's diet?

5. In what way are female lemurs dominant to males?

6. Why is the aye-aye near extinction in the wild?

7. In what way do the captive lemurs behave like wild lemurs?

Menu for a Monkey

Karen B. Strier

The muriquis' diet may reveal the medical riches of a South American forest.

The muriquis were on the move again, swinging hand over hand through the trees in single file as fast as I could count them. I stumbled in pursuit down the overgrown trail, skipping over protruding roots in an effort to avoid falling flat on my face. The monkeys were already out of sight by the time I reached the valley bottom and began the steep climb up the opposite side. But as I stopped on the crest of the ridge to catch my breath, excited neighs and chirps coming from a large fig tree on the slope below gave away the muriquis' location. Less urgently now, I left the trail and made my way through the dense undergrowth to a spot where I could sit and watch the entire group almost at eye level.

The canopy of the tree was laden with fruit—the muriquis would enjoy a respite of several days following the difficult trek they had made that morning. They would camp out here, feasting on the abundant ripe figs until the fruit was nearly depleted and it was time for them to search for their next meal. Then they might lead me on another long, high-speed chase through the forest or meander at a more leisurely pace, eating leaves along the way, until they discovered another fruit tree where they would camp out again.

After studying the same group of muriquis, or woolly spider monkeys, over the past decade, I have grown accustomed to what at first had seemed to be their unpredictable behavior. Part of my early confusion was the result of how little was known about this primate when I first traveled to their homeland, the Atlantic forest of southeastern Brazil. But scattered observations by a handful of scientists, as well as anatomical descriptions of museum specimens, had raised an intriguing question.

Muriquis are the largest monkeys in the New World, with adults of both sexes weighing twenty pounds or more. Their large bodies signal that they, like many other large-bodied primates, have a relatively low metabolism. This allows them to subsist on leaves, a food that is easily obtained in large quantities but is low in readily available energy. Their well-developed jaws and chewing muscles and sharp, crested molars enable them to break open the leaves' tough cell walls, releasing the nutrients stored inside and making them easier to

From *Natural History*, March 1993, "Menu for a monkey", pp. 34–43 by Karen Strier. Reprinted from Natural History, March/1993; copyright © Natural History Magazine, Inc., 1993.

digest. In this respect, muriquis resemble howler monkeys, which live throughout much of Central and South America.

Yet muriquis do not share the howlers' slow, quadrupedal method of climbing through the trees. Instead, they swing through the branches by their arms, an energetically costly mode of travel, better suited to tracking widely dispersed but energy-rich food sources, such as fruit, rather than the more ubiquitous leaves. This "suspensory" locomotion is a trait that muriquis share with their closest cousins, the spider monkeys, which live in Central America and in the Amazon basin. According to primatologist John Cant, spider monkeys can specialize in eating fruit because they can cut down on travel time.

To reconcile the evidence of seemingly contradictory feeding adaptations, I set out in 1982 to study muriquis in the wild at the 3.5-square-mile forest at Fazenda Montes Claros in Minas Gerais, Brazil. I quickly discovered that what muriquis eat is only one of the notable characteristics of this species, for unlike nearly all other primates, muriquis live a social life strikingly free of aggression. Fights never break out within groups over access to food or the best feeding sites, and there is no discernible pecking order. Group members simply wait patiently for their turn to eat, and they avoid feeding so closely together as to interfere with one another.

The rules of etiquette among muriquis extend well beyond their courteous dining manners, for relations between the sexes are egalitarian. The muriquis live in groups that include several adults of both sexes, as opposed, for example, to just females and one adult male. Among most other primates that live in such groups, the males are better equipped than the females for combat, being larger and having bigger canines. The males typically compete for mates, establishing a hierarchy by fighting among themselves. The dominant male can monopolize the mating scene and can bully the females into sexual liaisons.

But the muriqui males and females are similar in size, so males can't dominate the females. And it is futile for males to fight among themselves for mates, since females are free to choose peaceful mates. All this appears to result from the muriquis' mixed diet. Because the monkeys rely at times on eating nothing but leaves, males and females are relatively large. At the same time, the need for agility in the long-distance pursuit of fruit limits how much bigger males can become.

Since a single male cannot dominate the group, the male muriquis' strategy is for close male relatives, brothers as well as fathers and sons, to stick together in a tolerant group. Instead of competing among themselves, they cooperate to prevent encroachments from other groups of males, while taking advantage of whatever sexual opportunities the females throw their way. So even if a male muriqui does not have offspring of his own, he is assured that the similar genes of a close relative will be passed on to the next generation.

It took me a long time to crack the code of muriqui social behavior because muriquis do no reach sexual maturity until they are about seven years old. By this age, nearly all the females born in the principal group I was observing had migrated out. The nexus of the society consists of the associations among the older males born to the group, their mothers and younger brothers, and young immigrant females.

In the past ten years, this muriqui group has more than doubled in size, from twenty-two members to the current forty-nine, each one distinguishable by its natural markings. Important social changes have coincided with this population growth, including a greater tendency for this once-cohesive group to split into smaller, temporary mixed-sex groups. Eventually it may divide permanently, but so far the entire group still tends to reunite whenever large concentrations of fruits, such as figs or the deliciously sweet wild mangoes, are discovered.

In recording the monkeys' diet, I observed pronounced variation from month to month, owing to seasonal differences in rainfall and available food. Over an annual cycle, the muriquis at Fazenda Montes Claros devote roughly half of their feeding time to leaves; one-third to fruit; one-tenth to flowers and flower products such as pollen and nectar; and the remainder to bark, bamboo, ferns, and grasses, which they come to the ground to eat. But despite the high contribution of leaves to their overall diet, muriquis almost always prefer to eat fruits and flowers, settling down to a protracted banquet whenever they can.

The pursuit of energy-rich fruits and flowers appears to dictate the muriquis' far-ranging movements. When these foods are scarce, muriquis travel faster and farther to find them. In contrast, leaves are usually eaten haphazardly when the monkeys are shifting from one fruit source to another and are paid little more than passing attention unless fruit is in short supply. But by consuming both types of food, the muriquis have evolved a successful adaptation to the Atlantic forest, which because of its distance from the equator is more seasonal than, for example, the Amazon basin, where energy-rich fruit is available year round.

In its adaptation, the muriqui differs from the brown howler monkey, which occupies the same Atlantic forest habitat and lives a lazier life, filling up mainly on leaves. The muriquis' digestive system cannot handle such a limited diet. Howler monkeys have elongated intestines relative to their body size, and there is ample time for nutrients from leaves to be absorbed as food travels slowly through their gut. Muriquis also have proportionately long intestines, but food passes through them much more rapidly. In a study of captive animals, primatologist Katharine Milton found that food passed through a muriqui's digestive tract more than twice as fast as it did through a howler monkey's. In the wild, muriquis defecate every few hours throughout the day, whereas the howler monkeys defecate just once after waking in the morning and once before nightfall.

While the muriquis' faster digestion prevents them from subsisting on leaves alone, it also provides an advantage: they don't have to be as careful as howlers about what leaves they eat. Primatologist Kenneth Glander found that although Costa Rican howler monkeys eat substantial quantities of foliage, they are highly selective about what leaves they forage on, avoiding those with high levels of tannins and compounds such as alkaloids and phenolics, which can be anything from mildly to severely toxic. Plants produce these often unpalatable chemicals to defend themselves against insects and other animals that might consume them.

Howler monkeys must be extremely choosy about their foods because their more deliberate digestive systems make them vulnerable to absorbing toxic compounds along with essential nutrients, but the muriquis' quick processing means that plant tannins and toxins, as well as many nutrients, are excreted before they can be absorbed. Ecologist Mark Leighton and chemist David Marks analyzed some thirty muriqui foods I had collected from the forest—fruits, leaves, and flowers—and found them to be unusually high in tannins and phenolics when compared with similar foods eaten by other monkeys and apes in other tropical forests. And when we compared the plants normally available at the same times of year, we found no evidence that the monkeys selected the ones with lower levels of tannins or other harmful compounds.

These biochemical and physiological data made sense of my observations that muriquis generally prefer fruits over leaves despite the greater effort required to find them. Ripe, fleshy fruits, in particular, are usually easier to digest than leaves and thus, ounce for ounce, are a better source of nutrients and energy for a primate with such a rapid food-passing rate.

Sorting out muriqui feeding habits could have marked the end of my study, but by 1989 two new questions had begun to intrigue me. With the help of Brazilian students who follow the muriquis year round, I had accumulated enough demographic data to detect a consistent birth season during the dry months, from May to September. I wondered whether this might be related to the muriquis' seasonal diet. And after reading two separate accounts of chimpanzees consuming plants with medicinal properties when they were suffering from intestinal parasites, I wondered whether the high level of the defensive plant compounds in the muriquis' diet provided them with similar protection.

These questions could be explored simultaneously because they shared a common denominator—diet. But how could I examine the effects of diet on reproduction, when female muriquis showed no visible signs of ovulation or pregnancy? And how could I detect parasitic infections, when the parasites were hidden in the gut? Capturing the monkeys—to take blood samples to measure ovarian hormones or to probe their intestines—was out of the question. The muriquis are an endangered species, and I did not want to subject them to possibly harmful procedures, nor did it seem worthwhile to disturb them and thus risk interfering with the long-term behavioral study.

After considering all kinds of sophisticated approaches, I realized that the solution to this dilemma lay in a naturally abundant and renewable resource: the muriquis' feces. To examine ovarian hormone levels, I began collaborating with reproductive endocrinologist Toni Ziegler, who developed a technique to monitor muriqui feces for estrogen and progesterone. And biologist Michael Stuart, whose specialty is identifying parasites in dung, has helped me in investigating muriqui intestinal parasite infections. By following recognized individuals until they defecated, I could collect the fecal samples needed for these studies and also keep track of what the muriquis were eating. Phytochemist Eloy Rodriguez is analyzing muriqui plant foods for steroids and bioactive compounds, and by combining the results from these studies, we will ultimately be able to evaluate the relationships between muriqui diet, reproduction, and parasite infections.

While simple in theory, my role in these investigations has not been easy. The biochemical analyses of the plant foods require gathering a grocery bag full of leaves or fruit from each plant species, and doing this after the muriquis have swarmed through one of their feeding trees is not as simple as it sounds. Collecting fresh fecal samples from identified individuals is equally laborious. The feces themselves are not so unpleasant to collect as one might suppose because they carry an aromatic scent from the cinnamon leaves that muriquis consume. The challenge, rather, is to get almost directly underneath the targeted individual at the moment of defecation so that the greenish brown dung can be spotted before it is camouflaged after hitting the ground.

Occasionally the feces land neatly in my glove, but more often they splatter uselessly in the tangled vegetation—or else fall alongside another muriqui's feces, so that I cannot be sure whose is whose. So even though the muriquis defecate often and, in the case of adults, abundantly each time, getting a clean sample sometimes means tailing one muriqui for up to six hours without pause.

The rewards for these efforts are new findings as promising and intriguing as everything else we have learned about muriquis. At Fazenda Montes Claros, October is the onset of both the rainy season and the muriquis' mating season, and at this time the muriquis' feeding behavior changes. From late September to mid-October, when edible fruit abounds, the monkeys eat mainly the leaves of just two species in the legume family, *Apuleia leiocarpa* and *Platypodium elegans*. And in contrast to the casual treatment they give most other leaves, the muriquis camp out at these leaf sources, behaving as if they were preferred fruits.

Preliminary analyses suggest that these leaves may contain some antimicrobial substances and are exceptionally low in the tannins so prevalent in other muriqui foods. The chemical role of tannins is to bind proteins and make them more difficult to digest, rendering plants less attractive as food sources. By eating these leaves instead of the fruits available at this time, both male and female muriquis may get an important surge in protein, fortifying them for the upcoming mating season.

During this same critical time of year, muriquis also alter their behavior by making speedy excursions away from the central part of the forest, where they usually hang out, to the periphery, where the forest gives way to surrounding pasture. Once there, they leap across gaps in the canopy to reach the fruit of another species of legume, *Enterolobium contortisiliquum*, whose common name is monkey ear. Uncharacteristically, both male and female muriquis abandon the monkey ear trees long before the fruits are depleted, suggesting that they only need a taste to be satisfied.

What they are seeking in these fruits is unknown, but monkey ear fruits contain stigmasterol, a steroid used in the laboratory synthesis of progesterone. We don't know yet whether this plant hormone also stimulates steroid production in muriquis or whether it is excreted without consequence. But recent studies, including one by anthropologist Pat Whitten, indicate that plant hormones can regulate reproduction in some animals. Thus stigmasterol, or some other hormone lurking in the muriquis' diet, may turn out to be linked to the monkeys' seasonal fertility.

That plants regulate muriqui reproduction remains a highly speculative proposition, but that they combat parasites is more apparent. Our first analysis showed that the muriquis at Fazenda Montes Claros were completely free of intestinal parasites, a discovery so startling that we repeated the fecal sampling during different seasons in subsequent years and looked at samples from the local howler monkeys for comparison. We also collected feces from another population of muriquis inhabiting the much larger and more pristine forest at Carlos Botelho State Park in the state of São Paulo.

The subsequent analyses confirmed and extended our original findings: No parasites were found in the muriquis and howler monkeys at Fazenda Montes Claros, while at Carlos Botelho at least three species of parasites were identified and nearly 90 percent of the monkeys sampled were infected. Such marked variation could result from any number of differences between the two sites, but it may be more than mere coincidence that many of the plants eaten by both muriquis and howler monkeys at Fazenda Montes Claros are the same species used by Amazonian peoples for controlling intestinal worms and other parasites. If these plants are effective in humans, there is every reason to believe that they are similarly effective in muriquis, even if in muriquis the effects are incidental rather than intentional. Far fewer of these medicinal plant species have been identified at the São Paulo forest; this may explain why parasite infections are more prevalent there.

These pharmacological clues have set an urgent agenda for the next decade of muriqui research. Our ability to explore the medicinal properties of plants in Brazil's Atlantic forest is jeopardized by continued habitat destruction. In the past century, the Atlantic forest has been reduced to less than 5 percent of its original area, threatening rare plants, and the monkeys that depend on them, with permanent extinction. While traditional peoples of the Amazon have survived long enough to impart to us some of their knowledge of forest plants, the indigenous human societies of the Atlantic forest are long gone. The muriquis and other monkeys may provide humans with their best guides to the forest's medicinal value.

Article 11: Menu for a Monkey

1. Where do the muriqui monkeys live?

2. How does muriqui body size relate to their metabolism? What kind of food would we expect them to eat?

3. How do the muriquis move through the trees?

4. What is the social structure of the muriquis? How does this relate to the relationships between males and females?

5. How does their diet affect their social behavior?

6. What causes the muriquis to travel?

7. How do the digestive capabilities of the muriqui relate to the types of leaves they can eat?

8. Briefly describe two reasons why the author was collecting feces for study.

9. Why is the author concerned about the destruction of the rainforest?

12

What are Friends for?

Barbara Smuts

Virgil, a burly adult male olive baboon, closely followed Zizi, a middle-aged female easily distinguished by her grizzled coat and square muzzle. On her rump Zizi sported a bright pink swelling, indicating that she was sexually receptive and probably fertile. Virgil's extreme attentiveness to Zizi suggested to me—and all rival males in the troop—that he was her current and exclusive mate.

Zizi, however, apparently had something else in mind. She broke away from Virgil, moved rapidly through the troop, and presented her alluring sexual swelling to one male after another. Before Virgil caught up with her, she had managed to announce her receptive condition to several of his rivals. When Virgil tried to grab her, Zizi screamed and dashed into the bushes with Virgil in hot pursuit. I heard sounds of chasing and fighting coming from the thicket. Moments later Zizi emerged from the bushes with an older male named Cyclops. They remained together for several days, copulating often. In Cyclops's presence, Zizi no longer approached or even glanced at other males.

From *Natural History*, February 1987, "What are Friends for?", pp. 36–44 by Barbara Smuts. Reprinted from Natural History, February/1987; copyright © Natural History Magazine, Inc., 1987.

Primatologists describe Zizi and other olive baboons *(Papio cynocephalus anubis)* as promiscuous, meaning that both males and females usually mate with several members of the opposite sex within a short period of time. Promiscuous mating behavior characterizes many of the larger, more familiar primates, including chimpanzees, rhesus macaques, and gray langurs, as well as olive, yellow, and chacma baboons, the three subspecies of savanna baboon. In colloquial usage, promiscuity often connotes wanton and random sex, and several early studies of primates supported this stereotype. However, after years of laboriously recording thousands of copulations under natural conditions, the Peeping Toms of primate fieldwork have shown that, even in promiscuous species, sexual pairings are far from random.

Some adult males, for example, typically copulate much more often than others. Primatologists have explained these differences in terms of competition: the most dominant males monopolize females and prevent lower-ranking rivals from mating. But exceptions are frequent. Among baboons, the exceptions often involve scruffy, older males who mate in full view of younger, more dominant rivals.

A clue to the reason for these puzzling exceptions emerged when primatologists began to question an implicit assumption of the dominance hypothesis—that females were merely passive objects of male competition. But what if females were active arbiters in this system? If females preferred some males over others and were able to express these preferences, then models of mating activity based on male dominance alone would be far too simple.

Once researchers recognized the possibility of female choice, evidence for it turned up in species after species. The story of Zizi, Virgil, and Cyclops is one of hundreds of examples of female primates rejecting the sexual advances of particular males and enthusiastically cooperating with others. But what is the basis for female choice? Why might they prefer some males over others?

This question guided my research on the Eburru Cliffs troop of olive baboons, named after one of their favorite sleeping sites, a sheer rocky outcrop rising several hundred feet above the floor of the Great Rift Valley, about 100 miles northwest of Nairobi, Kenya. The 120 members of Eburru Cliffs spent their days wandering through open grassland studded with occasional acacia thorn trees. Each night they retired to one of a dozen sets of cliffs that provided protection from nocturnal predators such as leopards.

Most previous studies of baboon sexuality had focused on females who, like Zizi, were at the peak of sexual receptivity. A female baboon does not mate when she is pregnant or lactating, a period of abstinence lasting about eighteen months. The female then goes into estrus, and for about two weeks out of every thirty-five-day cycle, she mates. Toward the end of this two-week period she may ovulate, but usually the female undergoes four or five estrous cycles before she conceives. During pregnancy, she once again resumes a chaste existence. As a result, the typical female baboon is sexually active for less than 10 percent of her adult life. I thought that by focusing on the other 90 percent, I might learn something new. In particular, I suspected that routine, day-to-day relationships between males and pregnant or lactating (nonestrous) females might provide clues to female mating preferences.

Nearly every day for sixteen months, I joined the Eburru Cliffs baboons at their sleeping cliffs at dawn and traveled several miles with them while they foraged for roots, seeds, grass, and occasionally, small prey items, such as baby gazelles or hares (see "Predatory Baboons of Kekopey," *Natural History*, March 1976). Like all savanna baboon troops, Eburru Cliffs functioned as a cohesive unit organized around a core of related females, all of whom were born in the troop. Unlike the females, male savanna baboons leave their natal troop to join another where they may remain for many years, so most of the Eburru Cliffs adult males were immigrants. Since membership in the troop remained relatively constant during the period of my study, I learned to identify each individual. I relied on differences in size, posture, gait, and especially, facial features. To the practiced observer, baboons look as different from one another as human beings do.

As soon as I could recognize individuals, I noticed that particular females tended to turn up near particular males again and again. I came to think of these pairs as friends. Friendship among animals is not a well-documented phenomenon, so to convince skeptical colleagues that baboon friendship was real, I needed to develop objective criteria for distinguishing friendly pairs.

I began by investigating grooming, the amiable simian habit of picking through a companion's fur to remove dead skin and ectoparasites (see "Little Things That Tick Off Baboons," *Natural History*, February 1984). Baboons spend much more time grooming than is necessary for hygiene, and previous research had indicated that it is a good measure of social bonds.

Although eighteen adult males lived in the troop, each nonestrous female performed most of her grooming with just one, two, or occasionally, three males. For example, of Zizi's twenty-four grooming bouts with males, Cyclops accounted for thirteen, and a second male, Sherlock, accounted for all the rest. Different females tended to favor different males as grooming partners.

Another measure of social bonds was simply who was observed near whom. When foraging, traveling, or resting, each pregnant or lactating female spent a lot of time near a few males and associated with the others no more often than expected by chance. When I compared the identities of favorite grooming partners and frequent companions, they overlapped almost completely. This enabled me to develop a formal definition of friendship: any male that scored high on both grooming and proximity measures was considered a friend.

Virtually all baboons made friends; only one female and three males who had most recently joined the troop lacked such companions. Out of more than 600 possible adult female-adult male pairs in the troop, however, only about one in ten qualified as friends; these really were special relationships.

Several factors seemed to influence which baboons paired up. In most cases, friends were unrelated to each other, since the male had immigrated from another troop. (Four friendships, however, involved a female and an adolescent son who had not yet emigrated. Unlike other friends, these related pairs never mated.) Older females tended to be friends with older males; younger females with younger males. I witnessed occasional May–December romances, usually involving older females and young adult males. Adolescent males and females were strongly rule-bound, and with the exception of mother-son pairs, they formed friendships only with one another.

Regardless of age or dominance rank, most females had just one or two male friends. But among males, the number of female friends varied greatly from none to eight. Although high-ranking males enjoyed priority of access to food and sometimes mates, dominant males did not have more female friends than low-ranking males. Instead it was the older males who had lived in the troop for many years who had the most friends. When a male had several female friends, the females were often closely related to one another. Since female baboons spend a lot of time near their kin, it is probably easier for a male to maintain bonds with several related females at once.

When collecting data, I focused on one nonestrous female at a time and kept track of her every movement toward or away from any male; similarly, I noted every male who moved toward or away from her. Whenever the female and male moved close enough to exchange intimacies, I wrote down exactly what happened. When foraging together, friends tended to remain a few yards apart. Males more often wandered away from females than the reverse, and females, more often than males, closed the gap. The female behaved as if she wanted to keep the male within calling distance, in case she needed his protection. The male, however, was more likely to make approaches that brought them within actual touching distance. Often, he would plunk himself down right next to his friend and ask her to groom him by holding a pose with exaggerated stillness. The female sometimes responded by grooming, but more often, she exhibited the most reliable sign of true intimacy: she ignored her friend and simply continued whatever she was doing.

In sharp contrast, when a male who was not a friend moved close to a female, she dared not ignore him. She stopped whatever she was doing and held still, often glancing surreptitiously at the intruder. If he did not move away, she sometimes lifted her tail and presented her rump. When a female is not in estrus, this is a gesture of appeasement, not sexual enticement. Immediately after this respectful acknowledgement of his presence, the female would slip away. But such tense interactions with nonfriend males were rare, because females usually moved away before the males came too close.

These observations suggest that females were afraid of most of the males in their troop, which is not surprising: male baboons are twice the size of females, and their canines are longer and sharper than those of a lion. All Eburru Cliffs males directed both mild and severe aggression toward females. Mild aggression, which usually involved threats and chases but no body contact, occurred most often during feeding competition or when the male redirected aggression toward a female after losing a fight with another male. Females and juveniles showed aggression toward other females and juveniles in similar circumstances and occasionally inflicted superficial wounds. Severe aggression by males, which involved body contact and sometimes biting, was less common and also more puzzling, since there was no apparent cause.

An explanation for at least some of these attacks emerged one day when I was watching Pegasus, a young adult male, and his friend Cicily, sitting together in the middle of a small clearing. Cicily moved to the edge of the clearing to feed, and a higher-ranking female, Zora, suddenly attacked her. Pegasus stood up and looked as if he were about to intervene when both females disappeared into the bushes. He sat back down, and I remained with him. A full ten minutes later, Zora appeared at the edge of the clearing; this was the first time she had come into view since her attack on Cicily. Pegasus instantly pounced on Zora, repeatedly grabbed her neck in his mouth and lifted her off the ground, shook her whole body, and then dropped her. Zora screamed continuously and tried to escape. Each time, Pegasus caught her and continued his brutal attack. When he finally released her five minutes later she had a deep canine gash on the palm of her hand that made her limp for several days.

This attack was similar in form and intensity to those I had seen before and labeled "unprovoked." Certainly, had I come upon the scene after Zora's aggression toward Cicily, I would not have understood why Pegasus attacked Zora. This suggested that some, perhaps many, severe attacks by males actually represented punishment for actions that had occurred some time before.

Whatever the reasons for male attacks on females, they represent a serious threat. Records of fresh injuries indicated that Eburru Cliffs adult females received canine slash wounds from males at the rate of one for every female each year, and during my study, one female died of her injuries. Males probably pose an even greater threat to infants. Although only one infant was killed during my study, observers in Botswana and Tanzania have seen recent male immigrants kill several young infants.

Protection from male aggression, and from the less injurious but more frequent aggression of other females and juveniles, seems to be one of the main advantages of friendship for a female baboon. Seventy times I observed an adult male defend a female or her offspring against aggression by another troop member, not infrequently a high-ranking male. In all but six of these cases, the defender was a friend. Very few of these confrontations involved actual fighting; no male baboon, subordinate or dominant, is anxious to risk injury by the sharp canines of another.

Males are particularly solicitous guardians of their friends' youngest infants. If another male gets too close to an infant or if a juvenile female plays with it too roughly, the friend may intervene. Other troop members soon learn to be cautious when the mother's friend is nearby, and his presence provides the mother with a welcome respite from the annoying pokes and prods of curious females and juveniles obsessed with the new baby. Male baboons at Gombe Park in Tanzania and Amboseli Park in Kenya have also been seen rescuing infants from chimpanzees and lions. These several forms of male protection help to explain why females in Eburru Cliffs stuck closer to their friends in the first few months after giving birth than at any other time.

The male-infant relationship develops out of the male's friendship with the mother, but as the infant matures, this new bond takes on a life of its own. My co-worker Nancy Nicolson found that by about nine months of age, infants actively sought out their male friends when the mother was a few yards away, suggesting that the male may function as an alternative caregiver. This seemed to be especially true for infants undergoing unusually early or severe weaning. (Weaning is generally a gradual, prolonged process, but there is tremendous variation among mothers in the timing and intensity of weaning. See "Mother Baboons," *Natural History*, September 1980). After being rejected by the mother, the crying infant often approached the male friend and sat huddled against him until its whimpers subsided. Two of the infants in Eburru Cliffs lost their mothers when they were still quite young. In each case, their bond with the mother's friend subsequently intensified, and—perhaps as a result—both infants survived.

A close bond with a male may also improve the infant's nutrition. Larger than all other troop members, adult males monopolize the best feeding sites. In general, the personal space surrounding a feeding male is inviolate, but he usually tolerates intrusions by the infants of his female friends, giving them access to choice feeding spots.

Although infants follow their male friends around rather than the reverse, the males seem genuinely attached to their tiny companions. During feeding, the male and infant express their pleasure in each other's company by sharing spirited, antiphonal grunting duets. If the infant whimpers in distress, the male friend is likely to cease feeding, look at the infant, and grunt softly, as if in sympathy, until the whimpers cease. When the male rests, the infants of his female friends may huddle behind him, one after the other, forming a "train," or, if feeling energetic, they may use his body as a trampoline.

When I returned to Eburru Cliffs four years after my initial study ended, several of the bonds formed between males and the infants of their female friends were still intact (in other cases, either the male or the infant or both had disappeared). When these bonds involved recently matured females, their long-time male associates showed no sexual interest in them, even though the females mated with other adult males. Mothers and sons, and usually maternal siblings, show similar sexual inhibitions in baboons and many other primate species.

The development of an intimate relationship between a male and the infant of his female friend raises an obvious question: Is the male the infant's father? To answer this question definitely we would need to conduct genetic analysis, which was not possible for these baboons. Instead, I estimated paternity probabilities from observations of the temporary (a few hours a day) exclusive mating relationships, or consortships, that estrous females form with a series of different males. These estimates were apt to be fairly accurate, since changes in the female's sexual swelling allow one to pinpoint the timing of conception to within a few days. Most females consorted with only two or three males during this period, and these males were termed likely fathers.

In about half the friendships, the male was indeed likely to be the father of his friend's most recent infant, but in the other half he was not—in fact, he had never been seen mating with the female. Interestingly, males who were friends with the mother but not likely fathers nearly always developed a relationship with her infant, while males who had mated with the female but were not her friend usually did not. Thus friendship with the mother, rather than paternity, seems to mediate the development of male-infant bonds. Recently, a similar pattern was documented for South American capuchin monkeys in a laboratory study in which paternity was determined genetically.

These results fly in the face of a prominent theory that claims males will invest in infants only when they are closely related. If males are not fostering the survival of their own genes by caring for the infant, then why do they do so? I suspected that the key was female choice. If females preferred to mate with males who had already demonstrated friendly behavior, then friendships with mothers and their infants might pay off in the future when the mothers were ready to mate again.

To find out if this was the case, I examined each male's sexual behavior with females he had befriended before they resumed estrus. In most cases, males consorted considerably more often with their friends than with other females. Baboon females typically mate with several different males, including both friends and nonfriends, but prior friendship increased a male's probability of mating with a female above what it would have been otherwise.

This increased probability seemed to reflect female preferences. Females occasionally overtly advertised their disdain for certain males and their desire for others. Zizi's behavior, described above, is a good example. Virgil was not one of her friends, but Cyclops was. Usually, however, females expressed preferences and aversions more subtly. For example, Delphi, a petite adolescent female, found herself pursued by Hector, a middle-aged adult male. She did not run away or refuse to mate with him, but whenever he wasn't watching, she looked around for her friend Homer, an adolescent male. When she succeeded in catching Homer's eye, she narrowed her eyes and flattened her ears against her skull, the friendliest face one baboon can send another. This told Homer she would rather be with him. Females expressed satisfaction with a current consort partner by staying close to him, initiating copulations, and not making advances toward other males. Baboons are very sensitive to such cues, as indicated by an experimental study in which rival hamadryas baboons rarely challenged a male-female pair if the female strongly preferred her current partner. Similarly, in Eburru Cliffs, males were less apt to challenge consorts involving a pair that shared a long-term friendship.

Even though females usually consorted with their friends, they also mated with other males, so it is not surprising that friendships were most vulnerable during periods of sexual activity. In a few cases, the female consorted with another male more often than with her friend, but the friendship survived nevertheless. One female, however, formed a strong sexual bond with a new male. This bond persisted after conception, replacing her previous friendship. My observations suggest that adolescent and young adult females tend to have shorter, less stable friendships than do older females. Some friendships, however, last a very long time. When I returned to Eburru Cliffs six years after my study began, five couples were still together. It is possible that friendships occasionally last for life (baboons probably live twenty to thirty years in the wild), but it will require longer studies, and some very patient scientists to find out.

By increasing both the male's chances of mating in the future and the likelihood that a female's infant will survive, friendship contributes to the reproductive success of both partners. This clarifies the evolutionary basis of friendship-forming tendencies in baboons, but what does the friendship mean to a baboon? To answer this question we need to view baboons as sentient beings with feelings and goals not unlike our own in similar circumstances. Consider, for example, the friendship between Thalia and Alexander.

The affair began one evening as Alex and Thalia sat about fifteen feet apart on the sleeping cliffs. It was like watching two novices in a singles bar. Alex stared at Thalia until she turned and almost caught him looking at her. He glanced away immediately, and then she stared at him until his head began to turn toward her. She suddenly became engrossed in grooming her toes. But as soon as Alex looked away, her gaze returned to him. They went on like this for more than fifteen minutes, always with split-second timing. Finally, Alex managed to catch Thalia looking at him. He made the friendly eyes-narrowed, ears-back face and smacked his lips together rhythmically. Thalia froze, and for a second she looked into his eyes. Alex approached, and Thalia, still nervous, groomed him. Soon she calmed down, and I found them still together on the cliffs the next morning. Looking back on this event months later, I realized that it marked the beginning of their friendship. Six years later, when I returned to Eburru Cliffs, they were still friends.

If flirtation forms an integral part of baboon friendship, so does jealousy. Overt displays of jealousy, such as chasing a friend away from a potential rival, occur occasionally, but like humans, baboons often express their emotions in more subtle ways. One evening a colleague and I climbed the cliffs and settled down near Sherlock, who was friends with Cybelle, a middle-aged female still foraging on the ground below the cliffs. I observed Cybelle while my colleague watched Sherlock, and we kept a running commentary. As long as Cybelle was feeding or interacting with females, Sherlock was relaxed, but each time she approached another male, his body would stiffen, and he would stare intently at the scene below. When Cybelle presented politely to a male who had recently tried to befriend her, Sherlock even made threatening sounds under his breath. Cybelle was not in estrus at the time, indicating that male baboon jealousy extends beyond the sexual arena to include affiliative interactions between a female friend and other males.

Because baboon friendships are embedded in a network of friendly and antagonistic relationships, they inevitably lead to repercussions extending beyond the pair. For example, Virgil once provoked his weaker rival Cyclops into a fight by first attacking Cyclops's friend Phoebe. On another occasion, Sherlock chased Circe, Hector's best friend, just after Hector had chased Antigone, Sherlock's friend.

In another incident, the prime adult male Triton challenged Cyclops's possession of meat. Cyclops grew increasingly tense and seemed about to abandon the prey to the younger male. Then Cyclops's friend Phoebe appeared with her infant Phyllis. Phyllis wandered over to Cyclops. He immediately grabbed her, held her close, and threatened Triton away from the prey. Because any challenge to Cyclops now involved a threat to Phyllis as well, Triton risked being mobbed by Phoebe and her relatives and friends. For this reason, he backed down. Males frequently use the infants of their female friends as buffers in this way. Thus, friendship involves costs as well as benefits because it makes the participants vulnerable to social manipulation or redirected aggression by others.

Finally, as with humans, friendship seems to mean something different to each baboon. Several females in Eburru Cliffs had only one friend. Louise and Pandora, for example, groomed their friend Virgil and no other male. Then there was Leda, who, with five friends, spread herself more thinly than any other female. These contrasting patterns of friendship were associated with striking personality differences.

Louise and Pandora were unobtrusive females who hung around quietly with Virgil and their close relatives. Leda seemed to be everywhere at once, playing with infants, fighting with juveniles, and making friends with males. Similar differences were apparent among the males. Some devoted a great deal of time and energy to cultivating friendships with females, while others focused more on challenging other males. Although we probably will never fully understand the basis of these individual differences, they contribute immeasurably to the richness and complexity of baboon society.

Male-female friendships may be widespread among primates. They have been reported for many other groups of savanna baboons, and they also occur in rhesus and Japanese Macaques, capuchin monkeys, and perhaps in bonobos (pygmy chimpanzees). These relationships should give us pause when considering popular scenarios for the evolution of male-female relationships in humans. Most of these scenarios assume that, except for mating, males and females had little to do with one another until the development of a sexual division of labor, when, the story goes, females began to rely on males to provide meat in exchange for gathered food. This, it has been argued, set up new selection pressures favoring the development of long-term bonds between individual males and females, female sexual fidelity, and as paternity certainly increased, greater male investment in the offspring of these unions. In other words, once women began to gather and men to hunt, presto—we had the nuclear family.

This scenario may have more to do with cultural biases about women's economic dependence on men and idealized views of the nuclear family than with the actual behavior of our hominid ancestors. The nonhuman primate evidence challenges this story in at least three ways.

First, long-term bonds between the sexes can evolve in the absence of a sexual division of labor of food sharing. In our primate relatives, such relationships rest on exchanges of social, not economic, benefits.

Second, primate research shows that highly differentiated, emotionally intense male-female relationships can occur without sexual exclusivity. Ancestral men and women may have experienced intimate friendships long before they invented marriage and norms of sexual fidelity.

Third, among our closest primate relatives, males clearly provide mothers and infants with social benefits even when they are unlikely to be the fathers of those infants. In return, females provide a variety of benefits to the friendly males, including acceptance into the group and, at least in baboons, increased mating opportunities in the future. This suggests that efforts to reconstruct the evolution of hominid societies may have overemphasized what the female must supposedly do (restrict her mating to just one male) in order to obtain male parental investment.

Maybe it is time to pay more attention to what the male must do (provide benefits to females and young) in order to obtain female cooperation. Perhaps among our ancestors, as in baboons today, sex and friendship went hand in hand. As for marriage—well, that's another story.

ID#_____   NAME_____

Article 12: What Are Friends For?

1. The author notes that although promiscuity is usually related to random copulation, recent primate field studies have shown that copulation is _____.

2. What is the assumption underlying the dominance hypothesis? Is this valid?

3. What questions was the author trying to answer in her study of the Eburru Cliffs baboon troop?

4. What two measures allowed the author to determine whether or not baboons were friends?

5. Describe how the following factors influenced baboon pairings:
   - Relatedness

   - Age

   - Sex

   - Dominance

6. Are females generally afraid of males? Why or why not?

7. What does the female baboon gain from the friendship in terms of:
   - Protection?

   - Infant care?

8. How often is the male the father of the female's infant? Is he more or less likely to form a male-infant bond if he is the father?

9. What benefits does the male derive from the friendship?

10. What does the study of baboon friendships tell us about male-female relationships in humans?

Called "Trimates," Three Bold Women Shaped Their Field

Virginia Morell, Patricia Kahn, Toomas Koppel and Dennis Normile

Melissa Remis, a doctoral candidate at Yale University, has just returned from a 3-year study of lowland gorillas in the Central African Republic, a study that involved some terrifying moments. Remis' aim was to "habituate" the gorillas to her presence, persuading them she was a nonthreatening creature, which would enable her to study their normal behavior patterns. But lowland gorillas don't accept strangers easily. The 400-pound males would charge her, screaming at the top of their lungs. In response, Remis crouched submissively and clung to a treetrunk, praying for the courage not to run, which would disrupt months of patient work. "It's like a wall of sound coming at you. You do everything you can to not move. You hold on to the tree, you hold on to your guide [to prevent him from challenging the gorilla], and you say to yourself over and over again, 'Don't move. Don't move. Don't move.'"

Reprinted *Science 260/no 5106*; 420–425 with permission from The American Association for the Advancement of Science. Copyright © 1993 AAAS.

Through these ordeals (which happened repeatedly), Remis drew on two sources of inner strength. "I knew that I could do it," she says, "because Jane and Dian had done it before me." Jane and Dian are Jane Goodall and Dian Fossey, who with their lesser-known colleague Birute Galdikas, are known as the "Trimates," the founding mothers of contemporary field primatology. "Without them, I don't think I ever would have dreamed this big," adds Remis.

Remis isn't the only one who was encouraged to "dream big" by Goodall, Fossey, and Galdikas. North American primatology, two decades ago a male preserve, is today more than 50% female. But it wasn't just in numbers that the three women had a huge impact on their scientific discipline. Their methods of living among primates (Goodall with chimpanzees, Fossey with gorillas, Galdikas with orangutans) opened the eyes of their male colleagues. "You have to understand," explains Sherwood Washburn, professor emeritus of anthropology at the University of California, Berkeley, "at that time [the early 1960s] it was not a question of if you had a scientific report, but of whether you could see the animals at all. Before Jane, you were excited even if all you saw was an arm or backside disappearing into the bush. But to sit with the animals, as she did, without them running away, was almost unthinkable."

Using these methods, the Trimates provided ground-breaking insights into the great ape societies—insights some insiders in the field think could not have come from a male approach. In all three cases, the payoff came from the women's capacity to empathize with their subjects, seeing them as individuals whose life histories influenced the structure of the group. At the time, male primatologists were quick to dismiss results acquired by way of this method as female sentimentality. Today, after many battles, the significance of the individual personality in primate groups is taken for granted, and the three women are seen as pathbreakers. "They were the pioneers," says John Mitani, a primatologist at the University of Michigan at Ann Arbor. "And because of that, if you want to study these animals today, you inevitably must look at their research."

Can Science Empathize?

In the eyes of Louis Leakey, the renowned paleoanthropologist who launched the three women's studies, the Trimates had two important virtues. For one, none of them had much specialized training. "He wanted someone with a mind uncluttered and unbiased by theory, who would make the study for no other reason than a real desire for knowledge," Goodall wrote in *In the Shadow of Man*, her first popular book.

Their second virtue, for Leakey, was their gender. Leakey thought women were better than men when it came to studying wild primates, says Mary Smith, a senior editor at the National Geographic who worked closely with Leakey and his ape ladies. Leakey, Smith says, "trusted women for their patience, persistence, and perception—traits which he thought made them better students of primate behavior."

Leakey himself was perceptive enough to see those qualities in each of the Trimates, whom he met over a span of more than a decade. Goodall came first, shortly after she arrived in Kenya from England in 1957, aged 24. She contacted Leakey, curator of Nairobi's Coryndon Natural History Museum (today the National Museums of Kenya), on a friend's advice. Leakey offered her a job as a secretary but soon afterward confided that he had bigger things in mind: If she was willing to go, he would find funds to send her to Tanzania to study chimpanzees there. Goodall accepted with alacrity.

In June 1960, she stepped into the forest at Gombe Stream on the shores of Lake Tanganyika, where her determination and skill in watching quickly produced results. Only 3 months into her study, she observed behaviors no researcher had ever reported: chimpanzees feasting on a wild piglet they had killed; chimpanzees hunting monkeys; chimpanzees using tools made from twigs to extract termites from their nests.

That last finding blew apart anthropology's conception of primates—and human beings. "I was at the meeting in London in 1962 when Jane first came back and made that amazing announcement about chimps making tools in the wild," says Alison Jolly, a primatologist at Princeton University. "She essentially redefined what it is to be a human being. We'd all been brought up on 'man-the-tool-maker' and this just took it apart. Everyone knew that things would never be the same again."

Still, primatology was a bastion of male domination—and Goodall came under attack. The ruling animal behaviorists expected the animals to be numbered and placed in general categories, such as "the male" and "the female." Goodall chose to recognize chimpanzees as individuals instead. "I named the animals and used words like 'individual,' 'emotion,' and 'personality,'" she recalls. That was the key to her method: Goodall watched as life histories unfolded, believing that these lives—rather than theories or experiments—held the key to social structure. "Letting nature, including the animal, go its own way, I think is more female—at least in our society," notes Jolly. "It requires a certain kind of patience to put up with something you can't control."

The leading lights of the field considered this tendency unscientific and sentimental. Like Fossey and Galdikas later, Goodall met with hostility from other researchers. The Trimates "all labored at times under a silent ostracism," says Geza Teleki, a primatologist and the chairman of the Washington D.C.-based Committee for the Care and Conservation of Chimpanzees. "And other times it came right out into the open. There were some meetings where scientists really laid into them in a nasty way, insinuating that what they were doing was not appropriate science."

In time, Goodall convinced other primatologists that what she was doing was indeed "appropriate science"—after she had learned some lessons herself. Says her doctoral advisor, Robert Hinde of Cambridge University: "My role with Jane was to teach her how to do science. Her role with me was to open my eyes to the idiosyncracies of the individuals and to see that these were crucial to an understanding of the animals." Even empathy, the most "female" of traits, came to be seen by male primatologists as an important facet of observing primates in the wild. "Empathy is very important in primatology," says Frans de Waal, a zoologist at the Yerkes Regional Primate Research Center in Atlanta. "It helps you to ask questions and to predict what your animals are going to do."

Most of the remaining scientific critics were silenced in 1986 by Goodall's book *The Chimpanzees of Gombe*. A compendium of 25 years of research, filled with charts and graphs, the book demonstrated that she, too, could make "objective" generalizations about chimpanzees. But the essence of her work remained the perception of individual personalities within the primate group. And some female researchers admire her specifically for persisting in a "female" approach against the discouragement of the male scientific culture. "To succeed at a science, a woman has to do what a man does as well or better, it's why women are very hesitant to approach a field in a more female way," says Barbara Smuts, a primatologist at the University of Michigan, Ann Arbor. "Jane was a sterling exception. She never shied from addressing the chimpanzees' emotional nature, but went ahead and wrote what she saw."

Complex Woman

In 1966, when Leakey decided Dian Fossey should be the second Trimate, Goodall was already famous and Leakey was searching for a second Jane Goodall to study gorillas. He found someone considerably more complex psychologically. Fossey, 33, was a physical therapist at a children's hospital in Kentucky who had a passion for African wildlife. Approaching Leakey after a lecture at the University of Kentucky at Louisville, she convinced him she was a worthy successor to Goodall.

Eight months after that meeting, with funds from the Wilkie Foundation (which had also sponsored Goodall), Fossey was on her way to the Congo, where she encountered disaster. Her study was disrupted by civil war, she was taken captive, held in a cage for public display, and may have been raped. Undaunted, Fossey set out again, this time for Rwanda, where she established the Karisoke Centre for Mountain Gorilla Research. Though she did not witness behaviors as sensational as those Goodall reported from Gombe, Fossey saw things primatologists had never viewed:

female gorillas transferring between groups; males killing infants to bring females into heat; gorillas eating their own dung to recycle nutrients.

Those findings formed the basis for Fossey's 1976 Cambridge dissertation, written, like Goodall's, under Hinde. Because so little was known about the gorillas at the time, her dissertation "really established the baseline" for primatologists' understanding of the species, says George Schaller, an eminent zoologist who in 1959 made the first study of wild mountain gorillas. Adds Phyllis Jay Dolhinow, a biological anthropologist at the University of California, Berkeley, "She contributed a vast amount of information about what was largely an unknown ape. Her paradigms were not fashionable, not quantitative, but that's okay. She was an accurate reporter and reported it well."

For Fossey, as for Goodall, the individuality of the apes was paramount. At Cambridge, Fossey forced herself to fit data into the required statistical format, but it was an excruciating experience, and after her thesis she wrote only four scientific articles. Instead of observing objectively, Fossey, whose own human contacts were tenuous, plunged further into the life of the gorilla band. By the end, she had so thoroughly habituated the animals by imitating their behaviors that she was able to sit among them as if she were a gorilla.

This integration into the gorilla group is a direct outgrowth of the empathy that made Goodall's and Fossey's work possible. But as Fossey [crossed the] line from dispassionate observer to participant in gorilla social life (tickling infants, letting the gorillas rummage in her belongings and groom her), she grew less interested in science. The final straw for her was the fact that the gorillas (then numbering only 250) were in danger of being wiped out by poachers and civilization itself. Analyzing age groups, mapping the animals' ranges, sampling dung, listing preferred foods—all work Fossey had done—seemed pointless when the gorillas themselves were in danger of disappearing.

Ultimately, Fossey gave up data collection altogether for what she termed "active conservation": patrolling the park for snares and poachers. Research assistants at her camp who did not follow suit were belittled. Says Kelly Stewart, a primatologist at the University of California, Davis, who worked with Fossey at Karisoke, "If anyone did anything other than going out on antipoaching patrols, she labeled them as selfish. And compared to her, other people were more interested in their own research and less in the conservation. But that was her whole life."

In 1977, poachers killed her favorite gorilla, Digit. "That tragedy practically unhinged her," says Mary Smith. "She became dangerous to herself and the Rwandans, because of her volcanic temper and her methods of interrogating alleged poachers." In 1979, the Rwandan government asked her to leave the country. She returned in 1983 only to be murdered at Karisoke by an unknown assailant 2 years later.

If Goodall's story raises the question of whether empathy can have a role in science, Fossey's raises the issue of what values scientists heed. Many studies have shown that a key difference between men and women is that men often place a high value on theoretical values—knowledge for its own sake—while women tend to evaluate knowledge according to its usefulness. In Fossey's case, the two types of values were intertwined from the beginning—since her scientific interest in the gorillas was triggered by a passion for wildlife and a desire to make a difference in the world.

Ultimately, her concern for the gorillas overrode her scientific values—an experience not uncommon among field primatologists, who often study endangered species. "It's the current dilemma for many scientists: whether one has the obligation to do something useful for the world or to remain purely theoretical," says Teleki. Adds Schaller: "Whether or not one approves of her methods and her goals, Fossey was the one who made the world aware of the plight of the gorillas. Her commitment was critical to their survival."

Publish or Perish?

In some ways Birute Galdikas had the most difficult scientific task of the three Trimates. Unlike chimpanzees or gorillas, orangutans are solitary creatures; observing their interactions is an exceedingly tricky business. Not only do the animals seldom mingle, they live high in the trees and rarely descend to ground level, which is often a swamp. It wasn't until Galdikas had been in the rain forests of Indonesia for a week that she saw her first orangutans, a mother and an infant. The apes were high overhead in the forest canopy. "To follow them, you would have had to just jump in the swamp, which was neck-deep there, and that's when I thought, Gee, this is going to be really hard."

But Galdikas had time and patience—and a passion for studying wild orangutans. She had nurtured that dream long before she met Leakey, in 1969, when he delivered a lecture at University of California, Los Angeles (UCLA), where she was a graduate student in anthropology. Galdikas approached him after the lecture, and her enthusiasm made it clear to him that she deserved a place in the lineage founded by Goodall and Fossey. It took Leakey some time to raise funds, but he ultimately secured enough from several sources to send Galdikas and her then-husband, photographer Rod Brindamour, on their way to Indonesia's Tanjung Puting reserve.

Once there, it wasn't just the solitary nature of the orangs that made study difficult. Orangutans lead slow-paced lives: Females are 15 before they bear their first infant—making a mockery of rapid publication. And the apes didn't welcome her. Instead, they hurled branches and defecated on her when she approached. But Galdikas wasn't in a hurry. "I never pressed them," she says. "I would stop so that they would see that I was not really dangerous, and the next time they would be more relaxed." Nevertheless, it took 12 years for her to habituate one of the orangutans to her presence.

As it had been for Goodall and Fossey, the scientific payoff from Galdikas' patient effort was substantial. The most academically oriented of the Trimates, Galdikas did not shy from modern data collecting techniques or statistics, drawing on those for her highly praised 1978 doctoral thesis from UCLA. In the thesis Galdikas recorded interactions quite different from the little that was then known about orangutans. She saw adolescent orangs traveling together; subadults sometimes forcibly copulating with females; and males and females spending time together in lengthy consortships. She also packed her doctoral study with statistical correlations, identified the orangs' calls, and catalogued every plant and insect they ate.

That would seem to be a highly promising start for a scientific career, and Galdikas' research could easily have led to a traditional University position; but this was not her goal. Though she has part-time appointments at Simon Fraser University in Vancouver, British Columbia, and at the Universitas Nasional in Jakarta, Galdikas' career is—like those of Goodall and Fossey and some other women scientists—more maverick and marginal than those of many male researchers. Like Fossey, Galdikas has grown increasingly concerned with conservation, and now runs her research center, Camp Leakey, primarily with the aid of Earthwatch, the conservation group, rather than with funding from mainstream scientific organizations.

Yet that hasn't been entirely by choice. Scientific funding agencies have become reluctant to support her work because in recent years she hasn't published much and what she has published often relies on data that was collected during her first years of study. "I always support her grant applications," says Peter Rodman, a biological anthropologist at the University of California, Davis. "But there are many things about the life histories of these animals that we'd like her to share. We really haven't heard about them since her thesis." That kind of complaint angers Galdikas. "Those who say I haven't published haven't been in the swamps up to their armpits. Besides, it shouldn't be the quantity of papers, but the quality," she adds, noting that her recent study of birth intervals among the orangutans is highly regarded.

Galdikas' retort—that quality is more important than quantity—is one that may reflect deep-rooted differences in how male and female researchers approach science. Several studies have shown that women publish fewer scientific papers than men do, and although there are differences of opinion about why that is so, many female researchers—and some males as well—believe it is because women are more concerned with thoroughness and with justifying each publication than with the overall number of their publications.

Galdikas' scientific trajectory, like that of Fossey and Goodall, may also reflect another key difference between men and women in scientific research. Males, conditioned practically from birth to think of themselves in terms of career success, bring those expectations to science. They tend to evaluate research topics, collaborations, and jobs in terms of rapid career payoff. It is unlikely that a promising young male researcher would have been willing to invest 12 years habituating a single orangutan, because of the risk that, if there weren't a huge payoff, his career would be in ruins. Galdikas' slowness in publishing—in fact, her overall indifference to conventional academic standards—is what made her scientific success possible.

The Female Style

The question of whether the successes of Jane Goodall, Dian Fossey, and Birute Galdikas were due to their gender is not easy to resolve. It may be tempting to think, with Louis Leakey, that females are patient and singularly perceptive observers. Yet that point of view may simply reflect his own male biases. The qualities the Trimates showed in the field might have had more to do with being scientific outsiders than with being women.

No matter which is true, the Trimates have had an enormous impact on the field of primatology. Not only have they spawned a vast number of students who went on to become major players in primatology, their early studies provided the core of what is known about chimpanzees, gorillas, and orangutans. Perhaps most important, says George Schaller, the Trimates taught science that the great apes are "true individuals." Says Schaller: "They have given us an empathy with our closest relatives, and that is the only thing that will save these animals in the end." . . .

Further Reading

"Jane Goodall" (no author cited), *Current Biography*, Nov 1991 v. 52 n. 11 p. 18(6). This article presents a summary of the pioneering research of Jane Goodall and her observations of chimpanzee behavior in the wild.

Orangutan Odyssey by Birute Galdikas and Nancy Briggs. This book presents an informative and comprehensive view of the research of Birute Galdikas among the orangutans in the wild.

"A Passion for the Primitive: Dian Fossey among the Animals" by Marianna Torgovnick, *Yale Review*, Oct 1996 v. 84 n. 4 p. 1(24). The author recounts the research of the late Dian Fossey and her passion for the preservation of gorillas in their natural habitat.

ID#_____   NAME_____

Article 13: Called "Trimates," Three Bold Women Shaped Their Field

1. What was different about the women's approach to field primatology as compared to their male counterparts?

2. According to Louis Leakey, what two important virtues did each woman have and how did these virtues help the women succeed?

3. What surprising behaviors did Goodall see in her study of wild chimpanzees?

4. Why were many animal behaviorists critical of Goodall's approach?

5. What were some obstacles faced by Dian Fossey when she arrived in the Congo to study gorillas?

6. Why did Fossey give up data collection and scientific research?

7. Name two reasons why Birute Galdikas' orangutan research was more difficult than Goodall or Fossey?

8. Galdikas believes that "quality is more important than quantity." How does this reflect the differences in how male and female researchers approach science?

Got Culture?

Craig Stanford

On my first trip to East Africa in the early 1990s, I stood by a dusty, dirt road hitchhiking. I had waited hours in rural Tanzania for an expected lift from a friend who had never shown up, leaving me with few options other than the kindness of strangers. I stood with my thumb out, but the cars and trucks roared by me, leaving me caked in paprika-red dust. I switched to a palm-down gesture I had seen local people using to get lifts. Voilá; on the first try a truck pulled over and I hopped in. A conversation in Kiswahili with the truck driver ensued and I learned my mistake. Hitchhiking with your thumb upturned may work in the United States, but in Africa the gesture can be translated in the way that Americans understand the meaning of an extended, declarative middle finger. Not exactly the best way to persuade a passing vehicle to stop. The universally recognized symbol for needing a lift is not so universal.

Much of culture is the accumulation of thousands of such small differences. Put a suite of traditions together—religion, language, ways of dress, cuisine, and a thousand other features—and you have a culture. Of course cultures can be much simpler too. A group of toddlers in a day care center possesses its own culture, as does a multi-national corporation, suburban gardeners, inner city gang members. Many elements of a culture are functional and hinged to individual survival: thatched roof homes from the tropics would work poorly in Canada, nor would harpoons made for catching seals be very useful in the Sahara. But other features are purely symbolic. Brides in western culture wear white to symbolize sexual purity. Brides in Hindu weddings wear crimson, to symbolize sexual purity. Whether white or red is more pure is nothing more than a product of the long-term memory and mindset of the two cultures. And the most symbolic of cultural traditions, the one that has always been considered a bailiwick of humanity only, is language. The words "white" and "red" have an entirely arbitrary relationship to the colors themselves. They are simply code names.

Arguing about how to define culture has long been a growth industry among anthropologists. We argue about culture the way the Joint Chiefs of Staff argue about national security: as though our lives depended on it. But given that culture requires symbolism and some linguistic features, can we even talk about culture in other animals?

From *Significant Others* by Craig Stanford. Copyright © by Craig Stanford. Reprinted by permission of Basic Books, a member of Perseus Books, L.L.C.

In 1996 I was attending a conference near Rio de Janeiro when the topic turned to culture. As a biological anthropologist with a decade of field research on African great apes, I offered my perspective on the concept of culture. Chimpanzees, I said with confidence, display a rich cultural diversity. Recent years have shown that each wild chimpanzee population is more than just a gene pool. It is also a distinct culture, comprising a unique assortment of learned traditions in tool use, styles of grooming and hunting, and other features of the sort that can only be seen in the most socially sophisticated primates. Go from one forest to another and you will run into a new culture, just as walking between two human villages may introduce you to tribes who have different ways of building boats or celebrating marriages.

At least that's what I meant to say. But I had barely gotten the word "culture" past my lips when I was made to feel the full weight of my blissful ignorance. The cultural anthropologists practically leaped across the seminar table to berate me for using the words "culture" and "chimpanzee" in the same sentence. I had apparently set off a silent security alarm, and the culture-theory guards came running. How dare you, they said, use a human term like "cultural diversity" to describe what chimpanzees do? Say "behavioral variation," they demanded. "Apes are mere animals, and culture is something that only the human animal can claim. Furthermore, not only can humans alone claim culture, culture alone can explain humanity." It became clear to me that culture, as understood by most anthropologists, is a human concept, and many passionately want it to stay that way. When I asked if this was not just a semantic difference—what are cultural traditions if not learned behavioral variations?—they replied that culture is symbolic, and what animals do lacks symbolism.

When Jane Goodall first watched chimpanzees make simple stick tools to probe into termite mounds, it became clear that tool cultures are not unique to human societies. Of course many animals use tools. Sea otters on the California coast forage for abalones, which they place on their chests and hammer open with stones. Egyptian vultures use stones to break the eggs of ostriches. But these are simple, relatively inflexible lone behaviors. Only among chimpanzees do we see elaborate forms of tools made and used in variable ways, and also see distinct chimp tool cultures across Africa. In Gombe National Park in Tanzania, termite mounds of red earth rise two meters high and shelter millions of the almond-colored insects. Chimpanzees pore over the mounds, scratching at plugged tunnels until they find portals into the mound's interior. They will gently insert a twig or blade of grass into a tunnel until the soldier termites latch onto the tools with their powerful mandibles, then they'll withdraw the probe from the mound. With dozens of soldier and worker termites clinging ferociously to the twig, the chimpanzee draws the stick between her lips and reaps a nutritious bounty.

Less than a hundred kilometers away from Gombe's termite-fishing apes is another culture. Chimpanzees in Mahale National Park live in a forest that is home to most of the same species of termites, but they practically never use sticks to eat them. If Mahale chimpanzees forage for termites at all, they use their fingers to crumble apart soil and pick out their insect snacks. However, Mahale chimpanzees love to eat ants. They climb up the straight-sided trunks of great trees and poke Gombe-like probes into holes to obtain wood-boring species. As adept as Gombe chimpanzees are at fishing for termites, they practically never fish for these ants, even though both the ants and the termites occur in both Gombe and Mahale.

Segue two thousand kilometers westward, to a rainforest in Côte d'Ivoire. In a forest filled with twigs, chimpanzees do not use stick tools. Instead, chimpanzees in Taï National Park and other forests in western Africa use hammers made of rock and wood. Swiss primatologists Christophe and Hedwige Boesch and their colleagues first reported the use of stone tools by chimpanzees twenty years ago. Their subsequent research showed that Taï chimpanzees collect hammers when certain species of nut-bearing trees are in fruit. These hammers are not modified in any way as the stone tools made by early humans were; they are hefted, however, and appraised for weight and smashing value before being carried back to the nut tree. A nut is carefully positioned in a depression in the tree's above-ground root buttresses (the anvil) and struck with precision by the tool-user. The researchers have seen mothers instructing their children on the art of tool use, by assisting them in placing the nut in the anvil in the proper way.

So chimpanzees in East Africa use termite- and ant-fishing tools, and West African counterparts use hammers, but not vice versa. These are subsistence tools; they were almost certainly invented for food-getting. Primatologist William McGrew of Miami University of Ohio has compared the tool technologies of wild chimpanzees with those of traditional human hunter—gatherer societies. He found that in at least some instances, the gap between chimpanzee technology and human technology is not wide. The now-extinct aboriginal Tasmanians, for example, possessed no complex tools or weapons of any kind. Though they are an extreme example, the Tasmanians illustrate that human culture need not be technologically complex.

As McGrew first pointed out, there are three likeliest explanations for the differences we see among the chimpanzee tool industries across Africa. The first is genetic: perhaps there are mutations that arise in one population but not others that govern tool making. This seems extremely unlikely, just as we would never argue that Hindu brides wear red while western brides wear white due to a genetic difference between Indians and westerners. The second explanation is ecological: maybe the environment in which the chimpanzee population lives dictates patterns of tool use. Maybe termite-fishing sticks will be invented in places where there are termites and sticks but not rocks and nuts, and hammers invented in the opposite situation. But a consideration of each habitat raises doubts. Gombe is a rugged, rock-strewn place where it is hard to find a spot to sit that is not within arm's reach of a few stones, but Gombe chimpanzees do not use stone tools. The West African chimpanzees who use stone tools live, by contrast, in lowland rainforests that are nearly devoid of rocks. Yet they purposely forage to find them. The tool-use pattern is exactly the opposite of what we would expect if environment and local availability accounted for differences among chimpanzee communities in tool use.

British psychologist Andrew Whiten and his colleagues recently conducted the first systematic survey of cultural differences in tool use among the seven longest-term field studies, representing more than a century and a half of total observation time. They found thirty-nine behaviors that could not be explained by environmental factors at the various sites. Alone with humans in the richness of their behavior repertoire, chimpanzee cultures show variations that can only be ascribed to learned traditions. These traditions, passed from one generation to the next through observation and imitation, are a simple version of human culture.

But wait. I said earlier that human culture must have a symbolic element. Tools that differ in form and function, from sticks to hammers to sponges made of crushed leaves, are all utterly utilitarian. They tell us much about the environment in which they are useful but little about the learned traditions that led to their creation. Human artifacts, on the other hand, nearly always contain some purely symbolic element, be it the designs carved into a piece of ancient pottery or the "Stanley" logo on my new claw hammer. Is there anything truly symbolic in chimpanzee culture, in the human sense of an object or behavior that is completely detached from its use?

Male chimpanzees have various ways of indicating to a female that they would like to mate. At Gombe, one such courtship behavior involves rapidly shaking a small bush or branch several times, after which a female in proximity will usually approach the male and present her swelling to him. But in Mahale, males have learned to use leaves in their courtship gesture. A male plucks a leafy stem from a nearby plant and noisily uses his teeth and fingers to tear off its leaves. Leaf-clipping is done mainly in the context of wanting to mate with a particular female, and appears to function as a purely symbolic signal of sexual desire (it could also be a gesture of frustration). A second leafy symbol is leaf-grooming. Chimpanzees pick leaves and intently groom them with their fingers, as seriously as though they were grooming another chimpanzee. And this may be the function; leaf-grooming may signal a desire for real grooming from a social partner. Since the signal for grooming involves grooming, albeit of another object, this gesture is not symbolic in the sense that leaf-clipping is. But its distribution across Africa is equally spotty; leaf-grooming is commonly practiced in East African chimpanzee cultures but is largely absent in western Africa.

These two cases of potentially symbolic behavior may not seem very impressive. After all, the briefest consideration of human culture turns up a rich array of symbolism, from language to the arts. But are all human creatures highly symbolic? If we use language and other forms of symbolic expression as the criterion for culture, then how about a classroom full of two-year-old toddlers in a day care center? They communicate by a very simple combination of gestures and half-formed sentences. Toddlers have little symbolic communication or appreciation for art and are very little different from chimpanzee in their cultural output. We grant them human qualities because we know they will mature into symbol-using, linguistically expert adults, leaving chimpanzees in the dust. But this is no reason to consider them on a different plane from the apes when both are fifteen months old.

Chimpanzee societies are based on learned traditions passed from mother to child and from adult males to eager wannabe males. These traditions vary from place to place. This is culture. Culture is not limited, however, to those few apes that are genetically ninety-nine percent human. Many primates show traditions. These are usually innovations by younger members of a group, which sweep rapidly through the society and leave it just slightly different than before. Japanese primatologist have long observed such traditions among the macaques native to their island nation. Researchers long ago noticed that a new behavior had arisen in one population of Japanese macaque monkeys living on Koshima Island just offshore the mainland. The monkeys were regularly tossed sweet potatoes, rice and other local treats by the locals. One day Imo, a young female in the group, took her potato and carried it to the sea, where she washed it with salty brine before eating it. This behavior rapidly spread throughout the group, a nice example of innovation happening in real time so that researchers could observe the diffusion. Later, other monkeys invented the practice of scooping up rice offered them with the beach sand it was scattered on, throwing both onto the surf and then scraping up the grains that floated while the sand sank.

At a supremely larger scale, such innovations are what human cultural differences are all about. Of course, only in human cultures do objects such as sweet potatoes take on the kind of symbolic meaning that permits them to stand for other objects and thus become a currency. Chimpanzees lack the top-drawer cognitive capacity needed to invent such a currency. Or do they? Wild chimpanzees hunt for a part of their living. All across equatorial Africa, meat-eating is a regular feature of chimpanzee life, but its style and technique vary from one forest to another. In Taï National Park in western Africa, hunters are highly cooperative; Christophe Boesch has reported specific roles such as ambushers and drivers as part of the apes' effort to corral colobus monkeys in the forest canopy. At Gombe in East Africa, meanwhile, hunting is like a baseball game; a group sport performed on an individual basis. This difference may be environmentally influenced; perhaps the high canopy rain forest at Taï requires cooperation more than the broken, low canopy forest at Gombe. There is a culture of hunting in each forest as well, in which young and eager male wannabes copy the predatory skills of their elders. At Gombe, for instance, chimpanzees relish wild pigs and piglets in addition to monkeys and small antelope. At Taï, wild pigs are ignored even when they stroll in front of a hunting party.

There is also a culture of sharing the kill. Sharing of meat is highly nepotistic at Gombe; sons who make the kill share with their mothers and brothers but snub rival males. They also share preferentially with females who have sexual swellings, and with high-ranking females. At Taï, the captor shares with the other members of the hunting party whether or not they are allies or relatives; a system of reciprocity seems to be in place in which the golden rule works. I have argued that since the energy and time that chimpanzees spend hunting is rarely paid back by the calories, protein and fat gotten from a kill, we should consider hunting a social behavior done at least partly for its own sake. When chimpanzees barter a limited commodity such as meat for other services—alliances, sex, grooming—they are engaging in a very simple and primitive form of currency exchange. Such an exchange relies on the ability of the participants to remember the web of credits and debts owed one another and to act accordingly. It may be that the two chimpanzee cultures two thousand kilometers apart have developed their distinct uses of meat as a social currency. In one place meat is used as a reward for cooperation, in the other as a manipulative tool of nepotism. Such systems are commonplace in all human societies, and their roots may be seen in chimpanzees' market economy, too.

I have not yet considered one obvious question. If tool use and other cultural innovations can be so valuable to chimpanzees, why have they not arisen more widely among primates and other big-brained animals? Although chimpanzees are adept tool-users, their very close relatives the bonobos are not. Bonobos do a number of very clever things—dragging their hands beside them as they wade through streams to catch fish is one notable example—but they are not accomplished technicians. Gorillas don't use tools at all, and orangutans have only recently been observed to occasionally use sticks as probing tools in their rainforest canopy world.

Other big-brained animals fare even worse. Wild elephants don't use their wonderfully dexterous trunks to manipulate tools in any major way, although when you're strong enough to uproot trees you may not have much use for a pokey little probe. Dolphins and whales, cognitively gifted though they may be, lack the essential anatomical ingredient for tool manufacture—a pair of nimble hands. Wild bottlenose dolphins have been observed to carry natural sponges about on their snouts to ferret food from the sea bottom, the only known form of cetacean tool use. But that may be the limit of how much a creature that lacks any grasping appendages can manipulate its surroundings.

So to be a cultural animal, it is not enough to be big-brained. You must have the anatomical prerequisites for tool cultures to develop. Even if these are in place, there is no guarantee that a species will generate a subsistence culture in the form of tools. Perhaps environmental necessity dictates which ape species use tools and which don't, except it is hard to imagine that bonobos have much less use for tools than chimpanzees do. There is probably a strong element of chance involved. The chance that a cultural tradition—tool use, hunting style or grooming technique—will develop may be very small in any given century or millennium. Once innovated, the chance that the cultural trait will disappear—perhaps due to the death of the main practitioners from whom everyone learned the behavior—may conversely be great. Instead of a close fit between the environment and the cultural traditions that evolve in it—which many scholars believe explains cultural diversity in human societies—the roots of cultural variation may be much more random. A single influential individual who figures out how to make a better mousetrap, so to speak, can through imitation spread his mousetrap through the group and slowly into other groups.

We tend to think of cultural traditions as highly plastic and unstable compared to biological innovation. It takes hundreds of generations for natural selection to bring about biological change, whereas cultural change can happen in one lifetime, even in a few minutes. Because we live in a culture in which we buy the newest cell phone and the niftiest handheld computer—we fail to appreciate how conservative traditions like tool use can be. *Homo erectus*, with a brain nearly the size of our own, invented a teardrop-shaped stone tool called a hand axe a million and a half years ago. It was presumably used for butchering carcasses, though some archaeologists think it may have also been a weapon. Whatever its purpose, more than a million years later those same stone axes were still being manufactured and used. Fifty thousand generations passed without a significant change in the major piece of material culture in a very big-brained and intelligent human species. *That's* conservatism and it offers us two lessons. First, if it ain't broke don't fix it: when a traditional way of making a tool works and the environment is not throwing any curves your way, there may be no pressure for a change. Second, we see a human species vastly more intelligent than an ape (*Homo erectus'* neocortical brain volume was a third smaller than a modern human's, but two and a half times larger than a chimpanzee's) whose technology didn't change at all. This tells us that innovations, once made, may last a very long time without being either extinguished or improved upon. It suggests that chimpanzee tool cultures may have been in place for all of the five million years since their divergence from our shared ancestor.

The very word *culture*, as William McGrew has pointed out, was invented for humans, and this has long blinded cultural theorists to a more expansive appreciation of the concept. Whether apes have culture or not is not really the issue. The heart of the debate is whether scholars who study culture and consider it their intellectual territory will accept a more expansive definition. In purely academic arguments like this one, the power lies with the party who owns the key concepts of the discipline. They define concepts however they choose, and the choice is usually aimed at fencing off their intellectual turf from all others.

Primatologists are latecomers to the table of culture, and they have had to wait their turn before being allowed to sit. We should be most interested in what the continuum of intelligence tells us about the roots of human behavior, not whether what apes do or don't do fits any particular, rigid definition of culture. When it comes to human practices, from building boats to weddings to choosing mates, we should look at the intersections of our biology and our culture for clues about what has made us who we are.

ID#_____ NAME_____

Article 14: Got Culture?

1. What does the author list as the two elements of culture?

2. What aspect of culture pertains only to humanity?

3. Why were the cultural anthropologists so upset with the author's claim that chimpanzees have culture?

4. What do the cultural anthropologists call what chimpanzees do?

5. Describe one example of regional variation in chimpanzee tool cultures.

6. Does the author believe human culture must be technologically complex? What example does he give?

7. The three possible explanations for the differences seen in chimpanzee tool use are
   _____ , _____ , and _____ .

8. Describe one example of symbolism in chimpanzee culture.

9. Describe one example of traditions in the Japanese macaque.

10. Besides a large brain, what anatomical characteristic must exist for tool cultures to develop?

11. What does the author feel is really at the heart of the debate over primate culture?

Tooling through the Trees
Carl Zimmer

Carel van Schaik had a dilemma. In August 1993 he was sitting in a crude shelter in the Suaq Balimbing swamp in Sumatra, deciding whether he should make the place his scientific home. Van Schaik, a primatologist at Duke University, studies orangutans. Suaq had a lot of them—as many as 20 individuals per square mile. But Suaq is a godforsaken place. Never mind the prevalence of malaria, dengue fever, and typhoid—simply following the orangutans as they moved high overhead in the trees required wading through thigh-high muck. Every day was an exercise in exhaustion.

"We were sitting there in our little shelter, thinking, 'Well, the place certainly has a lot of orangutans,'" says van Schaik. "But it was such a terribly deep swamp. We were really tearing our hair out, wondering whether we should stay there or not. And then Ibrahim, one of my Indonesian assistants, just dropped in a little observation: 'You know, boss, I saw something really weird today. I don't know what to make of it. Sarah'—one of our orangutans—'was putting a stick in her mouth and then hammering away at a tree with it.'

"I said, 'What?'"

Sketchy as Ibrahim's news was, van Schaik began to wonder if he had actually seen something never witnessed before: a wild orangutan using a tool. Slogging through Suaq suddenly seemed worth the effort.

Toolmaking was once considered a hallmark of the unique intelligence of human beings. Researchers began to question that notion, however, as they discovered that wild chimpanzees, our closest relatives, use a number of tools, including sticks to get termites out of nests, and stones to crack open nuts. Moreover, they don't just use whatever happens to be lying around—they tailor their tools to fit a particular job.

The last common ancestor of chimps and humans lived 6 million years ago. Gorillas split off from the ancestor of chimps and humans 8 million years ago, and while they sometimes play with tools in captivity, they never use them in the wild. Orangutans, which branched away from the other apes 14 to 16 million years ago, have a different story. Captive orangutans have been taught to wield hammers, screwdrivers, and keys (among zookeepers they're notorious as lock-picking escape artists), and even to make stone-flake knives. But since they needed a human to teach them and had never been seen to use tools in the wild, it appeared they weren't in the same league

From *Discover Magazine*, 1995, Volume 16 by Carl Zimmer. Copyright © 1995 by Discover Magazine. Reprinted by permission.

as chimps. "Animals do a lot of things in captivity that they will never do in the wild. It's the difference between having the capacity to do something and having the actual skill," says van Schaik. Researchers believed that the ability to make and use tools was something that only emerged in our chimplike ancestors.

Van Schaik and his coworkers came back to Suaq in January 1994, built a boardwalk through the swamp to make their lives a little easier, and began following up on Ibrahim's report. They quickly discovered that the Suaq orangutans used tools for a number of purposes. As Ibrahim had seen, sometimes an ape will break off a branch about a foot long, snap off the twigs, fray one end, and put the other end in its mouth. Holding on to a tree trunk with its arms and legs, the orangutan rams the stick into a hole containing a termite nest. It then flicks out the broken-up chunks—full of delectable larvae and pupae—and eats them. The Suaq orangutans also use sticks to scare out ants from tree colonies. "But the most common use is when they go for honey," says van Schaik. "They put a stick in and poke through some nest wall and move it around and catch the honey, pull it out, turn it around and stick the other end in their mouth, and then go back in." If the stick is too long to use comfortable, they snap off one end.

Orangutans also use tools to eat fruit. When the fruit of the Neesia tree ripens, its hard, ridged husk softens until it falls open. Inside are seeds that the orangutans love, but they are surrounded by fiberglass-like hairs that, as van Schaik can personally attest, "hurt like hell." A Neesia-eating orangutan will select a five-inch stick, strip off its bark, and then carefully collect the hairs with it. Once the fruit is safe, the ape pops the seeds out with the stick or with its fingers.

Every adult orangutan van Schaik's team has followed for more than five minutes at Suaq uses tools. "It's clearly a routine thing, a population-wide, year-round phenomenon," says van Schaik. "It's not the idiosyncrasy of one genius."

On the other hand, other orangutan populations don't seem to do it. One reason may be ecological: the trees in Suaq are especially riddled with insects, and the orangutans there depend heavily on insects for food, so they're under pressure to figure out how to get bugs out of trees. Yet there are similar swamps in Borneo where researchers have not seen orangutans use tools. Van Schaik thinks cultural factors may play a role, too. In any given population, some genius does have to figure out how to use sticks first. In Borneo, says van Schaik, the inventor may simply not have been born yet; in other environments, an individual orangutan may have invented tools only to have its peers ignore the skill because it was superfluous there.

It's possible, of course, that the very first invention of tools among orangutans happened relatively recently in Suaq. Van Schaik thinks that's unlikely. Of the four types of great apes, he points out, three—chimps, orangs, and humans—have now been observed to use tools in the wild. The simplest explanation, says van Schaik, is that the apes' common ancestor did, too. Gorillas, the fourth great ape, lost the skill because they developed an easy diet of leaves and nettles that made tools pointless. But by the time humans evolved, toolmaking was a long-established art. "We don't have to see early hominids as these heroes that invented 10,000 different things in five minutes," says van Schaik. "There may have been little that was new there—they already had the capacity and most likely the skill."

Van Schaik's observations complement a growing body of research that suggests the real quantum leap of intelligence did not happen 6 million years ago among the earliest hominids but 16 million years ago among the earliest great apes. It was then, in this view, that animals first evolved insight—an ability to make connections between concepts, recognize cause and effect, and plan actions. The sort of thinking required for using tools, for symbolic communication, for empathy—for all these supposedly quintessentially human gifts—may be far older than we imagined.

Further Reading

"The Red Ape's Surprise: Tool-making Wild Orangutans Rival Chimps in Creativity" by Carel van Schaik and Caroline Dopyera, *Wildlife Conservation*, Jan–Feb 1997 v. 100 n. 1 p. 37(7). This article presents additional evidence of the manufacturing of sophisticated tools among orangutans in the wild.

"Orangutans in the Wild" by Cheryl Knott, *National Geographic*, August 1998 v. 194 n. 2 p. 30(28). The author presents data collected on how the availability of food affects the movement and behavior of orangutans in the wild.

ID#_____   NAME_____

Article 15: Tooling through the Trees

1. Why is it so difficult to study orangutans at Suaq?

2. What discovery made the team decide to study the Suaq orangutans?

3. What kinds of tools are used by captive orangutans?

4. List the four types of tools used by wild orangutans at the Suaq site. Include in your answer what the tools are used for.

5. Does Van Schaik think this tool use is a recent phenomenon? Why or why not?

16

Which of Our Genes Make Us Human?

Ann Gibbons

We humans like to think of ourselves as special, set apart from the rest of the animal kingdom by our ability to talk, write, build complex structures, and make moral distinctions. But when it comes to genes, humans are so similar to the two species of chimpanzee that physiologist Jared Diamond has called us "the third chimpanzee." A quarter-century of genetic studies has consistently found that for any given region of the genome, humans and chimpanzees share at least 98.5% of their DNA. This means that a very small portion of human DNA is responsible for the traits that make us human, and that a handful of genes somehow confer everything from an upright gait to the ability to recite poetry and compose music.

But what are these genes, so few in number yet so powerful in effect? Until now there has been little funding or research to track them down, and the primate genome has been almost virgin territory. "You could write everything we knew about the genetic differences in a one-sentence article," quips neuroscientist Thomas Insel, director of the Yerkes Regional Primate Research Center of Emory University in Atlanta.

Now that is changing, as a persistent band of geneticists and evolutionary biologists launches new studies to find differences in the genes, chromosomes, and biochemistry of humans and chimpanzees. Next month, researchers will report finding the first significant biochemical variation between humans and other apes: Humans lack a particular form of a ubiquitous cell surface molecule found in all other apes. Other teams are reporting newfound differences in the arrangements of DNA on the chromosomes of humans and other primates.

And new sequencing projects are starting to compare primate and human DNA base by base. Two new centers—at Yerkes and in Leipzig—opened simultaneously last year to study the molecular evolution of the great apes; next month, at an international meeting in Chicago, researchers will push for an organized, international primate genome project (see sidebar). Because primates are less susceptible than humans to

Reprinted *Science* 281: 1432–1434 with permission from The American Association for the Advancement of Science. Copyright © 1998 AAAS.

certain diseases, including cancer and AIDS, the sequence differences are of more than evolutionary interest and are already drawing commercial attention. One Denver, Colorado, biotech company has already submitted patents on key human and chimp genes.

For the moment, no one can tie the few known molecular variations with the familiar litany of chimp-human differences, such as body hair, language, or brain size. But the leaders of genomic and evolutionary research alike say that now is the time to explore those links. "This is one of the major questions that those of us interested in our own biology would like to ask—what does that 1.5% difference look like?" says Francis Collins, director of the National Human Genome Research Institute.

Vive La Difference

That question was first raised in print in a landmark 1975 paper by geneticist Mary-Claire King and the late biochemist Allan Wilson, both then of the University of California, Berkeley. They surveyed protein and nucleic acid studies and found that the average human protein was more than 99% identical to its chimpanzee counterpart; the coarse DNA hybridization methods of the time showed that the average nucleic acid sequence was almost as similar. Thus, King and Wilson concluded, humans and chimpanzees were genetically as similar as sibling species of other organisms, such as fruit flies or mice.

This left a great paradox: Our DNA is almost identical to that of our chimp cousins, but we don't look or act alike. "The molecular similarity between chimpanzees and humans is extraordinary because they differ far more than many other sibling species in anatomy and way of life," the pair wrote.

What's more, much of the DNA in any organism is so-called "junk DNA" that has no apparent function, and mutations in these regions do not change the function of genes. Thus, many of the genetic differences between humans and chimps probably don't affect the organisms at all. The challenge is to find those few mutations that do make a difference—either by altering genes that code for proteins or by changing how genes are regulated, King and Wilson said.

But although many labs have since confirmed that our nuclear DNA is 98% to 99% identical to that of chimpanzees, few have taken on the quest to find the differences that matter. "It was one of those fields that fell through the cracks," says Ajit Varki, a glycobiologist at the University of California, San Diego (UCSD), who has recently surveyed the known differences between humans and apes.

The tools and funds for sequencing large amounts of DNA rapidly weren't available until recently. And this line of work required a bold shift in thinking for most labs. "Most people in comparative genetics ask what's similar and conserved," says molecular evolutionist Caro-Beth Stewart at the State University of New York, Albany, who trained with Wilson. "Just a few of us have been trying to ask: What's different? What makes us human?"

The Biochemical Trail

One way to answer that question is to start with biochemical differences, and then trace them back to their genetic origins. That approach has yielded its first big payoff, to be reported in the October [1998] issue of the *American Journal of Physical Anthropology*. After studying tissues and blood samples from the great apes and 60 humans from diverse ethnic groups, Varki and his colleagues Elaine Muchmore and Sandra Diaz at UCSD were surprised to find that human cells are missing a particular form of sialic acid, a type of sugar, found in all other mammals studied so far, including the great apes. "Now you've got something that is changing the surfaces of all cells in the body," says Varki.

The sialic acid molecule is found on the surface of every cell in the body, and previous work has shown that it can take on a surprising variety of roles. In some cases, it acts as a receptor for messages from other cells, but pathogens including those that cause cholera, influenza, and malaria also use it to gain a foothold on the cell. Chimpanzees are not as susceptible as humans to some of these pathogens, and the researchers speculate that this molecular change may be part of the reason why. There are even hints that sialic acid may be involved in cellular communication during brain development and function, says Varki.

The chimp and mammalian form of sialic acid, known as *N*-glycolyl-neuraminic acid (Neu5Gc), is modified from the basic form of the compound (called Neu5Ac) by the addition of an oxygen atom. But the human form is simply the basic acid, lacking the additional oxygen atom. That changes the shape of the molecule in a region that could alter how it is recognized by other molecules, whether pathogens or cellular messengers, says Varki. Other researchers are intrigued: "I think this is really nice work," says Svante Pääbo, a molecular geneticist at the University of Munich and leader of a German effort to sequence ape genomes. "It's really the first difference [in the expression of a gene product] that has come up."

In recent months, Varki's team has traced this difference back to a gene that codes for a hydroxylase enzyme in apes, which adds the extra oxygen atom. Humans are missing a 92-base pair section of this gene, according to new results from a team of Japanese researchers, led by glycobiologists Akemi Suzuki and Yasunori Kozutsumi at Tokyo Metropolitan Institute. Varki's lab has a paper in press in the *Proceedings of the National Academy of Sciences* that includes similar studies on the gene in the great apes; they are now also working on human fossils with Pääbo's lab to see if this change was recent in humans.

Yet the question still remains: Does this biochemical difference matter? No one has yet identified a specific function altered by the loss of this particular version of the molecule. "Until we know what this gene does, I remain skeptical of its importance," says Harvard University molecular anthropologist Maryellen Ruvolo. In search of clues, Kozutsumi is raising mice where the hydroxylase enzyme gene is knocked out, as it is in humans, to see if they produce the similar form of sialic acid seen in humans—and if they have any anatomical or behavioral differences. "Maybe their mice will speak," jokes Varki, whose own lab is raising transgenic mice that overexpress hydroxylase in the brain to see if it affects anatomy or behavior.

But Ruvolo doesn't expect dramatic results: "Somehow, I can't believe that switching off the expression of this gene in adult humans is responsible for a myriad of important changes in human evolution." Most researchers, including Varki, agree that the difference won't come down to a single genetic change. "There won't be one magic gene that makes us human," says King, now at the University of Washington, Seattle.

Remodeling Chromosomes

Another tactic for finding the key differences is to start with chromosomes, because even a simple karyotype—a picture of the chromosomes—reveals that other apes have 24 pairs of chromosomes while humans have 23 pairs. While 18 of the 23 pairs are virtually identical in humans and other apes, it has long been known that the remaining pairs have segments that have been reshuffled since the great apes went their separate ways. In recent years, several labs in the United States and Germany have been homing in on this chromosomal remodeling.

For example, the gene mutated in a rare human disorder called adrenoleukodystrophy—made famous by the movie *Lorenzo's*

Pushing a Primate Genome Project

Paleoanthropologists have long mined the stones and bones left by ancient humans for evidence of our past. But locked in the DNA of apes in zoos and tropical forests is an untapped treasure trove of clues about how we became human. "All sorts of attention is lavished on every new early human fossil out of Africa," says Edwin McConkey, a molecular biologist at the University of Colorado, Boulder. "But chimpanzees are astonishingly close to us genetically. Isn't it time to study these living links as well?"

McConkey is one of the leaders of a push for an international program to sequence DNA from chimpanzees and other great apes. The effort would supplement existing searches for the key molecular differences that set humans apart from our primate relatives (see main text). And now is the time to act, McConkey and molecular evolutionist Morris Goodman of Wayne State University in Detroit argued in a recent article in *Trends in Genetics*. . . . A group of influential researchers makes the case for such a project, pointing to the current ability to scan genomes quickly and the ballooning amount of human genetic data. "All the technology is in place now," says Mary-Claire King, a geneticist at the University of Washington, Seattle.

Genome leaders say they are on board, although in the United States no one is talking about funding anywhere near the scale of the $1.5 billion Human Genome Project. "The timing is right for some pilot projects" to lay the groundwork for a complete primate genome project perhaps 5 years from now, says Francis Collins, director of the National Human Genome Research Institute (NHGRI). But while American scientists are talking about a project, work is already under way in Germany, where the German human genome project has awarded $1.1 million to the newly formed Max Planck Institute for Evolutionary Studies in Leipzig for comparative studies of human and primate genomes. They've already started with an effort to sequence comparable segments of DNA from six chromosomes in humans and chimpanzees, says Svante Pääbo, a molecular geneticist at the University of Munich who heads the work. "I think the majority of primate comparative genomics in the next few years is going to be done in Germany at Leipzig," says McConkey.

Other groups are gearing up in the United States, including one at Yerkes Regional Primate Research Center in Atlanta, where researchers opened a Living Links Center with $250,000 from Emory University to compare chimpanzees and humans using genetic, neuroanatomical, behavioral, and cognitive approaches. No sequencing is under way yet, but the center is negotiating an agreement with a Denver biotech firm, GenoPlex Inc., to do high-volume DNA screening. "What's strange is that several people have had the same idea at exactly the same time," says Thomas Insel, director of Yerkes.

So far, researchers have done little more than prove the worth of their tools and affirm the overall similarity of the human and chimp genomes. But the pilot projects are promising. For example, Collins's team at NHGRI tested DNA chips—a DNA-scanning technology made by Affymetrix of Santa Clara, California—to compare the sequence of a 3400-base pair segment of the human breast cancer gene *BRCA1* with the same gene in chimpanzees, gorillas, and orangutans. Using a large segment of human DNA as a reference on the chip, the researchers searched for sequence variations in the same gene in other apes. The technology was remarkably fast and accurate, Collins's group reported in February in *Nature Genetics*. "The DNA chip worked very well," says Collins. "It's a way to look at primate sequences faster than sequencing each primate's DNA de novo" and should keep down the cost of a full-scale primate genome effort once DNA chips become more affordable.

But chips aren't the only candidate technology, says Collins: "Other people are playing with gel-based methods and mass spectrometry." When the methods are refined and more affordable in 5 years or so, he predicts that human genome sequencing will have yielded a list of hot genes to study in primates, such as those that help equip humans for language, higher order brain function, and upright walking. Says King: "It's the next logical step of the Human Genome Project." —A.G.

Oil—turns up on the X chromosome in chimpanzees and humans. But nonfunctioning copies of it also have been found in different places in the chimpanzee and human genomes. Chromosomes 4, 9, and 12 have also been remodeled differently in chimps and humans, according to work published last month in *Genomics* by human geneticists David Nelson and Elizabeth Nickerson of Baylor College of Medicine in Houston. For example, the researchers spotted a chunk of DNA that sits on chromosome 4 in all apes and humans, but in chimpanzees it has moved to a new spot on the same chromosome and been inverted. The translocated chunk includes a gene called *AF4*, which codes for a transcription factor—and is mutated in some forms of acute leukemia in humans. Because apes are much less prone to certain cancers, including leukemia, this is an intriguing finding, raising the possibility that the inversion alters the factor's expression in chimps and so helps protect them from leukemia, says Nelson.

Still, the functional significance of this and other chromosomal differences between humans and other apes is unknown. One possibility, says Nelson, is that similar remodeling disrupted specific genes in our primate ancestors, altering human physiology or function. Because sperm and eggs can't mingle their genetic material unless the chromosomes line up properly, he adds that such rearrangements could have created a reproductive barrier between our ancestors and other primates—the first step in creating new species like our own.

But others, such as Pääbo, think that chromosomal rearrangements at influential sites are rare and so are skeptical that they play a major role in the differences between chimp and human. Pääbo and King think instead that the most promising research avenue is to identify small sequence differences that subtly change the expression of genes that regulate the timing of development, such as those that code for transcription factors that might lengthen the growth period of the brain and, hence, allow more complex brain structure in human fetuses.

The sequencing efforts that may reveal these differences are now under way. Pääbo's group in Munich and Leipzig has sequenced a 10,156–base pair segment of DNA in the X chromosome of humans and chimpanzees, confirming again that they are about 99% similar. Now they're seeking differences in the expression of the identified genes in the brain and in the immune system.

And at GenoPlex Inc., a Denver-based company founded last year by University of Colorado Health Sciences Center geneticists Jim Sikela and Tom Johnson, researchers have come up with a rapid method to find meaningful sequencing differences between humans and chimps. After sequencing a stretch of DNA in each species, they count two different types of nucleotide differences: those that change the structure and function of a protein product, and silent substitutions that don't. If the ratio of replacement to silent substitutions is high, they consider that the gene sequence is likely to have undergone a functional change that was selected for in humans.

Preliminary results suggest that they have found uniquely human genes involved in AIDS susceptibility and learning and memory, says Walter Messier, an evolutionary biologist at the company. The firm has submitted patents on novel uses of these gene sequences, which they hope may become targets for new drugs.

Much of this work is in its infancy, but researchers say they are poised on the verge of a brave new world where they will be able to identify and tinker with the DNA that makes us human—and will face new ethical dilemmas. "What happens if scientists identify a human gene that controls development of the larynx—a gene that might give chimpanzees the anatomy needed for speech?" asks Edwin McConkey, a molecular biologist at the University of Colorado, Boulder. "Can you imagine the ethical debate involved in whether or not to create transgenic chimps? It will open a real Pandora's box."

ID#_____ NAME_____

Article 16: Which of Our Genes Make Us Human?

1. What percentage of the genome is shared between humans and chimpanzees?

2. Why has a Denver biotech company already submitted patents for human and chimpanzee genes?

3. What did the UCSD team find on human cells that was different from other mammals? Why is this significant?

4. Do most researchers believe that the differences between humans and chimpanzees will come down to a single genetic change?

5. Humans have _____ chromosomes, while the apes have _____ chromosomes.

6. How might chromosome rearrangements create a reproductive barrier between apes and humans?

7. What two uniquely human genes were discovered through Sikela and Johnson's work with DNA sequencing?

98% Alike? (What Our Similarity to Apes Tells Us about Our Understanding of Genetics)

Jonathan Marks

It's not too hard to tell Jane Goodall from a chimpanzee. Goodall is the one with long legs and short arms, a prominent forehead, and whites in her eyes. She's the one with a significant amount of hair only on her head, not all over her body. She's the one who walks, talks, and wears clothing.

A few decades ago, however, the nascent field of molecular genetics recognized an apparent paradox: However easy it may be to tell Jane Goodall from a chimpanzee on the basis of physical characteristics, it is considerably harder to tell them apart according to their genes.

More recently, geneticists have been able to determine with precision that humans and chimpanzees are over 98 percent identical genetically, and that figure has become one of the most well-known factoids in the popular scientific literature. It has been invoked to argue that we are simply a third kind of chimpanzee, together with the common chimp and the rarer bonobo; to claim human rights for nonhuman apes; and to explain the roots of male aggression.

Using the figure in those ways, however, ignores the context necessary to make sense of it. Actually, our amazing genetic similarity to chimpanzees is a scientific fact constructed from two rather more mundane facts: our familiarity with the apes and our unfamiliarity with genetic comparisons.

To begin with, it is unfair to juxtapose the differences between the bodies of people and apes with the similarities in their genes. After all, we have been comparing the bodies of humans and chimpanzees for 300 years, and we have been comparing DNA sequences for less than 20.

Now that we are familiar with chimpanzees, we quickly see how different they look from us. But when the chimpanzee was a novelty, in the 18th century, scholars were struck by the overwhelming similarity of human and ape bodies. And why not? Bone for bone, muscle for muscle, organ for organ, the bodies of humans and apes differ only in subtle ways. And yet, it is

From *The Chronicle of Higher Education*, May 12, 2000, Volume 46 by Jonathan Marks. Copyright © 2000 by Jonathan Marks. Reprinted by permission.

impossible to say just how physically similar they are. Forty percent? Sixty percent? Ninety-eight percent? Three-dimensional beings that develop over their lifetimes don't lend themselves to a simple scale of similarity.

Genetics brings something different to the comparison. A DNA sequence is a one-dimensional entity, a long series of A, G, C, and T subunits. Align two sequences from different species and you can simply tabulate their similarities; if they match 98 out of 100 times, then the species are 98 percent genetically identical.

But is that more or less than their bodies match? We have no easy way to tell, for making sense of the question "How similar are a human and a chimp?" requires a frame of reference. In other words, we should be asking: "How similar are a human and a chimp, compared to what?"

Let's try and answer the question. How similar are a human and a chimp, compared to, say, a sea urchin? The human and chimpanzee have limbs, skeletons, bilateral symmetry, a central nervous system; each bone, muscle, and organ matches. For all intents and purposes, the human and chimpanzee aren't 98 percent identical, they're 100 percent identical.

On the other hand, when we compare the DNA of humans and chimps, what does the percentage of similarity mean? We conceptualize it on a linear scale, on which 100 percent is perfectly identical and 0 percent is totally different. But the structure of DNA gives the scale a statistical idiosyncrasy.

Because DNA is a linear array of those four bases—A, G, C, and T—only four possibilities exist at any specific point in a DNA sequence. The laws of chance tell us that two random sequences from species that have no ancestry in common will match at about one in every four sites.

Thus even two unrelated DNA sequences will be 25 percent identical, not 0 percent identical. (You can, of course, generate sequences more different than that, but greater differences would not occur randomly.) The most different two DNA sequences can be, then, is 75 percent different.

Now consider that all multicellular life on earth is related. A human, a chimpanzee, and the banana the chimpanzee is eating share a remote common ancestry, but a common ancestry nevertheless. Therefore, if we compare any particular DNA sequence in a human and a banana, the sequence would have to be more than 25 percent identical. For the sake of argument, let's say 35 percent. In other words, your DNA is over one-third the same as a banana's. Yet, of course, there are few ways other than genetically in which a human could be shown to be one-third identical to a banana.

That context may help us to assess the 98 percent DNA similarity of humans and chimpanzees. The fact that our DNA is 98 percent identical to that of a chimp is not a transcendent statement about our natures, but merely a decontextualized and culturally interpreted datum.

Moreover, the genetic comparison is misleading because it ignores qualitative differences among genomes. Genetic evolution involves much more than simply replacing one base with another. Thus, even among such close relatives as human and chimpanzee, we find that the chimp's genome is estimated to be about 10 percent larger than the human's; that one human chromosome contains a fusion of two small chimpanzee chromosomes; and that the tips of each chimpanzee chromosome contain a DNA sequence that is not present in humans.

In other words, the pattern we encounter genetically is actually quite close to the pattern we encounter anatomically. In spite of the shock the figure of 98 percent may give us, humans are obviously identifiably different from, as well as very similar to, chimpanzees. The apparent paradox is simply a result of how mundane the apes have become and how exotic DNA still is.

Another way in which humans and apes are frequently conflated is phylogenetically. Humans, the argument runs, fall within a group that comprises chimpanzees, gorillas, and orangutans—the great apes. We are genetically more closely related to chimpanzees than they are to orangutans. Because we fall within the ape group, we are ourselves apes.

True, but again we need to look at the context.

Traditional zoological classifications incorporate two evolutionary processes: descent and divergence. The category of great apes is marked by the divergence of humans from it. It is, in taxonomic parlance, paraphyletic: The group is missing some close relatives that fall within it and is an artificial amalgam of the species left behind.

Two other famous paraphyletic categories are invertebrates, a motley assortment of things that didn't evolve a backbone; and reptiles, the diverse scaly creatures that the birds left behind.

More to the point, consider the coelacanth, which by virtue of its limb structure is more closely related to tetrapods—animals with four limbs—than to other fish, such as trout. Therefore, fish are also a paraphyletic category, an assemblage of vertebrates that didn't evolve four limbs. Tetrapods are a phylogenetic subset of fish, although they have diverged extensively from their aquatic relatives.

Humans, of course, are tetrapods. Because of that fact, and because tetrapods share an ancestry with fish—including both the closely related coelacanth and the distant trout—the conclusion should be obvious: Humans are indeed apes, but only in precisely the same way that humans are fish. We simply fall within a diverse group of creatures with broad, general similarities to one another, from whom our ancestors radically diverged.

Our apeness, like our fishness, is not a profound revelation about human nature, but merely an artifact of the way we classify things.

Genetics has the power to make a familiar fact seem unfamiliar and to give biases and opinions the ring of scientific authority. Social and political activists have invoked genetics over the full course of the last century and will undoubtedly continue to do so over the course of this one. It is thus of the utmost importance that we regard genetic data in a cultural and critical framework and place them intellectually where the study of heredity intersects the study of human systems of meaning.

In a recent issue of *Anthropology Today*, Gisli Palsson and Paul Rabinow analyzed the Iceland genome project and called for "a molecular anthropology that includes scientific, technological, political, cultural, and ethical dimensions." I agree that we need such a molecular anthropology, which should be informed by genetics and which should, at the same time, approach genetics with a critical, analytical, and ethnographic eye.

The time is ripe for such an interdisciplinary endeavor. Our place in nature is not determined by genetic data alone; it is a contested site on the boundary of godliness and animalness, between beast and angel. To make sense of the data requires both anthropological and biological knowledge.

ID#_____ NAME_____

Article 17: 98% Alike? (What Our Similarity to Apes Tells Us about Our Understanding of Genetics)

1. Why does the author suggest humans are "simply a third kind of chimpanzee?"

2. Rather than, "How similar are a human and a chimpanzee," what does the author believe we should be asking?

3. Why does the author feel the 98% alike genetic comparison is misleading?

4. What does Marks mean when he says humans are apes in the same way that humans are fish?

Section III:
Hominid Evolution

One of the most fascinating topics is the story of our origins. Who are we? How did we get here? What did our ancestors look like? How did they live? Were we the hunters or the hunted? When did we acquire language? What happened to the Neanderthals? Why do we look the way we do? These questions have fascinated humans for centuries, as the array of origin myths from all different societies can attest. Scientists have been searching for the answers to these questions for over a century and we are finding the answers slowly but surely. The articles included in this section begin with the very earliest hominid fossils and take us to the modern transition. They explore the morphology, or form, of our ancestors and their behavior. We find answers to the above questions, which have fascinated us for so long.

The first selection, *One Giant Step for Mankind*, describes the recent discovery of two highly significant early specimens, *Ardipithecus ramidus* and *Orrorin tugenensis*, and their place on the hominid line. Climate, diet and bipedalism are discussed. New evidence questions the importance of bipedalism as a defining characteristic of hominids.

The next two articles, *Hominid Hardware* and *Scavenger Hunt* examine the tool making ability and subsistence behavior of the early hominids. In the former, author Shanti Menon describes the earliest stone tools found in East Africa and the identity of the possible toolmaker. The latter article, written by Pat Shipman, describes her work into the question of hunting versus scavenging behavior in early hominids. Pat challenges the traditional idea of "Man the Hunter" by examining stone tool cut marks on fossil animal bone and comparing them to carnivore tooth marks under the scanning electron microscope. Her findings changed the way we looked at early hominid subsistence adaptations.

Doubting Dmanisi is another article by Pat Shipman, describing the discovery of the oldest humans on the Eurasian continent. These individuals, found in the last decade, represent specimens of *Homo erectus* that show a surprising resemblance to fossil forms from East Africa. They suggest a link to the African continent, perhaps to the exclusion of the Asian *Homo erectus* forms, turning our understanding of the evolution of *H. erectus* on its head.

Kate Wong's article, *Who Were the Neandertals?* is an excellent summary of the Neanderthal debate. She addresses the questions surrounding the Neanderthals demise, did they survive and compete and leave genes in later populations, or were they wiped out by modern human technology and behavior? The sidebars to this article also expand our understanding of the contentious issues surrounding these Pleistocene individuals. The most recent Neanderthal skeleton found, that of a child in Lagar Velho Portugal, challenges the idea that the Neanderthals went extinct without interbreeding. Neanderthal hunting ability, speech capabilities, tool culture, and interactions with modern humans are all discussed.

The replacement hypothesis and the multiregional hypothesis are contrasted for the origin of modern humans.

In a related article, selection 23, *Not Our Mom*, discusses the latest attempts to extract and analyze Neanderthal DNA and concludes that the Neanderthals were not, in fact, ancestral to modern humans.

Finally, Matt Cartmill's, *The Gift of Gab*, exposes us to a basic understanding of linguistic ability in humans and chimpanzees. He describes the anatomical specializations needed for language capability, but also focuses on the psychology and behavior. Past understanding of language ability and acquisition is challenged by current research into social interaction and brain enlargement.

One Giant Step for Mankind

Michael D. Lemonick and Andrea Dorfman

The region of Ethiopia called the Middle Awash, some 140 miles northeast of the capital of Addis Ababa, is a hot, harsh and inhospitable place—a rocky desert punctuated by tree-lined rivers, the occasional lake and patches of lava that are slowly being buried by sediments flushed out of the hills by the torrential rains that come along twice a year.

But between 5 million and 6 million years ago, the landscape here was very different. The same tectonic forces that racked the region with earthquakes and volcanic eruptions had also thrust the land up as much as a mile higher than it is today. As a result, the area was cooler and wetter and overgrown with trees, bushes and patches of grass. These fertile woodlands were rich in wildlife. Primitive elephants, giant bears, horses, rhinos, pigs, rats and monkeys lived here, along with dozens of other mammal species long since extinct.

And it was here too that nature indulged in what was perhaps her greatest evolutionary experiment. For it was in eastern Africa at about this time that a new type of primate arose—an animal not so different from its apelike ancestors except in one crucial respect: this creature stood on two legs instead of scurrying along chimplike on all fours. Its knuckle-walking cousins would stay low to the ground and never get much smarter. But while it wouldn't happen until millions of years in the future, this new primate's evolutionary descendants would eventually develop a large, complex brain. And from that would spring all of civilization, from Mesopotamia to Mozart to *Who Wants to Be a Millionaire*.

That's the broad outline, anyway. While this view of human evolution has generally been accepted by scientists for decades, no one has yet been able to say precisely when that first evolutionary step on the road to humanity happened, nor what might have triggered it.

But a discovery reported last week in the journal *Nature* has brought paleontologists tantalizingly close to answering both these questions. Working as part of an international team led by U.S. and Ethiopian scientists, a graduate student named Yohannes Haile-Selassie (no relation to the Emperor),

From *Time*, July 23, 2001, pp. 54–61. © 2001 TIME Inc. Reprinted by permission.

enrolled at the University of California, Berkeley, has found the remains of what appears to be the most ancient human ancestor ever discovered. It's a chimp-size creature that lived in the Ethiopian forests between 5.8 million and 5.2 million years ago—nearly a million and a half years earlier than the previous record holder and very close to the time when humans and chimps first went their separate evolutionary ways.

"Having a fossil in this region of time, very near the divergence point, is really exciting," says anthropologist C. Owen Lovejoy of Ohio's Kent State University. "Going all the way back to Darwin, people have speculated how, when and why humans stood up on two legs. For paleontologists, this find is a dream come true."

As is often the case with discoveries like this, Haile-Selassie was not specifically looking for the things he found. He had set out to better understand how the ancient ecosystems worked and evolved. "I didn't even think about finding hominids," he says. "All I wanted to do was collect enough vertebrate bones so that I could write my dissertation." In December 1997, though, at a place called Alayla, he spotted a piece of jawbone lying on the rock-strewn ground. "I picked up the mandible less than five minutes after we got there," he recalls, "but didn't realize I had something really special until a year later, when we found some more bones and I started the serious analysis."

In all, the team eventually found 11 specimens—from at least five different individuals—in a cluster of sites, including Haile-Selassie's partial lower jaw with associated teeth, several hand and foot bones, and pieces of three arm bones and a collarbone. Luckily, the fossils were trapped in sediments that were sandwiched between layers of volcanic ash, whose age can be accurately gauged by a technique known as argon-argon dating. (This layering is still visible in places that have not been so heavily eroded, enabling the scientists to trace the area's geologic history.) The verdict, confirmed by a second dating method and by the other primitive animals found with the hominid remains: most of the fossils are between 5.6 million and 5.8 million years old, although one toe bone is a few hundred thousand years younger.

It was the detailed anatomy of these fragmentary fossils, especially the teeth, that convinced Haile-Selassie that he had discovered a new human ancestor. Although apelike, the lower canines and upper premolars, in particular, display certain traits found only in the teeth of later hominids—the term scientists use to describe ourselves and our non-ape ancestors. They also differ in shape from the teeth of all known fossil and modern apes. Even the way in which the teeth had been worn down was telling. Explains Haile-Selassie's thesis adviser, Berkeley paleontologist Tim White: "Apes all sharpen their upper canines as they chew. Hominids don't." The new creature's back teeth are larger than a chimp's too, while the front teeth are narrower, suggesting that its diet included a variety of fibrous foods, rather than the fruits and soft leaves that chimps prefer.

When Haile-Selassie compared the newly discovered bones and teeth with those of *Ardipithecus ramidus*, a 4.4 million-year-old hominid found in the Middle Awash in the early 1990s that was the previous record holder, he realized that the two creatures were very similar. But the older one's teeth, while different from an ape's, do have a number of characteristics that are decidedly more apelike than those of the younger hominid.

On the basis of these minor but distinctive differences, Haile-Selassie decided to classify the new human ancestor as a subspecies, or variant, of *ramidus* and has given it the name *Ardipithecus ramidus kadabba*. (The name is derived from the local Afar language. *Ardi* means ground or floor;

ramid means root; and *kadabba* means basal family ancestor. In accordance with the sometimes bizarre nomenclature of science, the younger creature now gets renamed *Ardipithecus ramidus*.)

Haile-Selassie and his colleagues haven't collected enough bones yet to reconstruct with great precision what *kadabba* looked like. But they do know it was about the size of modern common chimpanzees, which when standing average about 4 ft. tall. That makes it roughly the same size as its close relative *A. ramidus ramidus* and about 20% taller than Lucy, the famous 3.2 million-year-old human ancestor discovered about 50 miles away in 1974 that is even further along the evolutionary track. The size of *kadabba's* brain and the relative proportions of its arms and legs were probably chimplike as well.

But unlike a chimp or any of the other modern apes that amble along on four limbs, *kadabba* almost certainly walked upright much of the time. The inch-long toe bone makes that clear. Two-legged primates (modern humans included) propel themselves forward by leaving the front part of their foot on the ground and lifting the heel. This movement, referred to as toeing off, causes the bones in the middle of the foot to take on a distinctive shape—a shape that is readily apparent in the ancient toe bones. "If you compare a chimp's foot bones with its hand bones, they look the same because they're used for the same thing"—that is, for grasping—Haile-Selassie explains. "Hominid fingers and toes don't look alike at all."

Exactly how this hominid walked is still something of a mystery, though with a different skeletal structure, its gait would have been unlike ours. Details of *kadabba's* lifestyle remain speculative too, but many of its behaviors undoubtedly resembled those of chimpanzees today. It probably still spent some time in trees. It probably lived in large social groups that would include both sexes. And rather than competing with one another for mates, the males may well have banded together to defend the troop against predators, forage for food and even hunt for game.

But that *kadabba* walked upright at all is hugely significant. Paleontologists have suspected for nearly 200 years that bipedalism was probably the key evolutionary transition that split the human line off from the apes, and fossil discoveries as far back as Java Man in the 1890s supported that notion. The astonishingly complete skeleton of Lucy, with its clearly apelike skull but upright posture, cemented the idea a quarter-century ago.

What's been much tougher to pin down is just why two-leggedness arose. The conventional wisdom has long focused on the fact that eastern Africa became significantly dryer about the time that humans first evolved. The change would have tended to favor grasslands over forests, and, so went the theory, our ancestors changed to take advantage of the new conditions. We learned to walk upright so that we could see over the tall grasses to spot predators coming; an upright posture, moreover, would offer a much smaller target for the oppressive heat of the grassland sun, and a larger target for cooling breezes.

The only trouble with this theory is that it's wrong. The earliest humans, it turns out, didn't live in grasslands. Dry climate or not, a companion paper published last week in *Nature* shows on the basis of other fossilized flora and fauna, as well as the chemistry of the ancient soil, that *Ardipithecus ramidus kadabba* lived in a well-forested environment. That's also the case with other extremely ancient hominids found during the past several years, including *Ardipithecus ramidus* and a species called *Orrorin tugenensis*, announced last December by French and Kenyan researchers. And while the ability to walk on two legs probably started out as an increasingly frequent behavior, evolution demands an explanation for why it persisted. On first blush, bipedalism just doesn't make much sense. For our earliest ancestors, it would have been slower than walking on all fours, while requiring the same amount of energy. Says Lovejoy bluntly: "It's unnatural. It's bizarre."

Yet the advantages of walking upright were somehow so great that the behavior endured through thousands of generations. Indeed, the anatomy of our ancestors underwent all sorts of basic changes to accommodate this new way of moving. Many of the changes help the body stay balanced by stabilizing the weight-bearing leg and keeping the upper torso centered over the feet. Lovejoy, who studies the anatomy and biomechanics of locomotion, thinks the changes may have improved coordination as well. "To walk upright in a habitual way, you have to do so in synchrony," he says. "If the ligaments and muscles are out of synch, that leads to injuries. And then you'd be cheetah meat."

By far the most crucial changes, according to Lovejoy, were those in the spine. The distance between chest and pelvis is longer in humans than in apes, allowing the lower spine to curve, which locates the upper body over the pelvis for balance. The pelvis grew broader, meanwhile, and humans developed a hip joint and associated muscles that stabilize the pelvis. Explains Lovejoy: "That's why a chimp sways from side to side as it walks upright and humans don't."

Changes also had to take place in the femur, or thighbone. For example, the femoral neck—the bent portion at the top of the bone—is broader in humans than it is in apes, which improves balance. The human knee is specialized for walking upright too: to compensate for the thighbone's being at an angle, there's a lump, or groove, at the end of the femur that prevents the patella from sliding off the joint. "A chimp doesn't have this groove because there is no angulation between the hip and the knee," Lovejoy says. "This change says you're a biped."

Finally, there's the foot. "What's important here is the arch," Lovejoy says. "It's a really important shock absorber. It's like wearing a good pair of running shoes." In order to create that arch, the chimp's opposable great toe became aligned with the others, and the toe's muscles and ligaments, which had been used for grasping and climbing, were repositioned under the foot. "The shape of the big toe is indicative of this. You can see it in Lucy's species," Lovejoy says, but not in the bone Haile-Selassie found, because it's from a different toe. "What we can see [in the new discovery's foot] is that the base of the bone adjacent to the knuckle has a distinct angle, showing that the creature walked step after step after step with its heel off the ground, using the front of its foot as a platform."

That's how it walked. *Why* it walked is tougher to understand, since motivation leaves behind no physical remains. But armed with knowledge about our ancestors' physical attributes and the environment that surrounded them, scientists have come up with several theories. Anthropologist Henry McHenry, of the University of California, Davis, for example, champions the idea that climate variation was part of the picture after all. When Africa dried out, say McHenry and his colleague Peter Rodman, the change left patches of forest widely spaced between open savannah. The first hominids lived mostly in these forest refuges but couldn't find enough food in any one place. Learning to walk on two legs helped them travel long distances over ground to the next woodsy patch, and thus to more food.

Meave Leakey, head of paleontology at the National Museums of Kenya and a member of the world's most famous fossil-hunting family, suspects the change in climate rewarded bipedalism for a different reason. Yes, the dryer climate made for more grassland, but our early ancestors, she argues, spent much of their time not in dense forest or on the savannah but in an environment with some trees, dense shrubbery and a bit of grass. "And if you're moving into more open country with grasslands and bushes and things like this, and eating a lot of fruits and berries coming off low bushes, there is a hell of an advantage to be able to reach higher. That's why the gerenuk [a type of antelope] evolved its long neck and stands on its hind legs, and why the giraffe evolved its long neck. There's strong pressure to be able to reach a wider range of levels."

But for Kent State's Lovejoy, the real answer is sex. Males who were best at walking upright would get more of it, leading to more offspring who were good on two legs, who in turn got more sex. His reasoning, first proposed nearly two decades ago, goes like this: like many modern Americans, monkeys and apes of both genders work outside the home—in the latter case, searching for food. Early humans, though, discovered the *Leave It to Beaver* strategy: if males handled the breadwinning, females could stay closer to home and devote more time to rearing the children, thus giving them a better shot at growing up strong and healthy.

And if you're going to bring home the bacon, or the Miocene equivalent, it helps to have your hands free to carry it. Over time, female apes would choose to mate only with those males who brought them food—presumably the ones who were best adapted for upright walking. Is that the way it actually happened? Maybe, but we may never know for sure. Leakey, for one, is unconvinced. "There are all sorts of hypotheses," she says, "and they are all fairy tales really because you can't prove anything."

If paleontologists argue about why bipedalism evolved, they're even more contentious over the organization of the human family tree. According to Haile-Selassie and his colleagues, the picture looks pretty straightforward from about 5.8 million years ago to the present. First comes *Ardipithecus ramidus kadabba*, the newest find. Then, more than a million years later, its descendant, the newly renamed *Ardipithecus ramidus*, appears. After that comes a new genus, called *Australopithecus* (where Lucy belongs), and finally, about 2 million years ago, the first members of the human genus Homo.

But not everyone buys the story. Indeed, the French and Kenyan team that presented a 6 million-year-old fossil last December insists that theirs, known as *Orrorin tugenensis* (or, more familiarly, Millennium Man because it was announced in 2000), is the true human ancestor and that *Ardipithecus* is nothing more than a monkey's uncle—or a chimp's great-great-grandfather, anyway. They even dismiss Lucy and her close kin, about as firmly entrenched in the human lineage as you can get, as evolutionary dead ends that left no living descendants.

No one disputes that this competing ancestor is 6 million years old and thus more ancient than *Ardipithecus*. What's still to be proved is that it's a hominid. Says Leakey: "If you read their paper, almost everything they say about the teeth suggests it's more apelike." And when they get to the femur, she says, they present no evidence disproving that it walked on all fours. Haile-Selassie makes precisely the same point. But Brigitte Senut of the National Museum of Natural History in Paris and Martin Pickford, chairman of paleoanthropology and prehistory at the Collège de France, co-leaders of the team that found *Orrorin*, dismiss the criticisms. Additional fossils found just last March, they say, along with the more detailed analysis they now have in hand of the earlier bones, will prove their case. "We are absolutely delighted about it," says Senut. "We had the possibility to show the evidence to some colleagues in South Africa recently, and just looking at the cast they said, '"Fantastic, it's a biped! And a better biped than Lucy."'

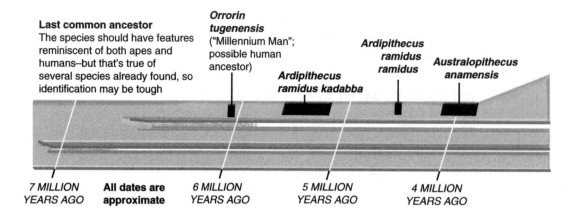

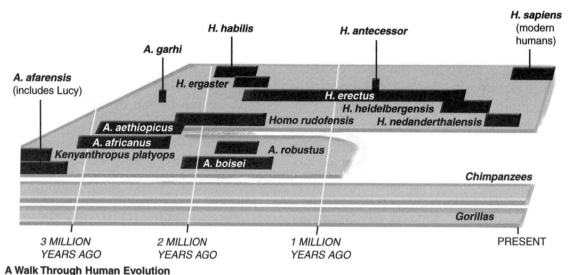

A Walk Through Human Evolution
The newest fossils have brought scientists tantalizingly close to the time when humans first walked upright—splitting off from chimpanzees. Their best guess is that it happened at least 6 million years ago

Even if they're right, though, establishing the precise path of human descent might be very hard. For most of the past 6 million years, multiple hominid species roamed the earth at the same time—including a mere 30,000 years ago, when modern humans and Neanderthals still coexisted. We still can't figure out exactly how Neanderthals relate to the human family; it's all the more difficult to know where these newly discovered species, with far fewer fossil remains to study, belong.

In the case of *Ardipithecus*, says Donald Johanson, professor of anthropology and director of the Institute of Human Origins at Arizona State University (and the man who discovered Lucy back in 1974), "when you put 5.5 million-year-old fossils together with 4.4 million-year-old ones as members of the same species, you're not taking into consideration that these could be twigs on a tree. Everything's been forced into straight line." Beyond that, he's dubious about categorizing the 5.2 million-year-old toe bone with the rest of the fossils: not only is it separated in time by several hundred thousand years, but it was also found some 10 miles away from the rest.

If *Orrorin* turns out to be a hominid, the same skepticism will apply to any claims about its pivotal position on the family tree. According to University of Tokyo paleontologist Gen Suwa, a co-discoverer of the 4.4 million-year-old *Ardipithecus ramidus ramidus*, *Orrorin* could well be ancestral to the new *Ardipithecus* remains, rather than the other way around. "There is nothing in the fossils," he says, "that would preclude such a position. But which side of the chimp-hominid split *Orrorin* occupies can be determined only by further analyses and new finds." Indeed, suggests Haile-Selassie, while *Orrorin* may be one of the earliest chimps or an ape that became extinct, it could also turn out to be the last common ancestor of humans and chimps—a creature paleontologists have been dreaming of finding for decades.

One of the most intriguing questions the new discoveries raise, says Bernard Wood, a professor of human origins at George Washington University, is whether bipedalism should still be considered the defining characteristic of being human. After all, all birds have wings, but not all creatures with wings are birds. It's already clear that eastern Africa was bubbling with evolutionary experiments 6 million years ago. Maybe two-legged walking evolved independently in several branches of the primate family. Says Wood: "This might be the first example of a creature it's not possible to label as hominid ancestor or chimp ancestor. But that doesn't make it the last common ancestor of both. I think it's going to be very hard to pin the tail on that donkey."

In the end, that may be the most exciting thing about these latest discoveries from the human race's birthing ground. Not that long ago, paleontologists were pretty certain we started on the road to becoming human by standing upright on the grassy savannah. Now that science is actually bringing in hard evidence, the story is getting more complicated—and more interesting. Clearly, there are still plenty of questions to ask, and plenty of surprises left to uncover, in the ancient sediments of eastern Africa.

—With reporting by Simon Robinson/Nairobi

ID#_____   NAME_____

Article 18: One Giant Step for Mankind

1. How was the climate of the Middle Awash at 5-6 ma different from today?

2. In 2001, graduate student Haile-Selassie found the remains of a human ancestor dating between _____ and _____ . Why are these dates significant?

3. Haile-Selassie's team found _____ specimens from at least _____ individuals.

4. How did the diet of *Ardipithecus ramidus kadabba* differ from that of a chimpanzee?

5. How do we know *A. r. kadabba* was bipedal?

6. Why are the traditional arguments for bipedalism, e.g. spotting predators, seeing over tall grasses, considered wrong today?

7. List three traits described by Lovejoy that are important for bipedalism.

8. What two reasons does Leakey give for disputing the hominid status of *Orrorin tugenensis*?

9. Why does Bernard Wood question whether bipedalism should be considered the defining characteristic of humans?

Hominid Hardware

Shanti Menon

The fist-size chunks of rock that Sileshi Semaw has collected from Gona, Ethiopia, over the past three years aren't much to look at—at least not to an untrained observer. But Semaw, a paleoanthropologist at Rutgers, possesses a highly trained eye, and as soon as he uncovered the first of his rocks he knew he had found something unique. The rocks—he has discovered about 3,000 of them in Gona—were shaped by the hands of human ancestors. And dating from more than 2.5 million years ago, they are the most ancient stone tools ever found.

Primitive hominids banged the rocks together to break off small, sharp-edged flakes for use as cutting and piercing tools. The resulting patterns on the cores, as the larger rocks are called, are unlike anything produced by natural erosion. Dating stone tools of such antiquity is often problematic—their age usually can't be easily determined from surrounding layers of sediments. But Semaw got lucky at the Gona site. Lying on top of the tools was a 2.52-million-year-old layer of volcanic ash, which was reliably dated by measuring the decay of its radioactive elements. And magnetic grains in the rock layer underneath the tools recorded a flip in Earth's magnetic field, called the Gauss-Matuyama transition, known to have occurred 2.6 million years ago. The tools, says Semaw, lay closer to the 2.6-million-year-old layer.

The simple flakes and cores Semaw found, made without much thought as to their final shape, are called Oldowan tools. They're named after Olduvai Gorge in Tanzania, where Mary Leakey discovered 1.8-million-year-old stone tools in the 1970s. Oldowan tools have since been found throughout East Africa, including a recent discovery of some 2.3-million-year-old tools in Hadar, not far from Gona. The tools Semaw discovered, though they push back the origins of the Oldowan industry by some 250,000 years, are practically indistinguishable from those at Olduvai—demonstrating that tool-making technology remained unchanged for nearly 1 million years.

"Quite a few archeologists believed that ancestral humans who lived prior to 2 million years ago were not as capable as those who lived at Olduvai Gorge," says Semaw. "But the evidence at Gona shows they were capable of making Oldowan tools. And the fact that we found thousands of tools around 2.6 million years ago implies that the hominids who made them weren't novices to toolmaking."

From *Discover Magazine*, May 1997 by Shanti Menon. Copyright © 1997 by Discover Magazine. Reprinted by permission.

But as to who those hominids were, Gona has yet to offer any clues. Semaw hasn't found any hominid remains at the site. Lucy and other members of her species, *Australopithecus afarensis*, roamed around nearby Hadar 3 million years ago. Researchers have recently discovered a 2.3-million-year-old jawbone at Hadar, which they attribute to an as yet unspecified species of our genus, *Homo*. But not much is known about what came after *afarensis* and before the sketchy early *Homo*. The Gona tools lie smack in the middle of a 700,000-year stretch in the Ethiopian fossil record marked by a paucity of evidence.

Some researchers are nevertheless willing to hazard a guess as to who might have fashioned the tools. Bernard Wood [at George Washington University] suggests that *Paranthropus aethiopicus* (also known as *Australopithecus boisei* or *A. aethiopicus*, depending on whom you're talking to) lived at the right time and in roughly the right place. But Semaw thinks that the tools were fashioned by some undiscovered early *Homo* species.

"*Aethiopicus* has really heavy jaws, built for chewing or crunching almost anything," says Semaw. "But the early *Homo* specimens we have are very lightly built compared with *aethiopicus*." Massive *aethiopicus*, sometimes affectionately referred to as the "Nutcracker," would not have needed tools to break open seeds or bones. But the more slender, delicate early *Homo*, Semaw suggests, would have been motivated to find a better way to process food. Until someone finds hominid remains at Gona, the creators of the world's oldest tools will remain anonymous.

ID#_____ NAME_____

Article 19: Hominid Hardware

1. Sileshi Semaw found stone tools in _____ that dated to _____ .

2. What techniques were used to date the stone tools?

3. What do these newly discovered tools resemble?

4. Do we know who made these tools? Why or why not?

5. Why does Semaw believe the tools were made by early *Homo*, rather than another hominid?

Scavenger Hunt

Pat Shipman

In both textbooks and films, ancestral humans (hominids) have been portrayed as hunters. Small-brained, big-browed, upright, and usually mildly furry, early hominid males gaze with keen eyes across the gold savanna, searching for prey. Skillfully wielding a few crude stone tools, they kill and dismember everything from small gazelles to elephants, while females care for young and gather roots, tubers, and berries. The food is shared by group members at temporary camps. This familiar image of Man the Hunter has been bolstered by the finding of stone tools in association with fossil animal bones. But the role of hunting in early hominid life cannot be determined in the absence of more direct evidence.

I discovered one means of testing the hunting hypothesis almost by accident. In 1978, I began documenting the microscopic damage produced on bones by different events. I hoped to develop a diagnostic key for identifying the postmortem history of specific fossil bones, useful for understanding how fossil assemblages were formed. Using a scanning electron microscope (SEM) because of its excellent resolution and superb depth of field, I inspected high-fidelity replicas of modern bones that had been subjected to known events or conditions. (I had to use replicas, rather than real bones, because specimens must fit into the SEM's small vacuum chamber.) I soon established that such common events as weathering, root etching, sedimentary abrasion, and carnivore chewing produced microscopically distinctive features.

In 1980, my SEM study took an unexpected turn. Richard Potts (now of Yale University), Henry Bunn (now of the University of Wisconsin at Madison), and I almost simultaneously found what appeared to be stone-tool cut marks on fossils from Olduvai Gorge, Tanzania, and Koobi Fora, Kenya. We were working almost side by side at the National Museums of Kenya, in Nairobi, where the fossils are stored. The possibility of cut marks was exciting, since both sites preserve some of the oldest known archaeological materials. Potts and I returned to the United States, manufactured some stone tools, and started "butchering" bones and joints begged from our local butchers. Under the SEM, replicas of these cut marks looked very different from replicas of carnivore tooth scratches, regardless of the species of carnivore or the type of

From *Natural History*, April 1984, "Scavenger Hunt", pp. 20 and 22-27 by Pat Shipman. Reprinted from Natural History, April/1984; copyright © Natural History Magazine, Inc., 1984.

tool involved. By comparing the marks on the fossils with our hundreds of modern bones of known history, we were able to demonstrate convincingly that hominids using stone tools had processed carcasses of many different animals nearly two million years ago. For the first time, there was a firm link between stone tools and at least some of the early fossil animals bones.

This initial discovery persuaded some paleoanthropologists that the hominid hunter scenario was correct. Potts and I were not so sure. Our study had shown that many of the cut-marked fossils also bore carnivore tooth marks and that some of the cut marks were in places we hadn't expected—on the bones that bore little meat in life. More work was needed.

In addition to more data about the Olduvai cut marks and tooth marks, I needed specific information about the patterns of cut marks left by known hunters performing typical activities associated with hunting. If similar patterns occurred on the fossils, then the early hominids probably behaved similarly to more modern hunters; if the patterns were different, then the behavior was probably also different. Three activities related to hunting occur often enough in peoples around the world and leave consistent enough traces to be used for such a test.

First, human hunters systematically disarticulate their kills, unless the animals are small enough to be eaten on the spot. Disarticulation leaves cut marks in a predictable pattern on the skeleton. Such marks cluster near the major joints of the limbs: shoulder, elbow, carpal joint (wrist), hop, knee, and hock (ankle). Taking a carcass apart at the joints is much easier than breaking or cutting through bones. Disarticulation enables hunters to carry food back to a central place or camp, so that they can share it with others or cook it or even store it by placing portions in trees, away from the reach of carnivores. If early hominids were hunters who transported and shared their kills, disarticulation marks would occur near joints in frequencies comparable to those produced by modern human hunters.

Second, human hunters often butcher carcasses, in the sense of removing meat from the bones. Butchery marks are usually found on the shafts of bones from the upper part of the front or hind limb, since this is where the big muscle masses lie. Butchery may be carried out at the kill site—especially if the animal is very large and its bones very heavy—or it may take place at the base camp, during the process of sharing food with others. Compared with disarticulation, butchery leaves relatively few marks. It is hard for a hunter to locate an animal's joints without leaving cut marks on the bone. In contrast, it is easier to cut the meat away from the midshaft of the bone without making such marks. If early hominids shared their food, however, there ought to be a number of cut marks located on the midshaft of some fossil bones.

Finally, human hunters often remove skin or tendons from carcasses, to be used for clothing, bags, thongs, and so on. Hide or tendon must be separated from the bones in many areas where there is little flesh, such as the lower limb bones of pigs, giraffes, antelopes, and zebras. In such cases, it is difficult to cut the skin without leaving a cut mark on the bone. Therefore, one expects to find many more cut marks on such bones than on the flesh-covered bones of the upper part of the limbs.

Unfortunately, although accounts of butchery and disarticulation by modern human hunters are remarkably consistent, quantitative studies are rare. Further, virtually all modern hunter-gatherers use metal tools, which leave more cut marks than stone tools. For these reasons I hesitated to compare the fossil evidence with data on modern hunters. Fortunately, Diane Gifford of the University of California, Santa Cruz, and her colleagues had recently completed a quantitative study of marks and damage on thousands of antelope bones processed by Neolithic (Stone Age) hunters in Kenya some 2,300 years ago. The data from Prolonged Drift, as the site is called, were perfect for comparison with Olduvai material.

Assisted by my technician, Jennie Rose, I carefully inspected more than 2,500 antelope bones from Bed I at Olduvai Gorge, which is dated to between 1.9 and 1.7 million years ago. We made high-fidelity replicas of every mark that we thought might be either a cut mark or a carnivore tooth mark. Back in the United States, we used the SEM to make positive identifications of the marks. (The replication and SEM inspection was time consuming, but necessary: only about half of the marks were correctly identified by eye or by light microscope.) I then compared the patterns of cut mark and tooth mark distributions on Olduvai fossils with those made by Stone Age hunters at Prolonged Drift.

By their location, I identified marks caused either by disarticulation or meat removal and then compared their frequencies with those from Prolonged Drift. More than 90 percent of the Neolithic marks in these two categories were from disarticulation, but to my surprise, only about 45 percent of the corresponding Olduvai cut marks were from disarticulation. This difference is too great to have occurred by chance; the Olduvai bones did not show the predicted pattern. In fact, the Olduvai cut marks attributable to meat removal and disarticulation showed essentially the same pattern of distribution as the carnivore tooth marks. Apparently, the early hominids were not regularly disarticulating carcasses. This finding casts serious doubt on the idea that early hominids carried their kills back to camp to share with others, since both transport and sharing are difficult unless carcasses are cut up.

When I looked for cut marks attributable to skinning or tendon removal, a more modern pattern emerged. On both the Neolithic and Olduvai bones, nearly 75 percent of all cut marks occurred on bones that bore little meat; these cut marks probably came from skinning. Carnivore tooth marks were much less common on such bones. Hominids were using carcasses as a source of skin and tendon. This made it seem more surprising that they disarticulated carcasses so rarely.

A third line of evidence provided the most tantalizing clue. Occasionally, sets of overlapping marks occur on the Olduvai fossils. Sometimes, these sets include both cut marks and carnivore tooth marks. Still more rarely, I could see under the SEM which mark had been made first, because its features were overlaid by those of the later mark, in much the same way as old tire tracks on a dirt road are obscured by fresh ones. Although only thirteen such sets of marks were found, in eight cases the hominids made the cut marks after the carnivores made their tooth marks. This finding suggested a new hypothesis. Instead of hunting for prey and leaving the remains behind for carnivores to scavenge, perhaps hominids were scavenging from the carnivores. This might explain the hominids' apparently unsystematic use of carcasses: they took what they could get, be it skin, tendon, or meat.

Man the Scavenger is not nearly as attractive an image as Man the Hunter, but it is worth examining. Actually, although hunting and scavenging are different ecological strategies, many mammals do both. The only pure scavengers alive in Africa today are vultures; not one of the modern African mammalian carnivores is a pure scavenger. Even spotted hyenas, which have massive, bone-crushing teeth well adapted for eating the bones left behind by others, only scavenge about 33 percent of their food. Other carnivores that scavenge when there are enough carcasses around include lions, leopards, striped hyenas, and jackals. Long-term behavioral studies suggest that these carnivores scavenge when they can and kill when they must. There are only two nearly pure predators, or hunters —the cheetah and the wild dog—that rarely, if ever, scavenge.

What are the costs and benefits of scavenging compared with those of predation? First of all, the scavenger avoids the task of making sure its meal is dead: a predator has already endured the energetically costly business of chasing or stalking animal after animal until one is killed. But while scavenging may be cheap, it's risky. Predators rarely give up their prey to scavengers without defending it. In such disputes, the larger animal, whether a scavenger or a predator, usually wins, although smaller animals in a pack may defeat a lone, larger animal. Both predators and scavengers suffer the dangers inherent in fighting for possession of a carcass. Smaller scavengers such as jackals or striped hyenas avoid disputes to some extent by specializing in darting in and removing a piece of a carcass without trying to take possession of the whole thing. These two strategies can be characterized as that of the bully or that of the sneak: bullies need to be large to be successful, sneaks need to be small and quick.

Because carcasses are almost always much rarer than live prey, the major cost peculiar to scavenging is that scavengers must survey much larger areas than predators to find food. They can travel slowly, since their "prey" is already dead, but endurance is important. Many predators specialize in speed at the expense of endurance, while scavengers do the opposite.

The more committed predators among the East African carnivores (wild dogs and cheetahs) can achieve great top speeds when running, although not for long. Perhaps as a consequence, these "pure" hunters enjoy a much higher success rate in hunting (about three-fourths of their chases end in kills) than any of the scavenger-hunters do (less than half of their chases are successful). Wild dogs and cheetahs are efficient hunters, but they are neither big enough nor efficient enough in their locomotion to make good scavengers. In fact, the cheetah's teeth are so specialized for meat slicing that they probably cannot withstand the stresses of bone crunching and carcass dismembering carried out by scavengers. Other carnivores are less successful at hunting, but have specializations of size, endurance, or (in the case of the hyenas) dentition that make successful scavenging possible. The small carnivores seem to have a somewhat higher hunting success rate than the large ones, which balances out their difficulties in asserting possession of carcasses.

In addition to endurance, scavengers need an efficient means of locating carcasses, which, unlike live animals, don't move or make noises. Vultures, for example, solve both problems by flying. The soaring, gliding flight of vultures expends much less energy than walking or cantering as performed by the part-time mammalian scavengers. Flight enables vultures to maintain a foraging radius two to three times larger than that of spotted hyenas, while providing a better vantage point. This explains why vultures can scavenge all of their food in the same habitat in which it is impossible for any mammal to be a pure scavenger. (In fact, many mammals learn where carcasses are located from the presence of vultures.)

Since mammals can't succeed as full-time scavengers, they must have another source of food to provide the bulk of their diet. The large carnivores rely on hunting large animals to obtain food when scavenging doesn't work. Their size enables them to defend a carcass against others. Since the small carnivores—jackals and striped hyenas—often can't defend carcasses successfully, most of their diet is composed of fruit and insects. When they do hunt, they usually prey on very small animals, such as rats or hares, that can be consumed in their entirety before the larger competitors arrive.

The ancient habitat associated with the fossils of Olduvai and Koobi Fora would have supported many herbivores and carnivores. Among the latter were two species of large saber-toothed cats, whose teeth show extreme adaptations for meat slicing. These were predators with primary access to carcasses. Since their teeth were unsuitable for bone crushing, the saber-toothed cats must have left behind many bones covered with scraps of meat, skin, and tendon. Were early hominids among the scavengers that exploited such carcasses?

All three hominid species that were present in Bed I times (*Homo habilis, Australopithecus africanus, A. robustus*) were adapted for habitual, upright bipedalism. Many anatomists see evidence that these hominids were agile tree climbers as well. Although upright bipedalism is a notoriously peculiar mode of locomotion, the adaptive value of which has been argued for years (See Matt Cartmill's article, "Four Legs Good, Two Legs Bad," *Natural History*, November 1983), there are three general points of agreement.

First, bipedal running is neither fast nor efficient compared to quadrupedal gaits. However, at moderate speeds of 2.5 to 3.5 miles per hour, bipedal *walking* is more energetically efficient than quadrupedal walking. Thus, bipedal walking is an excellent means of covering large areas slowly, making it an unlikely adaptation for a hunter but an appropriate and useful adaptation for a scavenger. Second, bipedalism elevates the head, thus improving the hominid's ability to spot items on the ground—an advantage both to scavengers and to those trying to avoid becoming a carcass. Combining bipedalism with agile tree climbing improves the vantage point still further. Third, bipedalism frees the hands from locomotive duties, making it possible to carry items. What would early hominids have carried? Meat makes a nutritious, easy-to-carry package; the problem is that carrying meat attracts scavengers. Richard Potts suggests that carrying stone tools or unworked stones for toolmaking to caches would be a more efficient and less dangerous activity under many circumstances.

In short, bipedalism is compatible with a scavenging strategy. I am tempted to argue that bipedalism evolved because it provided a substantial advantage to scavenging hominids. But I doubt hominids could scavenge effectively without tools, and bipedalism predates the oldest known stone tools by more than a million years.

Is there evidence that, like modern mammalian scavengers, early hominids had an alternative food source, such as either hunting or eating fruits and insects? My husband, Alan Walker, has shown that the microscopic wear on an animal's teeth reflects its diet. Early hominid teeth wear more like that of chimpanzees and other modern fruit eaters than that of carnivores. Apparently, early hominids ate mostly fruit, as the smaller, modern scavengers do. This accords with the estimated body weight of early hominids, which was only about forty to eighty pounds—less than that of any of the modern carnivores that combine scavenging and hunting but comparable to the striped hyena, which eats fruits and insects as well as meat.

Would early hominids have been able to compete for carcasses with other carnivores? They were too small to use a bully strategy, but if they scavenged in groups, a combined bully-sneak strategy might have been possible. Perhaps they were able to drive off a primary predator long enough to grab some meat, skin, or marrow-filled bone before relinquishing the carcass. The effectiveness of this strategy would have been vastly improved by using tools to remove meat or parts of limbs, a task at which hominid teeth are poor. As agile climbers, early hominids may have retreated into the trees to eat their scavenged trophies, thus avoiding competition from large terrestrial carnivores.

In sum, the evidence on cut marks, tooth wear, and bipedalism, together with our knowledge of scavenger adaptation in general, is consistent with the hypothesis that two million years ago hominids were scavengers rather than accomplished hunters. Animal carcasses, which contributed relatively little to the hominid diet, were not systematically cut up and transported for sharing at base camps. Man the Hunter may not have appeared until 1.5 to 0.7 million years ago, when we do see a shift toward omnivory, with a greater proportion of meat in the diet. This more heroic ancestor may have been *Homo erectus*, equipped with Acheulean-style stone tools and, increasingly, fire. If we wish to look further back, we may have to become accustomed to a less flattering image of our heritage.

ID#_____   NAME_____

Article 20: Scavenger Hunt

1. Shipman discovered that hominids were using stone tools to make cutmarks on bones. So why wasn't she convinced that early hominids were hunters?

2. Briefly describe the three activities modern hunters engage in and how they affect bones, which can be tested in fossil remains.

3. Why did Shipman compare the Olduvai remains to the Prolonged Drift remains?

4. Were the early hominids disarticulating the carcasses? What is the evidence?

5. Which came first: the tooth marks or the cut marks? What does this mean for "Man the Hunter?"

6. Would you expect a predator to have more speed or endurance? Why?

7. What three reasons does the author give to support the idea that bipedalism is compatible with a scavenging strategy?

8. What do studies of teeth tell us about the diet of early hominids?

Doubting Dmanisi

Pat Shipman

Why are some discoveries welcomed, whereas others are received with skepticism? I am prompted to ask this by recent developments in paleoanthropology. On the face of things, the story is an old one: International team finds startling new fossil human, oldest of its type in the region; experts agog. The catch is that the new find now being hailed merely echoes an earlier one in the same place, by many of the same researchers—but the early find was received with a "wait and see" attitude, of not outright disbelief. What makes the difference?

The original find, in 1991, was a primitive human mandible or jaw found at the then newly discovered fossil site of Dmanisi in the Republic of Georgia. A joint German-Georgian team of scientists and students excavated there for some months, recovering beautiful fossils of extinct species like saber-toothed cats, elephants and rhinos, along with some crude stone tools. On the last day—similar episodes are so common that the Last Day Find is practically a cliché—Antje Justus, a German graduate student, freed a partial skeleton of a saber-tooth cat from the sediments of her area of the dig. Lying directly underneath the extinct cat was the fossilized jaw of a primitive human, with a complete set of teeth. This was the find everyone had been hoping for all summer long.

In that moment, Dmanisi was transformed from being an interesting site to being one of major significance for human origins. Although the jaw itself could not be dated directly (as is often the case), its inferred age was impressive. The most recent record of the extinct animals found at Dmanisi turned out to be about 1.2 million years ago, while the fresh-looking lava lay underneath the fossil-bearing sediments was estimated to be about 1.8 million years old, according to preliminary radiometric dating. That meant that the owner of the Dmanisi mandible lived in the interval between 1.2 and 1.8 million years ago, making it the earliest evidence of *Homo erectus* from the Eurasian continent by a significant margin.

The first I heard of the find was in December of 1991, when Justus, paleontologist Leo Gabunia of the Republic of Georgia National Academy of Sciences, and dig director David Lordkipanidze of the Georgia State Museum traveled to a conference on *Homo erectus* at the Senckenberg Museum in Frankfurt, Germany. Gabunia and Justus gave a joint presentation briefly describing the site, the fauna, the tools, the

From *American Scientist*, November/December 2000 by Pat Shipman. Copyright © 2000 by Sigma Xi. Reprinted by permission.

jaw and the preliminary dates. They generously brought the original fossil with them, so that colleagues could examine it firsthand during the workshop portion of the conference.

I knew most of the conference participants, but Gabunia, Justus and Lordkipanidze seemed to have come out of nowhere, speaking of a site I couldn't find without an atlas. Gabunia is a quiet, silver-haired man who spoke in French so clear that even I understood the jaw's anatomy. Justus put the find in context, speaking in articulate English and looking even younger than she was. Lordkipanidze fell somewhere in the middle in terms of age and personality; his English was excellent, his enthusiasm palpable, and he was obviously knowledgeable. If they were even half right in what they were saying, this was a very important new find indeed.

Separated at Birth?

Like everyone else, I was eager to look at the jaw. I knew the African *erectus* specimens well, for my husband, Alan Walker, had co-directed the dig at Nariokotome, Kenya, which had yielded the most complete known skeleton of *Homo erectus* a few years before. (In 1991, as now, some researchers would call the Nariokotome and other early African specimens *Homo ergaster* to distinguish them from their presumed descendants in Eurasia, the fossils originally dubbed *Homo erectus*.) Whatever you want to call them, the specimens from Dmanisi and Nariokotome needed close comparison. When Gabunia put his fossil next to the cast of the Nariokotome jaw that Alan had brought, there was an almost visible spark of recognition. The two jaws were not just *similar*, they might have come from twins. Impulsively, Alan gave Gabunia the Nariokotome cast to take home with him, knowing there was none in the Republic of Georgia.

From then on, I was convinced the new jaw was *Homo erectus* and probably a very old one. The morphology, the date, the fauna were all right. No other Eurasian site had yielded hominids (human ancestors) anywhere near as old as the Dmanisi jaw; most were less than half a million years old. Only in Africa were there hominids dated to more than 1 million years, and the oldest *Homo erectus* (or *ergaster*, for those who preferred that term) in Africa was about 2 million years ago. By about 1 million years, *Homo erectus* had massively expanded its geographic range and was found in Java, somewhat later in China and later still in Europe. What propelled *Homo erectus* out of Africa into such a stunning dispersal? And why was there a time lag of almost 1 million years between the species' first evolutionary appearance in Africa and its invasion of Eurasia? It was an intriguing mystery.

In 1989, my husband and I had tackled this problem in a paper published in the *Journal of Human Evolution*. We interpreted *Homo erectus's* expanded brain size, increased body size and powerful strength relative to those of previous hominids as evidence that *Homo erectus* had a strikingly different diet from its predecessors. Earlier hominids were largely or exclusively vegetarian; we hypothesized that *Homo erectus* was the first efficient, regular hunter in human evolution. Only consistent access to very high-quality food would have enabled *erectus* mothers to bear and raise offspring with such nutritionally expensive characteristics.

Diets and Dates

To test our hypothesis, we made a prediction based on the energetic and ecological "rules" that govern the animal kingdom. If *Homo erectus* had indeed undergone a dietary shift from plant- to an animal-based diet, then the ecological consequences of becoming a predator should be visible in the fossil record. The most obvious repercussion of this dietary shift would have been a density dilemma. Predators must be

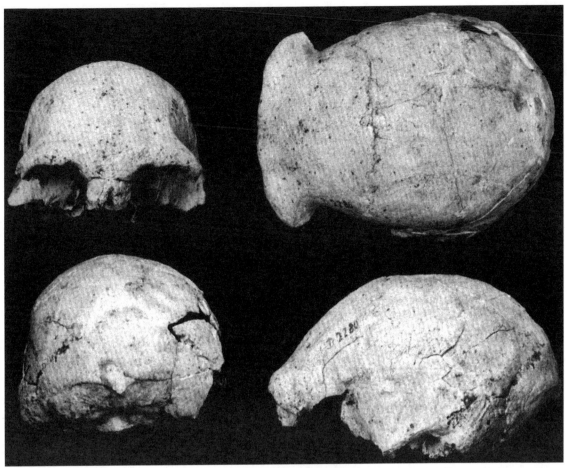

PHOTOGRAPHS OF PARTIAL SKULL AND FULL SKULL FOUND IN DMANISI, REPUBLIC OF GEORGIA BY GOURAM TSIBAKHASHVILI. Copyright © by David O. Lordkipanidze. Reprinted by permission.

Figure 1. Partial skull (*above four perspectives*) and full skull (*next page*) found in Dmanisi, the Republic of Georgia, confirm earlier claims for a 1.7-million-year-old dispersal of *Homo erectus* out of Africa. Many anthropologists were surprised by the fossils' antiquity and by their close anatomical resemblance to early African specimens of *Homo erectus*.

much more rare (less densely distributed across the landscape) than their prey. Violate this principle and you, as predator, risk starvation. There are two basic solutions to this problem. First, predators may, if time permits, evolve smaller bodies that require fewer or smaller bodies that require fewer or smaller prey. Second, the predators may lower their population density if they greatly expand their territory, in which case their depredations are spread across a wider range of prey populations. Could we see one of these solutions in the fossil record? Yes, gratifyingly, we could, for by spreading out of Africa across the Old World, *Homo erectus* had behaved just exactly as a newly predatory species ought to.

What we could not explain or understand was the troublesome time lag *before* the geographic expansion took place. Other colleagues suggested that perhaps *Homo erectus* was confined to Africa until some technological breakthrough occurred, the favorite being the invention of the Acheulian tool culture. We didn't like this idea much, for there is no obvious functional property of Acheulian tools that makes them superior to the earliest Oldowan tools, but we had no better alternative.

Thus, when Gabunia and Justus presented their finds at Senckenberg, every listener in the audience knew that the *Homo erectus* lineage hadn't gotten out of Africa until 1 million years ago. Many scholars

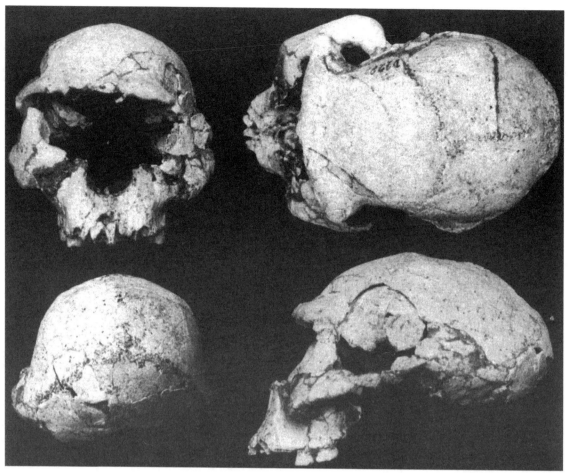

PHOTOGRAPHS OF PARTIAL SKULL AND FULL SKULL FOUND IN DMANISI, REPUBLIC OF GEORGIA BY GOURAM TSIBAKHASHVILI.
Copyright © by David O. Lordkipanidze. Reprinted by permission.

concluded that the Dmanisi jaw was not *Homo erectus* but a later species of *Homo* and figured that the date was wrong. What should have made us all suspicious was that proof that *Homo erectus* was confined to Africa prior to 1 million years ago was nothing more than a flimsy absence of evidence of the species in Eurasia.

I wonder, too, whether the identity of those presenting the work contributed to the general skepticism. Had three of the well-known and highly respected leaders of the field announced the Dmanisi finds, the general response might have been more favorable. As it was, Justus was only a student, and students are notoriously prone to oversell the importance of their finds; Gabunia and Lordkipanidze were mature scientists, but they had no reputation in paleoanthropology as far as Western Europeans and Americans were concerned.

Instead of focusing on the new Dmanisi material, most of the participants at the Senckenberg conference got drawn into a flaming debate over the taxonomic status of *Homo erectus* started by Milford Wolpoff of the University of Michigan, Alan Thorne of the University of Canberra and their colleagues. They argued forcefully that *Homo erectus* had no validity as a species and should be eliminated altogether. All members of the genus *Homo*, from about 2 million years ago to the present, were one highly variable, widely spread species, *Homo sapiens*, with no natural breaks or subdivisions. The subject of the conference, *Homo erectus*, didn't exist. It was a radical suggestion.

Tempers flared and voices grew loud. One European, shocked by the vehemence, said quietly to me that, in his country, such insults would be resolved with pistols at dawn.

Skulls

Although the Dmanisi jaw and its significance were largely overshadowed in 1991, excavations continued. In the summer of 1999, David Lordkipanidze sent word that there was something new and special from Dmanisi: "Skulls," he said enigmatically. We waited eagerly for more information. In May of 2000, a wonderful new paper appeared in *Science* by Gabunia and a host of colleagues, including Justus, Lordkipanidze and the German researchers who had worked with them from the beginning. Enlarging the team were two Americans—Carl Swisher III, and dating specialist, and Susan Antón, an expert on the skull of *Homo erectus*—and Marie-Antoinette de Lumley, a renowned archaeologist from the Laboratoire Museum National d'Histoire Naturelle.

Skulls it was. The paper announced two new skulls of *Homo erectus* from Dmanisi, one very complete and the other a partial skull missing the face. Anatomically, these specimens were very similar to the older, African specimens like Nariokotome, which the Dmanisi team called *Homo ergaster*, meaning the *ergaster* was no longer a strictly African form. The antiquity of Dmanisi was now firmly established at 1.7 million years, based on state-of-the-art radiometric and paleomagnetic studies by Swisher and colleagues; the date was supported by additional study of the faunal material. Finally, more than 1,000 stone artifacts excavated from Dmanisi confirmed that the tools were part of the Oldowan (or Mode I) culture.

This time, the new Dmanisi discoveries were widely hailed by the media who garnered many catchy quotes from major figures in paleoanthropology. "Fossil signs of first human migration are found," *The New York Times* cheered. "This has doubled again the age of humans in Europe, or at least at the gates of Europe," declared Giacomo Giacobini of the University of Turin, echoing an endorsement of Ofer Bar-Yosef of Harvard University, who has visited Dmanisi. "As soon as *Homo erectus* evolves in Africa, they're out," remarked Walker to a reporter. Ian Tattersall of the American Museum of Natural History added, "these guys [were] moving very, very fast." The million-year time lag simply evaporated, leaving in its place an impressively rapid outward dispersal from Africa.

Why are the claims for Dmanisi accepted now, when they were not in 1991? For one thing, the evidence itself is stronger. Skulls are more readily identifiable to species than are jaws when hominids are at issue. Bringing new experts onto the team, well known for their work in dating, morphology and archaeology, has also enhanced the credibility of the work.

Since 1991 the field's focus has shifted. The move to eliminate *Homo erectus* is largely defunct, and many anthropologists use *Homo ergaster* as an informal shorthand for "the earliest part of the evolving *ergaster/erectus* lineage." Moreover, the simple dichotomy that once linked early Africa-Oldowan and contrasted that complex with the late Eurasian-Acheulian has been dismantled. In 1994, Carl Swisher and colleagues produced evidence that the Javan *Homo erectus* sites may range in age from as much as 1.8 million years to roughly 50,000 years, making them both younger and older than previously thought. Scrappy fossils that may be *Homo erectus* have been found in China, too, dating to about 1.9 million years. Thus, "early" no longer implies "African." Similarly, though Oldowan tools once suggested great antiquity, they too have been found at younger sites, such as Gran Dolina at Atapuerca, Spain, some 780,000 years ago, whereas the oldest Acheulian sites in Eurasia are now as old as

1.5 million years. A whole series of finds and analyses has contributed to a new paradigm that makes the Dmanisi find more palatable.

This episode offers an important lesson about how science is done. When we scrutinize a colleague's work, we try to make an objective judgement. We evaluate the work against the holy grails of Replicability and Causality, but these are largely unattainable goals, at least for those working with fossils. Like most scientists, we tend to accord an extra dollop of credibility to studies conducted by colleagues known to have done reputable work.

But should the work of the young or the less known be held to higher standards than that of the great matriarchs and silverbacked males of the field? Skepticism is a cheap stance to adopt, for it is easier to cast doubt than to substantiate, especially if new techniques and new paradigms must be forged along the way. Science is a process of discovery, not confirmation. Let us allow for the occasional, delicious surprise that makes us rethink all we thought we knew.

ID#_____   NAME_____

Article 21: Doubting Dmanisi

1. The discovery of a _____ dated between _____ and _____ transformed the site of Dmanisi into a site of major significance for human evolution.

2. What did the jaw from Dmanisi resemble?

3. What three traits do Shipman and Walker think were evidence that *Homo erectus* had a different diet than previous hominids?

4. Why were the high quality foods important?

5. What behavioral change did *H. erectus* make that signifies its status as a predatory species?

6. What exciting discovery was made in 2000?

7. The stone tools excavated from Dmanisi are part of the _____ stone tool culture.

Who Were the Neandertals?

Kate Wong

It was such a neat and tidy story. No match for the anatomically modern humans who swept in with a sophisticated culture and technology, the Neandertals—a separate species—were quickly driven to extinction by the invading moderns. But neat and tidy stories about the past have a way of unraveling, and the saga of the Neandertals, it appears, is no exception. For more than 200,000 years, these large-brained hominids occupied Europe and western Asia, battling the bitter cold of glacial maximums and the daily perils of prehistoric life. Today they no longer exist. Beyond these two facts, however, researchers fiercely debate who the Neandertals were, how they lived and exactly what happened to them.

The steadfast effort to resolve these elusive issues stems from a larger dispute over how modern humans evolved. Some researchers posit that our species arose recently (around 200,000 years ago) in Africa and subsequently replaced archaic hominids around the world, whereas others propose that these ancient populations contributed to the early modern human gene pool. As the best known of these archaic groups, Neandertals are critical to the origins controversy. Yet this is more than an academic argument over certain events of our primeval past, for in probing Neandertal biology and behavior, researchers must wrestle with the very notion of what it means to be fully human and determine what, if anything, makes us moderns unique. Indeed, spurred by recent discoveries, paleoanthropologists and archaeologists are increasingly asking, How much like us were they?

Comparisons of Neandertals and modern humans first captured the attention of researchers when a partial Neandertal skeleton turned up in Germany's Neander Valley in 1856. Those remains—a heavily built skull with the signature arched browridge and massive limb bones—were clearly different, and Neandertals were assigned to their own species, *Homo neanderthalensis* (although even then there was disagreement: several German scientists argued that these were the remains of a crippled Cossack horseman). But it was the

Reprinted with permission. Copyright © 2000 by Scientific American, Inc. All rights reserved.

French discovery of the famous "Old Man" of La Chapell-aux-Saints some 50 years later that led to the characterization of Neandertals as primitive protohumans. Reconstructions showed them as stooped, lumbering, apelike brutes, in stark contrast to upright, graceful *Homo sapiens*. The Neandertal, it seemed, represented the ultimate "other," a dim-witted ogre lurking behind the evolutionary threshold of humanity.

Decades later reevaluation of the La Chapelle individual revealed that certain anatomical features had been misinterpreted. In fact, Neandertal posture and movement would have been the same as ours. Since then, paleoanthropologists have struggled to determine whether the morphological features that do characterize Neandertals as a group—such as the robustness of their skeletons, their short limbs and barrel chests, prominent browridges and low, sloping foreheads, protruding midfaces and chinless jaws—warrant designating them as a separate species. Researchers agree that some of these characteristics represent environment adaptations. The Neandertals' stocky body proportions, for example, would have allowed them to retain heat more effectively in the extremely cold weather brought on by glacial cycles. But other traits, such as the form of the Neandertal browridge, lack any clear functional significance and seem to reflect the genetic drift typical of isolated populations.

For those scholars who subscribe to the replacement model of modern human origins, the distinctive Neandertal morphology clearly resulted from following an evolutionary trajectory separate from that of moderns. But for years, another faction of researchers has challenged this interpretation, arguing that many of the features that characterized Neandertals are also seen in the early modern Europeans that followed them. "They clearly have a suite of features that are, overall, different, but it's a frequency difference, not an absolute difference," contends David W. Frayer, a paleoanthropologist at the University of Kansas. "Virtually everything you can find in Neandertals you can find elsewhere."

He points to one of the earliest-known modern Europeans, a fossil from a site in southwestern Germany called Vogelherd, which combines the skull shape of moderns with features that are typically Neandertal, such as the distinct space between the last molar and the ascending part of the lower jaw known as a retro-molar gap, and the form of the mandibular foramen–a nerve canal in the lower jaw. Additional evidence, according to Frayer and Milford H. Wolpoff of the University of Michigan, comes from a group of early moderns discovered in Moravia (Czech Republic) at a site called Mladec. The Mladec people, they say, exhibit characteristics on their skulls that other scientists have described as uniquely Neandertal traits.

Although such evidence was once used to argue that Neandertals could have independently evolved into modern Europeans, this view has shifted somewhat. "It's quite clear that people entered Europe as well, so the people that are there later in time are a mix of Neandertals and those populations coming into Europe," says Wolpoff, who believes the two groups differed only as much as living Europeans and aboriginal Australians do. Evidence for mixing also appears in later Neandertal fossils, according to Fred H. Smith, paleoanthropologist at Northern Illinois University. Neandertal remains from Vindija cave in northwestern Croatia reflect "the assimilation of some early modern features," he says, referring to their more modern-shaped browridges and the slight presence of a chin on their mandibles.

Those who view Neandertals as a separate species, however, maintain that the Vindija fossils are too fragmentary to be diagnostic and that any similarities that do exist can be attributed to convergent evolu-

> **Guide to Terminology**
>
> **Neandertal** can also be spelled Neanderthal. Around 1900 German orthography changed, and the silent "h" in certain words, such as "thal" (meaning "valley"), was dropped. This designation *Homo neanderthalensis* remains the same, but the common name can be spelled either way.
> **Paleolithic,** or Old Stone Age, is the period ranging from the beginning of culture to the end of the last glaciation. It is subdivided into Lower, Middle and Upper stages.
> **Mousterian** is a Middle Paleolithic, stone tool-based cultural tradition associated with Neandertals and with early moderns in the Near East.
> **Aurignacian** is an Upper Paleolithic cultural tradition associated with moderns that includes advanced tools and art objects.
> **Châtelperronian** is an Upper Paleolithic cultural tradition associated with Neandertals. It resembles both the Mousterian and the Aurignacian.

tion. These researchers likewise dismiss the mixing argument for the early moderns from Mladec. "When I look at the morphology of these people, I see robustness, I don't see Neandertal," counters Christopher B. Stringer of the Natural History Museum in London.

Another reason to doubt these claims for interbreeding, some scientists say, is that they contradict the conclusions reached by Svante Pääbo, then at the University of Munich, and his colleagues, who in July 1997 announced that they had retrieved and analyzed mitochondrial DNA (mtDNA) from a Neandertal fossil. The cover of the journal *Cell*, which contained their report, said it all: "Neandertals Were Not Our Ancestors." From the short stretch of mtDNA they sequenced, the researchers determined that the difference between the Neandertal mtDNA and living moderns' mtDNA was considerably greater than the differences found among living human populations. But though it seemed on the surface that the species question had been answered, undercurrents of doubt have persisted [see "Ancestral Quandary," by Kate Wong, News and Analysis, January 1998].

New fossil evidence from western Europe has intensified interest in whether Neandertals and moderns mixed. In January 1999 researchers announced the discovery in central Portugal's Lapedo Valley of a largely complete skeleton from a four-year-old child buried 24,500 years ago in the Gravettian style known from other early modern Europeans. According to Erik Trinkaus of Washington University, Cidália Duarte of the Portuguese Institute of Archaeology in Lisbon and their colleagues, the specimen, known as Lagar Velho 1, bears a combination of Neandertal and modern human traits that could only have resulted from extensive interbreeding between the two populations [see box "The Hybrid Child from Portugal"].

If the mixed ancestry interpretation for Lagar Velho 1 holds up after further scrutiny, the notion of Neandertals as a variant of our species will gain new strength. Advocates of the replacement model do allow for isolated instances of interbreeding between moderns and the archaic species, because some other closely related mammal species interbreed on occasion. But unlike central and eastern European specimens that are said to show a combination of features, the Portuguese child dates to a time when Neandertals are no longer thought to have existed. For Neandertal features to have persisted thousands of years after those people disappeared, Trinkaus and Duarte say, coexisting populations of Neandertals and moderns must have mixed significantly.

Their interpretation has not gone unchallenged. In a commentary accompanying the team's report in the *Proceedings of the National Academy of Sciences USA* last June, paleoanthropologists Ian Tattersall of the American Museum of Natural History

The Hybrid Child From Portugal
Erik Trinkaus and Cidália Duarte

On a chilly afternoon in late November 1998, while inspecting the Abrigo do Lagar Velho rockshelter in central Portugal's Lapedo Valley, two archeology scouts spotted loose sediment in a rodent hole along the shelter's back wall. Knowing that burrowing animals often bring deeper materials to the surface, one of the scouts reached in to see what might have been unearthed. When he withdrew his hand, he held in it something extraordinary: bones of a human child buried nearly 25,000 years ago.

Subsequent excavation of the burial, led by one of us (Duarte), revealed that the four-year-old had been ceremonially interred—covered with red ocher and laid on a bed of burnt vegetation, along with pierced deer teeth and a marine shell—in the Gravettian style known from modern humans of that time across Europe. Based on the abrupt cultural transition seen in archaeological remains from the Iberian Peninsula, it seemed likely that when moderns moved into the area after 30,000 years ago, they rapidly replaced the native Neandertals. So it stood to reason that this specimen, called Lagar Velho 1, represented an early modern child. In fact, it didn't occur to us at first that it could be anything else.

This wonderfully complete skeleton does have a suite of features that align it predominantly with early modern Europeans. These include a prominent chin and certain other details of the mandible (lower jaw), small front teeth, characteristic proportions and muscle markings on the thumb, the narrowness of the front of the pelvis, and several aspects of the shoulder blade and forearm bones. Yet intriguingly, a number of features also suggest Neandertal affinities—specifically the front of the mandible (which slopes backward despite the chin), details of the incisor teeth, the pectoral muscle markings, the knee proportions and the short, strong lower-leg bones. Thus, the Lagar Velho child appears to exhibit a complex mosaic of Neandertal and early modern human features.

This anatomical amalgam is not the result of any abnormalities. Taking normal human growth patterns into consideration, our analysis indicates that except for a bruised forearm, a couple of lines in the bones indicating times when growth was trivially arrested (by sickness or lack of food) and the fact that it died as a child, Lagar Velho 1 developed normally. The combination can only have resulted from a mixed ancestry—something that had not been previously documented for western Europe. We therefore conclude that Lagar Velho 1 resulted from interbreeding between indigenous Iberian Neandertals and early modern humans dispersing throughout Iberia sometime after 30,000 years ago. Because the child lived several millennia after Neandertals are thought to have disappeared, its anatomy probably reflects a true mixing of these populations during the period when they coexisted and not a rare chance mating between a Neandertal and an early modern human.

Fieldwork conducted last summer yielded major portions of the skull and most of the remaining teeth, along with more archaeological material. And in an effort to fully understand this remarkable specimen, we have organized a team of specialists to examine the skeleton further. Among the projects planned are CT scan analyses of the skull and limb bones and computer-based virtual reconstruction of the damaged skull. Rigorous study is necessary because the discovery of an individual with such a mosaic of features has profound implications. First, it rejects the extreme Out of Africa model of modern human emergence, which proposes that early moderns originating in Africa subsequently displaced all archaic humans in other regions. Instead the Lagar Velho child's anatomy supports a scenario that combines a dispersal of anatomically modern humans out of Africa with mixing between that population and the archaic populations it encountered. (The African ancestry of early modern Europeans is reflected in their relatively long lower-leg bones, a tropical adaptation. Lagar Velho 1, however, has the short shins of the cold-adapted Neandertals.)

Lagar Velho 1 also provides insights into the behavioral similarities of Neandertals and early modern humans. Despite the paleontological evidence indicating anatomical differences between these two groups, their overall adaptive patterns, social behaviors and means of communication (including language) cannot have contrasted greatly. To their contemporaries, the Neandertals were just another group of Pleistocene hunter-gatherers, fully as human as themselves.

in New York City and Jeffrey H. Schwartz of the University of Pittsburgh argued that Lagar Velho 1 is instead most likely "a chunky Gravettian child." The robust body proportions that Trinkaus and his colleagues view as evidence for Neandertal ancestry, Stringer says, might instead reflect adaptation to Portugal's then cold climate. But this interpretation is problematic, according to Jean-Jacques Hublin of France's CNRS, who points out that although some cold-adapted moderns exhibit such proportions, none are known from that period in Europe. Rather Hublin is troubled that Lagar Velho 1 represents a child, noting that "we do not know anything about the variation in children of a given age in this range of time."

Survival Skills

Taxonomic issues aside, much research has focused on Neandertal behavior, which remained largely misunderstood until recently. Neandertals were often portrayed as incapable of hunting or planning ahead, recalls archaeologist John J. Shea of the State University of New York at Stony Brook. "We've got reconstructions of Neandertals as people who couldn't survive a single winter, let alone a quarter of a million years in the worst environments in which humans ever lived," he observes. Analysis of animal remains from the Croatian site of Krapina, however, indicates that Neandertals were skilled hunters capable of killing even large animals such as rhinoceroses, according to University of Cambridge archaeologist Preston T. Miracle. And Shea's studies suggest that some Neandertals employed sophisticated stone-tipped spears to conquer their quarry—a finding supported last year when researches reported the discovery in Syria of a Neandertal-made stone point lodged in a neckbone of a prehistoric wild ass. Moreover, additional research conducted by Shea and investigations carried out by University of Arizona archaeologists Mary C. Stiner and Steven L. Kuhn have shown that Neandertal subsistence strategies varied widely with the environment and the changing seasons.

Such demonstrations refute the notion that Neandertals perished because they could not adapt. But it may be that moderns were better at it. One popular theory posits that modern humans held some cognitive advantage over Neandertals, perhaps a capacity for the most human trait of all: symbolic thought, including language. Explanations such as this one arose from observations that after 40,000 years ago, whereas Neandertal culture remained relatively static, that of modern Europeans boasted a bevy of new features, many of them symbolic. It appeared that only moderns performed elaborate burials, expressed themselves through body ornaments, figurines and cave paintings, and crafted complex bone and antler tools—an industry broadly referred to as Upper Paleolithic. Neandertal assemblages, in contrast, contained only Middle Paleolithic stone tools made in the Mousterian style.

Yet hints that Neandertals thought symbolically had popped up. Neandertal burials, for example, are well known across Europe, and several, it has been argued, contain grave goods. (Other researchers maintain that for Neandertals, interment merely constituted a way of concealing the decomposing body, which might have attracted unwelcome predators. They view the purported grave goods as miscellaneous objects that happened to be swept into the grave.) Evidence for art, in the form of isolated pierced teeth and engraved bone fragments, and red and yellow ocher, has been reported from a few sites, too, but given their relative rarity, researchers tend to assign alternative explanations to these items.

The possibility that Neandertals might have engaged in modern practices was taken more seriously in 1980, when researchers reported a Neandertal from the Saint-Césaire rock-shelter in Charente-

A Case for Neandertal Culture
João Zilhão and Francesco d'Errico

Ever since the discovery nearly 150 years ago of the specimen that defined the Neandertals, researchers have tended to deny Neandertals the behavioral capabilities of modern humans, such as the use of symbols or of complex techniques for tool manufacture. Instead Neandertals were characterized as subhuman, stuck in primitive technical traditions impervious to innovation. And when sophisticated cultural remains were linked to late Neandertals at several sites in western Europe, the evidence was explained away. The most spectacular of these sites, a cave in north-central France named Grotte du Renne (one in a string of sites collectively known as the Arcy-sur-Cure caves), yielded a wealth of complex bone and stone tools, body ornaments and decorated objects, found in association with Neandertal remains. Other sites in France and along the Cantabrian and Pyrenean mountain ranges bore similar artifacts made in this tradition, called the Châtelperronian.

Because early modern Europeans had a comparable industry known as Aurignacian—which often appears at the same sites that contain Châtelperronian materials—some researchers have suggested that the archaeological layers were disputed, mixing Aurignacian artifacts into the Neandertal-associated levels. Other scholars have interpreted this to mean that Neandertals picked up these ideas from moderns, either collecting or trading for items manufactured by moderns or imitating the newcomers' practices without really grasping the underlying symbolic nature of some of the objects.

Our reassessment of the evidence from the Grotte du Renne shows that the Neandertal-associated personal ornaments and tools found there did not result from a mixing of the archaeological strata, as demonstrated by the presence of finished objects and the byproducts of their manufacture in the same stratigraphic level. Moreover, the Châtelperronian artifacts recovered at the Grotte du Renne and other sites, such as Quinçay, in the Poitou-Charentes region of France, were created using techniques different from those favored by Aurignacians. With regard, for example, to the pendants—modified bear, wolf and deer teeth, among others—Neandertals carved a furrow around the tooth root so that a string of some sort could be tied around it for suspension, whereas Aurignacians pierced their pendants. As archaeologist François Lévêque and a colleague have described, even when, as they did on occasion,

---

Maritime, France, found in association with stone tools manufactured according to a cultural tradition known as the Châtelperronian, which was assumed to have been the handiwork of moderns. Then, in 1996, Hublin and his colleagues made an announcement that catapulted the Châtelperronian into the archaeological limelight. Excavations that began in the late 1940s at a site called the Grotte du Renne at Arcy-sur-Cure near Auxerre, France, had yielded numerous blades, body ornaments and bone tools and revealed evidence of huts and hearths—all hallmarks of the Upper Paleolithic. The scant human remains found amid the artifacts were impossible to identify initially, but using computer tomography to examine the hidden inner-ear region preserved inside an otherwise uninformative skull fragment, Hublin's team identified the specimen as Neandertal.

In response, a number of scientists suggested that Neandertals had acquired the modern-looking items either by stealing them, collecting artifacts discarded by moderns or perhaps trading for them. But this view has come under fire, most recently from archaeologists Francesco d'Errico of the University of Bordeaux and João Zilhão of the Portuguese Institute of Archaeology, who argue that the Châtelperronian artifacts at the Grotte du Renne and elsewhere, though superficially similar to those from the Aurignacian, reflect an older, different method of manufacture [see box "A Case for Neandertal Culture"].

Most researchers are now convinced that Neandertals manufactured the Châtelper-

Neandertals put a hole through a tooth, they took an unusual approach, puncturing the tooth. Moderns, on the other hand, preferred to scrape the tooth thin and then pierce it.

Similarly, the new knapping techniques and tool types that appear among late Neandertals at other sites in France, Italy and Spain fail to show any influence from the Aurignacian. Instead they maintain affinities with the preceding local traditions, of which they seem to represent an autonomous development.

If the Neandertals' Châtelperronian culture was an outcome of contact with moderns, then the Aurignacian should predate the Châtelperronian. Yet our reanalysis of the radiometric dates for the archaeological sequences reveals that apart from a few debatable instances of mixture, wherever both cultures are represented at the same site, the Châtelperronian always underlies the Aurignacian, suggesting its priority. Furthermore, consideration of the hundreds of datings available from this period in Europe and the Near East shows that wherever the context of the dated samples is well known, the earliest occurrences of the Aurignacian are apparently from no earlier than around 36,500 years ago. The same radiometric data, however, indicate that by then Neandertals were already moving toward modernity on their own. In other words, the Châtelperronian and other late Neandertal cultures, such as the Uluzzian of Italy, emerged in Europe around 40,000 years ago, long before any moderns established themselves in those areas.

That this autonomous development included the manufacture and use of symbolic objects created for visual display on the body, as are often observed in traditional societies, reflects various social roles within Neandertal cultures. Thus, "modern" behavior seems to have emerged in different groups of humans, as would happen later in history with the invention of agriculture, writing and state society.

An alternative explanation, taking into account the broadly simultaneous appearance of personal ornaments in many parts of the Old World, is that contacts between modern and archaic humans challenged each group's personal, social and biological identities, igniting an explosion of production of symbolic objects by all those involved. On the strength of the available data, however, we favor the hypothesis of independent invention.

Regardless of which is eventually proved correct, the behavioral barrier that seemed to separate moderns from Neandertals and gave us the impressions of being a unique and particularly gifted human type—the ability to produce symbolic cultures—has definitively collapsed.

---

ronian tools and ornaments, but what prompted this change after hundreds of thousands of years is unclear. Cast in this light, "it's more economical to see that as a result of imitation or acculturation from modern humans than to assume that Neandertals invented it for themselves," reasons Cambridge archaeologist Paul A. Mellars. "It would be an extraordinary coincidence if they invented all these things shortly before the modern humans doing the same things arrived." Furthermore, Mellars disagrees with d'Errico and Zilhão's proposed order of events. "The dating evidence proves to me that [Neandertals] only started to do these things after the modern humans had arrived in western Europe or at least in northern Spain," he asserts. (Unfortunately, because scientists have been unable to date these sites with sufficient precision, researchers can interpret the data differently.)

From his own work on the Grotte du Renne body ornaments, New York University archaeologist Randall White argues that these artifacts reflect manufacturing methods known—albeit at lower frequencies—from Aurignacian ornaments. Given the complicated stratigraphy of the Grotte du Renne site, the modern-looking items might have come from overlying Aurignacian levels. But more important, according to White, the Châtelperronian does not exist outside of France, Belgium, Italy and northern Spain. Once you look at the Upper Paleolithic from a pan-European perspective, he says, "the Châtelperronian becomes post-Aurignacian by a long shot."

Still, post-Aurignacian does not necessarily mean after contact with moderns. The earliest Aurignacian sites do not include any human remains. Researchers have assumed that they belonged to moderns because moderns are known from younger Aurignacian sites. But "who the Aurignacians were biologically between 40,000 and 35,000 years ago remains very much an unanswered question," White notes.

He adds that if you look at the Near East around 90,000 years ago, anatomically modern humans and Neandertals were both making Mousterian stone tools, which, though arguably less elaborate than Aurignacian tools, actually require a considerable amount of know-how. "I cannot imagine that Neandertals were producing these kinds of technologically complex tools and passing that on from generation to generation without talking about it," White declares. "I've seen a lot of people do this stuff, and I can't stand over somebody's shoulder and learn how to do it without a lot of verbal hints." Thus, White and others do not buy the argument that moderns were somehow cognitively superior, especially if Neandertals' inferiority meant that they lacked language. Instead it seems that moderns invented a culture that relied more heavily on material symbols.

Researchers have also looked to Neandertal brain morphology for clues to their cognitive ability. According to Ralph L. Holloway of Columbia University, all the brain asymmetries that characterize modern humans are found in Neandertals. "To be able to discriminate between the two," he remarks, "is, at the moment, impossible." As to whether Neandertal anatomy would have permitted speech, studies of the base of the skull conducted by Jeffrey T. Laitman of the Mount Sinai School of Medicine suggest that if they talked, Neandertals had a somewhat limited vocal repertoire. The significance of such physical constraints, however, is unclear.

Fading Away

If Neandertals possessed basically the same cognitive ability as moderns, it makes their disappearance additionally puzzling. But the recent redating of Neandertal remains from Vindija cave in Croatia emphasizes that this did not happen overnight. Smith and his colleagues have demonstrated that Neandertals still lived in central Europe 28,000 years ago, thousands of years after moderns had moved in [see box "The Fate of Neandertals"]. Taking this into consideration, Stringer imagines that moderns, whom he views as a new species, replaced Neandertals in a long, slow process. "Gradually the Neandertals lost out because moderns were a bit more innovative, a bit better able to cope with rapid environmental change quickly, and they probably had bigger social networks," he supposes.

On the other hand, if Neandertals were an equally capable variant of our own species, as Smith and Wolpoff believe, long-term overlap of Neandertals and the new population moving into Europe would have left plenty of time for mingling, hence the mixed morphology that these scholars see in late Neandertals and early moderns in Europe. And if these groups were exchanging genes, they were probably exchanging cultural ideas, which might account for some of the similarity between, say, the Châtelperronian and the Aurignacian. Neandertals as entities disappeared, Wolpoff says, because they were outnumbered by the newcomers. Thousands of years of interbreeding between the small Neandertal population and the larger modern human population, he surmises, diluted the distinctive Neandertal features, which ultimately faded away.

"If we look at Australians a thousand years from now, we will see that the European features have predominated [over those of native Australians] by virtue of many more Europeans," Wolpoff asserts.

The Fate of the Neandertals
Fred H. Smith

Strong evidence has accumulated in recent years that the emergence of modern humans in Europe resulted largely from the immigration of peoples into the continent, probably from the Near East, starting sometime between 40,000 and 30,000 years ago. Most researchers envision these early modern populations as having moved into Anatolia and the Balkans, then up through the plains and valleys of central Europe, and finally into northern and western Europe. Meanwhile the indigenous Neandertals, it was thought, were systematically pushed into more peripheral and undesirable parts of the landscape by these expanding populations of moderns. The Neandertals' last bastion appeared to be the Iberian Peninsula, where fossils from a Spanish site called Zafarraya have been dated to 32,000 years ago and tools attributed to Neandertals have been dated around 28,000 years ago. Many scholars argued that after this time no traces of Neandertals remained in Europe and that Neandertals did not make any biological contributions to early modern humans. It seemed that Neandertals were sent into complete extinction by a superior human species—us.

Now new evidence from an important site in northwestern Croatia calls aspects of this conventional wisdom into question. By performing accelerator mass spectrometry dating directly on two Neandertal specimens from Vindija cave, my colleagues and I have demonstrated that Neandertals were living in some of the most desirable real estate in central Europe as late as 28,000 years ago. These dates, the most recent known for Neandertal fossils, show that these humans were not quickly relegated to the periphery; they competed quite well with intruding modern populations for a long time.

This overlap of Neandertal and early modern peoples for several millennia in the heart of Europe allowed some of them. Work by my Croatian colleagues Ivor Karavanic of the University of Zagreb and Jakov Radovic of the Croatian Natural History museum has revealed a combination of Mousterian and Aurignacian tools in the same stratigraphic level as the dated Neandertal fossils, suggesting that Neandertals either made advanced implements or traded with moderns for them. Morphologically, the Vindija Neandertals look more modern than do most other Neandertals, which suggests that their ancestors interbred with early moderns.

The likelihood of gene flow between the groups is also supported by evidence that Neandertals left their mark on early modern Europeans. Fossils representing early modern adults from central European sites such as Vogelherd in southwestern Germany and Mladec in Moravia (Czech Republic) have features that are difficult to explain unless they have some Neandertal contribution to their ancestry. For example, Neandertals and early modern Europeans virtually all exhibit a projection of the back of the skull called an occipital bun (aspects of the shape and position of the buns differ between them because the overall skull shapes are not the same). Yet fossils from the Near Eastern sites of Skhul and Qafzeh, which presumably represent the ancestors of early modern Europeans, do not have this morphology. It is hard to explain how the growth phenomenon responsible for this bunning could reappear independently and ubiquitously in early modern Europeans. Instead it is far more logical to recognize this morphology as a link to the Neandertals. The Portuguese child discovered recently offers more intriguing clues [see box "The Hybrid Child from Portugal"].

I believe the evidence shows that the behavioral and biological interactions between Neandertal and early modern human populations were very complex—too complex for the origins of modern humans in Europe to have involved a simple, complete biological replacement of the Neandertals. Neandertals as organisms no longer exist, and Neandertal genes may not have persisted to the present day, but those genes were there in the beginnings of modern European biological history.

"Not by virtue of better adaptation, not by virtue of different culture, not by virtue of anything except many more Europeans. And I really think that's what describes what we see in Europe—we see the predominance of more people."

From the morass of opinions in this notoriously contentious field, one consensus emerges: researchers have retired the old vision of the shuffling, cultureless Neandertal. Beyond that, whether these ancient hominids were among the ancestors of living people or a very closely related species that competed formidably with our own for the Eurasian territory and eventually lost remains to be seen. In either case, the details will most likely be extraordinarily complicated. "The more we learn, the more questions arise, the knottier it gets," muses archaeologist Lawrence G. Straus of the University of New Mexico. "That's why simple explanations just don't cut it."

ID#_____   NAME_____

Article 22: Who Were the Neandertals?

1. What famous find led to the characterization of Neandertals as stooped, lumbering brutes? Is this an appropriate description? Why or why not?

2. The author reports that the stocky body proportions were due to _____ , while the large browridge is more likely due to _____ .

3. Name two sites where modern Europeans exhibit Neandertal traits.

4. What did the mitochondrial DNA studies conclude?

5. What evidence indicates that Lagar Velho had been ceremoniously interred?

6. List two features each that link Lagar Velho with moderns and with Neandertals. Are these the result of abnormal growth?

7. What do Trinkaus and Duarte conclude about Lagar Velho? What does this mean for overall adaptive patterns?

8. What does John Shea say about the hunting ability of the Krapina Neandertals?

9. Name two things that indicate Neandertals had symbolic thought.

10. In "A Case for Neandertal Culture", name two lines of evidence the authors suggest indicate Neandertal culture evolved independently from modern humans.

11. What does Laitman suggest about Neandertal speech capabilities?

12. How does Stringer's description of the fate of the Neandertals contrast with that of Wolpoff?

13. In "The Fate of the Neandertals", does Fred Smith support the replacement idea? Why or why not?

Not Our Mom

Robert Kunzig

A small stretch of DNA from a Neanderthal bone was described this past year, and it doesn't look like ours. The bone was the right humerus, or upper-arm bone, of the Neander Valley skeleton itself, discovered near Düsseldorf in 1856; the DNA was from the "control region" of mitochondrial DNA. The control region codes for nothing, and so natural selection ignores it; and sex does too, because unlike the DNA that makes us visibly who we are, the stuff in the cell nucleus, mitochondrial DNA is passed intact from mother—and only from mother—to child. In theory, the control region comes to each one of us out of the deep past, like a taste for chicken soup, via an endless bucket brigade of mothers, altered only by random mutations. If some of us had a Neanderthal in that maternal line, her imprint ought to be discernible. Svante Pääbo of the University of Munich and his colleagues looked at the DNA from their single Neanderthal, and they looked at DNA from more than 1,600 modern Europeans, Africans, Asians, native Americans and Australians, and Oceanians. They saw no evidence of a relation.

The work was widely hailed as a technical triumph—reassuring in a year when earlier reports of far more ancient DNA from insects in amber seemed to be crumbling. Few labs besides Pääbo's, it seems clear, would have been able to extract the Neanderthal DNA from liquefied bone samples that contained only some 50 copies of the target molecule. A graduate student named Matthias Krings did the hard work—amplifying the scarce DNA by means of the polymerase chain reaction, cloning it, and finally determining its sequence. "It was Krings who put in the 100-hour weeks," says Ralf Schmitz of the Rheinisches Amt für Bodendenkmalpflege, an agency responsible for archeology in the Rhineland. "When he saw there might be something in there, he just kept working until he was sure."

But it was Schmitz, a young archeologist, who made the project happen in the first place. In 1991 the Rheinisches Landesmuseum in Bonn authorized him to organize new studies of its prize fossil. Schmitz got in touch with Pääbo, who had extracted DNA from a 30,000-year-old horse buried in permafrost. At first Pääbo was discouraging: The chances of getting DNA out of a Neanderthal that was anywhere from 30,000 to 100,000 years old and that had not been frozen, he said, were very slim—too slim to convince the custodians of the fossil. "It's as if you're cutting

From *Discover Magazine*, January 1998 by Robert Kunzig. Copyright © 1998 by Discover Magazine. Reprinted by permission.

a piece out of the Mona Lisa to study the paint," says Schmitz. "You have to have good arguments for doing that."

By 1996, though, gene-extraction techniques had improved, Pääbo was willing, and Schmitz got permission. In June of that year, he and Heike Krainitzki, a professional bone preparator, entered the steel vault where the bones are stored in a steel box in a steel cabinet—the Landesmuseum keeps only the skullcap with the famous browridges on display. "The nervous tension was enormous," Schmitz recalls. "We were both very tense. Krainitzki didn't want anyone else to be there. A German TV network had wanted to broadcast it live, but she wouldn't do it." The two of them wore protective clothing and surgeons' masks to avoid contaminating the bone. With a goldsmith's saw Krainitzki cut a half-inch thick, eighth-of-an-ounce, half-moon slice from the right humerus—the bone that X-rays and other tests had shown was best preserved. She and Schmitz then immediately carried the slice to Munich. There Krings drilled tiny samples from the cortex; the hard calcium carbonate in that outer layer offers DNA more protection against the outside world than it gets in the marrow.

Five months later Schmitz was back in Munich. . . . Krings had extracted a bit of DNA that he thought was Neanderthal. He was now repeating the whole experiment with a separate hundredth-of-an-ounce bit of bone drilled from that half-moon slice. If he got the same DNA sequence again, he would be virtually certain he was not looking at a modern human contaminant. The results, Schmitz remembers, came in one November evening at 10:14 P.M. "It felt as if we had climbed Everest," he says. Later there would be another occasion for celebration: The results were confirmed by an independent laboratory, that of Mark Stoneking at Penn State, which got the same sequence from another bit of the Neanderthal bone.

Careful controls like that seem to have convinced the researchers' peers, after the paper was published last July, that Krings and his colleagues did indeed have the first bit of Neanderthal DNA and the oldest bit of DNA ever extracted from a human being. What sort of human the Neanderthal was, however, remains subject to debate. There are two main schools of thought. One holds that Neanderthals are our ancestors, or rather are ancestors primarily of modern Europeans; in this view modern humans evolved from archaic ones such as Neanderthals in different parts of the world simultaneously, all the while exchanging enough genes to remain part of the same species. The other view is that Neanderthals were a separate species that were replaced, after little or no fraternization, by modern humans, who began migrating out of Africa around 100,000 years ago.

The Neanderthal DNA does not resolve the issue—but it suggests Neanderthals were indeed a separate species, and thus it favors the out-of-Africa hypothesis. Krings's 379-nucleotide sequence differed at 27 positions, on average, from the modern human sequences, and it was no closer to Europeans than to any other moderns. Among themselves the modern sequences differed by an average of only eight places. Picture a crowd of modern humans huddled around a campfire, with nobody more than eight yards from the center; then the Neanderthal is 27 yards away, well outside the circle, in the shadows at the edge of the woods. By Pääbo's and Krings's calculations, *Homo sapiens* and *Homo neanderthalensis* must have evolved separately for more than half a million years to have become so different.

Of course, the researchers have only looked at one bit of DNA from one Neanderthal. Only when they or others have compared it with DNA from a second Neanderthal will the Munich result be fully convincing. It is fitting, though, that the first Neanderthal DNA came from the first

Neanderthal—and even from one of the bones that stayed the shovels of the miners in 1856, after they had already unwittingly tossed the skullcap and other bones out of Little Feldhofer Cave, down into the valley of the Düssel River. There is no Neander River, you see; the valley got its name in the late seventeenth century from a preacher and poet who often went there, a man named Joachim Neumann. In English his name would be Newman, but in the fashion of his day Neumann translated it into Greek, and it became Neander. A century and a half later, by a remarkable coincidence, the New Man Valley yielded a truly new man—a separate species of human, it now seems. It is wonderful, really, that after another century and a half, the Neanderthal Man himself should once again be in the news.

ID#_____   NAME_____

Article 23: Not Our Mom

1. How is mitochondrial DNA inherited?

2. What technological innovations occurred that allowed the team to study Neanderthal DNA?

3. Why did they choose the humerus?

4. Describe the two main schools of thought concerning the relationship of Neanderthals to modern humans.

5. What does the Neanderthal DNA tell us? Does the Neanderthal DNA suggest they are closely related to Europeans?

The Gift of Gab
Matt Cartmill

People can talk. Other animals can't. They can all communicate in one way or another—to lure mates, at the very least—but their whinnies and wiggles don't do the jobs that language does. The birds and beasts can use their signals to attract, threaten, or alert each other, but they can't ask questions, strike bargains, tell stories, or lay out a plan of action.

Those skills make *Homo sapiens* a uniquely successful, powerful, and dangerous mammal. Other creatures' signals carry only a few limited kinds of information about what's happening at the moment, but language lets us tell each other in limitless detail about what used to be or will be or might be. Language lets us get vast numbers of big, smart fellow primates all working together on a single task—building the Great Wall of China or fighting World War II or flying to the moon. It lets us construct and communicate the gorgeous fantasies of literature and the profound fables of myth. It lets us cheat death by pouring out our knowledge, dreams, and memories into younger people's minds. And it does powerful things for us inside our own minds because we do a lot of our thinking by talking silently to ourselves. Without language, we would be only a sort of upright chimpanzee with funny feet and clever hands. With it, we are the self-possessed masters of the planet.

How did such a marvelous adaptation get started? And if it's so marvelous, why hasn't any other species come up with anything similar? These may be the most important questions we face in studying human evolution. They are also the least understood. But in the past few years, linguists and anthropologists have been making some breakthroughs, and we are now beginning to have a glimmering of some answers.

We can reasonably assume that by at lease 30,000 years ago people were talking—at any rate, they were producing carvings, rock paintings, and jewelry, as well as ceremonial graves containing various goods. These tokens of art and religion are high-level forms of symbolic behavior, and they imply that the everyday symbol-handling machinery of human language must have been in place then as well.

Language surely goes back further than that, but archeologists don't agree on just how far. Some think that earlier, more basic human behaviors—hunting in groups, tending fires, making tools—also demanded language. Others think these activities

From *Discover Magazine*, November 1998 by Matt Cartmill. Copyright © 1998 by Matt Cartmill. Reprinted by permission.

are possible without speech. Chimpanzees, after all, hunt communally, and with human guidance they can learn to tend fires and chip flint.

Paleontologists have pored over the fossil bones of our ancient relatives in search of evidence for speech abilities. Because the most crucial organ for language is the brain, they have looked for signs in the impressions left by the brain on the inner surfaces of fossil skulls, particularly impressions made by parts of the brain called speech areas because damage to them can impair a person's ability to talk or understand language. Unfortunately, it turns out that you can't tell whether a fossil hominid was able to talk simply by looking at brain impressions on the inside of its skull. For one thing, the fit between the brain and the bony braincase is loose in people and other large mammals, and so the impression we derive from fossil skulls are disappointingly fuzzy. Moreover, we now know that language functions are not tightly localized but spread across many parts of the brain.

Faced with these obstacles, researchers have turned from the brain to other organs used in speech, such as the throat and tongue. Some have measured the fossil skulls and jaws of early hominids, tried to reconstruct the shape of their vocal tracts, and then applied the laws of acoustics to them to see whether they might have been capable of producing human speech.

All mammals produce their vocal noises by contracting muscles that compress the rib cage. The air in the lungs is driven out through the windpipe to the larynx, where it flows between the vocal cords. More like flaps than cords, these structures vibrate in the breeze, producing a buzzing sound that becomes the voice. The human difference lies in what happens to the air after it gets past the vocal cords.

In people, the larynx lies well below the back of the tongue, and most of the air goes out through the mouth when we talk. We make only a few sounds by exhaling through the nose—for instance, nasal consonants like *m* or *n*, or the so-called nasal vowels in words like the French *bon* and *vin*. But in most mammals, including apes, the larynx sticks farther up behind the tongue, into the back of the nose, and most of the exhaled air passes out through the nostrils. Nonhuman mammals make mostly nasal sounds as a result.

At some point in human evolution the larynx must have descended from its previous heights, and this change had some serious drawbacks. It put the opening of the windpipe squarely in the path of descending food, making it dangerously easy for us to choke to death if a chunk of meat goes down the wrong way—something that rarely happens to a dog or a cat. Why has evolution exposed us to this danger?

Some scientists think that the benefits outweighed the risks, because lowering the larynx improved the quality of our vowels and made speech easier to understand. The differences between vowels are produced mainly by changing the size and shape of the airway between the tongue and the roof of the mouth. When the front of the tongue almost touches the palate, you get the *ee* sound in *beet*; when the tongue is humped up high in the back (and the lips are rounded), you get the *oo* sound in *boot*, and so on. We are actually born with a somewhat ape-like throat, including a flat tongue and a larynx lying high up in the neck, and this arrangement makes a child's vowels sound less clearly separated from each other than an adult's.

Philip Lieberman of Brown University thinks that an ape-like throat persisted for some time in our hominid ancestors. His studies of fossil jaws and skulls persuade him that a more modern throat didn't evolve until some 500,000 years ago, and that some evolutionary lines in the genus *Homo* never did acquire modern vocal organs. Lieberman concludes that the Neanderthals, who lived in Europe until perhaps 25,000 years ago, belonged to a dead-end lineage that never developed our range of vowels, and that their speech—if they had any at all—would have been harder to understand than ours. Apparently, being easily understood wasn't terribly important to them—not important enough, at any rate, to outweigh the risk of inhaling a chunk of steak into a lowered larynx. This suggests that vocal communication wasn't as central to their lives as it is to ours.

Many paleoanthropologists, especially those who like to see Neanderthals as a separate species, accept this story. Others have their doubts. But the study of other parts of the skeleton in fossil hominids supports some of Lieberman's conclusions. During the 1980s a nearly complete skeleton of a young *Homo* male was recovered from 1.5-million-year-old deposits in northern Kenya. Examining the vertebrae attached to the boy's rib cage, the English anatomist Ann MacLarnon discovered that his spinal cord was proportionately thinner in this region than it is in people today. Since that part of the cord controls most of the muscles that drive air in and out of the lungs, MacLarnon concluded that the youth may not have had the kind of precise neural control over breathing movements that is needed for speech.

This year my colleague Richard Kay, his student Michelle Balow, and I were able to offer some insights from yet another part of the hominid body. The tongue's movements are controlled almost solely by a nerve called the hypoglossal. In its course from the brain to the tongue, this nerve passes through a hole in the skull, and Kay, Balow, and I found that this bony canal is relatively big in modern humans—about twice as big in cross section as that of a like-size chimpanzee. Our larger canal presumably reflects a bigger hypoglossal nerve, giving us the precise control over tongue movements that we need for speech.

We also measured this hole in the skulls of a number of fossil hominids. Australopithecines have small canals like those of apes, suggesting that they couldn't talk. But later *Homo* skulls, beginning with a 400,000-year-old skull from Zambia, all have big, humanlike hypoglossal canals. These are also the skulls that were the first to house brains as big as our own. On these counts our work supports Lieberman's ideas. We disagree only on the matter of Neanderthals. While he claims their throats couldn't have produced human speech, we find that their skulls also had human-size canals for the hypoglossal nerve, suggesting that they could indeed talk.

In short, several lines of evidence suggest that neither the australopithecines nor the early, small-brained species of *Homo* could talk. Only around half a million years ago did the first big-brained *Homo* evolve language. The verdict is still out on the language abilities of Neanderthals. I tend to think that they must have had fully human language. After all, they had brains larger than those of most modern humans, made elegant stone tools, and knew how to use fire. But if Lieberman and his friends are right about those vowels, Neanderthals may have sounded something like the Swedish chef on *The Muppet Show*.

We are beginning to get some idea of when human language originated, but the fossils can't tell us how it got started, or what the intermediate stages between animal calls and human language might have been like. When trying to understand the origin of a trait that doesn't fossilize, it's sometimes useful to look for similar but simpler versions of it in other creatures living today. With luck, you can find a series of forms that suggest how simple primitive makeshifts could have evolved into more complex and elegant versions. This is how Darwin attacked the problem of the evolution of the eye. Earlier biologists had pointed to the human eye as an example of a marvelously perfect organ that must have been specially created all at once in its final form by God. But Darwin pointed out that animal eyes exist in all stages of complexity, from simple skin cells that can detect only the difference between light and darkness, to pits lined with such cells, and so on all the way to the eyes of people and other vertebrates. This series, he argued, shows how the human eye could have evolved from simpler precursors by gradual stages.

Can we look to other animals to find simpler precursors of language? It seems unlikely. Scientists have sought experimental evidence of language in dolphins and chimpanzees, thus far without success. But even if we had no experimental studies, common sense would tell us that the other animals can't have languages like ours. If they had, we would be in big trouble because they would organize against us. They don't. Outside of Gary Larson's *Far Side* cartoons and George Orwell's *Animal Farm*, farmers don't have to watch their backs when they visit the cowshed. There are no conspiracies among cows, or even among dolphins and chimpanzees. Unlike human slaves or prisoners, they never plot rebellions against their oppressors.

Even if language as a whole has no parallels in animal communication, might some of its peculiar properties be foreshadowed among the beasts around us? If so, that might tell us something about how and in what order these properties were acquired. One such property is reference. Most of the units of human languages refer to things—to individuals (like *Fido*), or to types of objects (*dog*), actions (*sit*), or properties (*furry*). Animal signals don't have this kind of referential meaning. Instead, they have what is called instrumental meaning: this is, they act as stimuli that trigger desired responses from others. A frog's mating croak doesn't *refer* to sex. Its purpose is to get some, not to talk about it. People, too, have signals of this purely animal sort—for example, weeping, laughing, and screaming —but these stand outside language. They have powerful meanings for us but not the kind of meaning that words have.

Some animal signals have a focused meaning that looks a bit like reference. For example, vervet monkeys give different warning calls for different predators. When they hear the "leopard" call, vervets climb trees and anxiously look down; when they hear the "eagle" call, they hide in low bushes or look up. But although the vervets' leopard call is in some sense about leopards, it isn't a word for leopard. Like a frog's croak or human weeping, its meaning is strictly instrumental; it's a stimulus that elicits an automatic response. All a vervet can "say" with it is "*Eeek! A leopard!*"—not "I really hate leopard!" or "No leopards here, thank goodness" or "A leopard ate Alice yesterday."

In these English sentences, such referential words as *leopard* work their magic through an accompanying framework of nonreferential, grammatical words, which set up an empty web of meaning that the referential symbols fill in. When Lewis Carroll tells us in "Jabberwocky" that "the slithy toves did gyre and gimble in the wabe," we have no idea what he is talking about, but we do know certain things—for instance, that all this happened in the past and that there was more than one tove but only one wabe. We know these things because of the grammatical structure of the sentence, a structure that linguists call syntax. Again, there's nothing much like it in any animal signals.

But if there aren't any intermediate stages between animal calls and human speech, then how could language evolve? What was there for it to evolve from? Until recently, linguists have shrugged off these questions—or else concluded that language didn't evolve at all, but just sprang into existence by accident, through some glorious random mutation. This theory drives Darwinians crazy, but the linguists have been content with it because it fits neatly into some key ideas in modern linguistics.

Forty years ago most linguists thought that people learn to talk through the same sort of behavior reinforcement used in training an animal to do tricks: when children use a word correctly or produce a grammatical sentence, they are rewarded. This picture was swept away in the late 1950s by the revolutionary ideas of Noam Chomsky. Chomsky argued that the structures of syntax lie in unconscious linguistic patterns—so-called deep structures—that are very different from the surface strings of words that come out of our mouths. Two sentences that look different on the surface (for instance, "A leopard ate Alice" and "Alice was eaten by a leopard") can mean the same thing because they derive from a single deep structure. Conversely, two sentences with different deep structures and different meanings can look exactly the same on the surface (for example, "Fleeing leopards can be dangerous"). Any models of language learning based strictly on the observable behaviors of language, Chomsky insisted, can't account for these deep-lying patterns of meaning.

Chomsky concluded that the deepest structures of language are innate, not learned. We are all born with the same fundamental grammar hard-wired into our brains, and we are preprogrammed to pick up the additional rules of the local language, just as baby ducks are hardwired to follow the first big animal they see when they hatch. Chomsky could see no evidence of other animals' possessing this innate syntax machinery. He concluded that we can't learn anything about the origins of language by studying other animals and they can't learn language from us. If language learning were just a matter of proper training, Chomsky reasoned, we ought to be able to teach English to lab rats, or at least to apes.

As we have seen, apes aren't built to talk. But they can be trained to use sign language or to point to word-symbols on a keyboard. Starting in the 1960s, several experimenters trained chimpanzees and other great apes to use such signs to ask for things and answer questions to get rewards. Linguists, however, were unimpressed. They said that the apes' signs had a purely instrumental meaning: the animals were just doing tricks to get a treat. And there was no trace of syntax in the random-looking jumble of signs the apes produced; an ape that signed "You give me cookie please" one minute might sign "Me cookie please you cookie eat give" the next.

Duane Rumbaugh and Sue Savage-Rumbaugh set to work with chimpanzees at the Yerkes Regional Primate Research Center in Atlanta to try to answer the linguists' criticisms. After many years of mixed results, Sue made a surprising breakthrough with a young bonobo (or pygmy chimp) named Kanzi. Kanzi had watched his mother, Matata, try to learn signs with little success. When Sue gave up on her and started with Kanzi, she was astonished to discover that he already knew the meaning of 12 of the keyboard symbols. Apparently, he had learned them without any training or rewards. In the years that followed, he learned new symbols quickly and used them referentially, both to answer questions and to "talk" about things that he intended to do or had already done. Still more amazingly, he had a considerable understanding of spoken English—including its syntax. He grasped such grammatical niceties as case structures ("Can you throw a potato to the turtle?") and if-then implication ("You can have some cereal if you give Austin your monster mash to play with"). Upon hearing such sentences, Kanzi behaved appropriately 72 percent of the time—more than a 30-month-old human child given the same tests.

Kanzi is a primatologist's dream and a linguist's nightmare. His language-learning abilities seem inexplicable. He didn't need any rewards to learn language, as the old behaviorists would have predicted; but he also defies the Chomskyan model, which can't explain why a speechless ape would have an innate tendency to learn English. It looks as though some animals can develop linguistic abilities for reasons unrelated to language itself.

Neuroscientist William Calvin of the University of Washington and linguist Derek Bickerton of the University of Hawaii have a suggestion as to what those reasons might be. In their forthcoming book, *Lingua ex Machina*, they argue that the ability to create symbols—signs that refer to things—is potentially present in any animal that can learn to interpret natural signs, such as a trail of footprints. Syntax, meanwhile, emerges from the abstract thought required for a social life. In apes and some other mammals with complex and subtle social relationships, individuals make alliances and act altruistically towards others, with the implicit understanding that their favors will be returned. To succeed in such societies, animals need to choose trustworthy allies and to detect and punish cheaters who take but never give anything in return. This demands fitting a shifting constellation of individuals into an abstract mental model of social roles (debtors, creditors, allies, and so on) connected by social expectations ("If you scratch my back, I'll scratch yours"). Calvin and Bickerton believe that such abstract models of social obligation furnished the basic pattern for the deep structures of syntax.

These foreshadowings of symbols and syntax, they propose, laid the groundwork for language in a lot of social animals but didn't create language itself. That had to wait until our ancestors evolved brains big enough to handle the large-scale operations needed to generate and process complex strings of signs. Calvin and Bickerton suggest that brain enlargement in our ancestry was the result of evolutionary pressures that favored intelligence and motor coordination for making tools and throwing weapons. As a side effect of these selection pressures, which had nothing to do with communication, human evolution crossed a threshold at which language became possible. Big-brained, nonhuman animals like Kanzi remain just on the verge of language.

This story reconciles natural selection with the linguists' insistence that you can't evolve language out of an animal communication system. It is also consistent with what we know about language from the fossil record. The earliest hominids with modern-size brains also seem to be the first ones with modern-size hypoglossal canals. Lieberman thinks that these are also the first hominids with modern vocal tracts. It may be no coincidence that all three of these changes seem to show up together around half a million years ago. If Calvin and Bickerton are right, the enlargement of the brain may have abruptly brought language into being at this time, which would have placed new selection pressures on the evolving throat and tongue.

This account may be wrong in some of its details, but the story in its broad outlines solves so many puzzles and ties up so many loose ends that something like it must surely be correct. It also promises to resolve our conflicting views of the boundary between people and animals. To some people, it seems obvious that human beings are utterly different from any beasts. To others, it's just as obvious that many other animals are essentially like us, only with fewer smarts and more fur. Each party finds the other's view of humanity alien and threatening. The story of language origins sketched above suggests that both parties are right: the human difference is real and profound, but it is rooted in aspects of psychology and biology that we share with our close animal relatives. If the growing consensus on the origins of language can join these disparate truths together, it will be a big step forward in the study of human evolution.

ID#_____ NAME_____

Article 24: The Gift *of* Gab

1. What were paleontologists looking for when they studied the brain for keys to language ability? Did it work? Why or why not?

2. Compare the placement of the larynx in humans and chimpanzees. What does this mean for the passage of air through the larynx in each?

3. Why is it dangerous to have a larynx that has descended?

4. Does Lieberman think Neanderthals had language? Why or why not?

5. What did the author and his colleagues find in their study of the hypoglossal nerve?
   - In humans?

   - In Neanderthals?

   - In australopithecines?

6. What is the difference between referential meaning and inferential meaning?

7. Define: syntax.

8. Chomsky revolutionized linguistics by concluding that the deepest structures of language are _____ , not _____ .

9. Chomsky believed that there was no use in studying language in other animals. How did the work with Kanzi challenge this conclusion?

10. What did Calvin and Bickerton conclude about the ability to create symbols and development of syntax?

11. Why do Calvin and Bickerton think language ability is a side effect of brain enlargement?